# DRESSED IN
# TIME

# DRESSED IN TIME

A World View

## MARGARET MAYNARD

BLOOMSBURY VISUAL ARTS
LONDON • NEW YORK • OXFORD • NEW DELHI • SYDNEY

BLOOMSBURY VISUAL ARTS
Bloomsbury Publishing Plc
50 Bedford Square, London, WC1B 3DP, UK
1385 Broadway, New York, NY 10018, USA
29 Earlsfort Terrace, Dublin 2, Ireland

BLOOMSBURY, BLOOMSBURY VISUAL ARTS and the Diana logo are trademarks of
Bloomsbury Publishing Plc

First published in Great Britain 2022

Cover design by Charlotte Daniels
Cover image © John M. Lund / Getty Images

ISBN:   HB:       978-1-3500-3274-3
        PB:       978-1-3500-3275-0
        ePDF:     978-1-3500-3276-7
        eBook:    978-1-3500-3277-4

Typeset by RefineCatch Ltd, Bungay, Suffolk NR35 1EF
Printed and bound in India

To find out more about our authors and books, visit www.bloomsbury.com
and sign up for our newsletters.

# CONTENTS

# ILLUSTRATIONS

# PREFACE

This book is the culmination of a lifetime's obsession with garments in all their forms. Since childhood I have had an almost inexplicable fascination with dress and dressing up, from how clothes have been made to how they are worn and represented. Completing a fine arts degree in South Africa many years ago, with very limited knowledge of design history, I looked everywhere for employment, as do many young people. I had never seen a single original work of Classical, Renaissance, or Modern art, only reproductions in calendars and one or two oil paintings by local artists. I had never encountered a dress from the past, apart from my mother's old clothes. I had one asset, however. I never said no to opportunities. Acquiring a position to design costumes for a state opera company came from sheer persistence. It was something way over my head, resulting in a more than urgent need to study dress. The situation was sink or swim.

Over the years as a researcher, I have passed through a great many different phases of the historiography of dress and fashion history. I have watched its astonishing and quickening rate of scholarly expansion. At the start of my career, "costume history" equated to theater dress, and sometimes the wearing of deteriorated "period" clothes to at least *feel* historic. My epiphany was acceptance into an impressive, very new course at London University's Courtauld Institute of Art, London, taught by Stella Mary Newton, herself a former theatrical costume designer and fashion designer. I believe she kindly included me in her extremely small class because I could read an unusual language, Afrikaans.

I believe that Courtauld methods gave me my career. We were taught, above all, the intensive skill of looking at dress in art of all kinds. But I felt there was far more to the subject than dress in western Europe. My early belief in the power and complexities of what people wear around the world, the materials of their dress and social meanings, as well as aesthetics, has only expanded. These interests have been sustained over sixty-five years of looking at paintings, sculpture, surviving dress, textiles, and archaeological remains. A short period in Papua New Guinea opened my eyes further. My great regret is not having studied anthropology or archaeology, a lack highlighted by the achievements of Joanne B. Eicher, another of my mentors.

My primary intention in this book is to use time and the social world, as variously entwined with clothing, to suggest new perspectives for dress studies. I have deliberately decided to cover an extensive period of time in order to support my argument. The examples I use are naturally selective, with a slight emphasis on geographical areas with which I am familiar. As this is a book purporting to take a world view, I also felt impelled to consider body coverings of ancient peoples who lived in the "deep time" of prewritten history. One reason for this is that my childhood home was located relatively near the Sterkfontein Caves, one of the most productive paleoanthropological sites in the world and claimed by some as the "Cradle of Humankind."

My book shows that time is a crucial tool for researching all aspects of clothing. The making of garments, their wearing, repairing, trading, replicating, the feelings we have about them, even their ceasing to be worn, represent shifting ground around which relationships of identity are constantly formed, then dissolved and transferred to other networks and associations. Being largely object focused, I have chosen not to be drawn too far into theoretical arguments, although different understandings of time that lie at the center of theoretical concerns with dress are important. Dress (fashion) and fabrics are associated with a multitude of temporal values beyond their physicality. Given their proximity to the body, clothes are signposts to specific social, physical, and emotional attachments. These embrace memory, the imagination, subjectivity, and proprieties of behavior but also loss. We need to rethink calling dress or fashion "typical" of any era, decade, or year.

Before proceeding, I need to clarify my use of the term "time." I use it in connection with *social* time, not the interrelated theories of relativity which refer to the behavior of objects in space. It is generally agreed that time and space cannot be divorced, but my concern with relativities of time and dress means the issue of space is a less prominent ingredient; social and historical time are my primary concern.[1] In the late 1990s emerged a new interest in Western historical thinking, termed the "temporal turn," which reinvigorated a long-existing framework for changes in historical time.[2] Corfield has looked carefully at the relationship of time to history and agrees that appreciation of the long term is important. Life is not made up of self-contained moments; instead the past meshes seamlessly with the present and the future.[3] While favoring history over the long term (what she calls "through-time"), she urges historians to accept short-term focus studies that can be located within these longer-term frameworks, thus accepting interconnections between them. She argues traditional period divisions are outmoded, favoring focused discontinuities.[4] Her work confirms the fragility of any subjective discussion on time, and the degree to which meanings are relative.

Using time, primarily in its Western understanding but certainly not entirely, is to open up avenues of new research allowing us to explore meanings of clothes not just about wearing them and why but details of their complex after lives. Dress may not retain its original social uses and indeed can outlive the body as an artifact. But there is a lesser known or understood, even hidden life of clothes, and related material networks, that exist over time beyond their apparent use. Clothing has narratives that extend from their primary use into keeping places, and are assembled in new ways as they enter into the historical frameworks of museums. They are also discarded from their primary use in the West and their potentially polluting factors exported to impoverished nations like those in Africa.

Many culturally specific terms are used to describe what people use to cover, supplement and modify their bodies. Over time, they have entered into use and been replaced as their suitability and usefulness diminishes. The etymology of dress is in fact an important subject that has been little studied to date. There are many terms in common use for articles that supplement and modify the body. These are difficult to define and discussed briefly in Chapter 1. There are other generalized phrases used repetitively by historians of dress which I explore in detail in Chapter 3.

In fact, one of my intentions in this book is to use time to expose inappropriate terms that still prevail in writing about fashion, dress, and clothing. There is some irony that to date a discipline of such inventiveness has been weighed down by outmoded terminology. I have deliberately chosen to use a format where chapters are followed by shorter focus accounts that explore in detail aspects of the related chapter. These shorter pieces are intended to stimulate ideas, which could hopefully later be reframed differently by others. Time is my fundamental scaffolding and the main unifying link for my ideas throughout.

No dress, fashion, clothing, or body modifications lie outside social and cultural understandings of time. Clocks tell time but not *the* time. Different cultures and constituencies have and do consolidate and measure time in various ways.[5] Kristeva, for instance, envisaged two forms of feminine time, a third wave of feminism that created its own signifying spaces to replace male hegemony in the definition of identity.[6] But industrial, agricultural, and leisure time, as well as countless other activities, policies, and imaginaries, have been shaped into definable entities. First Nations peoples, burdened by the deep shadow of colonialism, were required to abide by times set by the new settlers, and being different from their own, living in this way often had dire results, clothing included.[7] Whatever the case, time lies at the heart of socio-cultural beliefs and practices that in various ways flow through to textiles, clothing, their making (and tools of fabrication), body ornamentation, valuing, preserving (treasuring), encountering, and technologies of wearing. Dress worldwide is culturally constituted by material and conceptual affirmation of the temporal, and concepts of time are found variously across great historical spans and geographic locations. Time and dress merge in the acts of making, remaking, trading, "handing down," and more.

Riello and McNeil suggest fashion can be used as a lens to observe the change and lack of continuities in history but should also be studied in its own right rather than in connection with other forms of historical change.[8] In their view, high fashion complicates time as a linear or cumulative phenomenon because of its cyclical practices, such as seasonal collections and annual catwalk shows. Their suggestion is that fashion, being a practice defined by change, becomes part of "a historical process that defines time itself," something with which I only partially agree.[9] Their views of the cyclical are useful to consider in the light of the work of leading cultural theorist of fashion, Susan B. Kaiser. She believes fashion is never finished but that time and space converge through the fashioned body, as demonstrated by complex entanglements of cultural experiences. Like Riello and McNeil, she does not hold with the idea that time is progressive or its routes linear, preferring the model of a "circuit of style-fashion-dress" where time and space are intertwined.[10]

But unlike Riello and McNeil, her position is, in part, more open ended than the purely cyclic as she suggests that journeys of style, production, and distribution can flow in multiple directions. Here she implies there are manifold routes which navigate and connect dress and associated meanings over time, twisting and turning through and beyond locations in many different ways.[11] By contrast, I suggest there are occasions when time and space are not interwoven and can be separated conceptually. There are other occasions when time and dress are so closely aligned that the relationships, networks, and other interconnections between the two are more entangled than Kaiser specifies. This is the reason I have chosen to consider time almost exclusively in this exploration of *Dressed in Time*. I feel strongly that fixed notions of progressive developments in dress need to be reconsidered and replaced with the idea of networks, processes, and social interactions. This shows multiple, often uncoordinated, periodicities coexist in the complexity of outfits people wear. Dress practices may then be seen to build on associations or dismantle them, and existing systems of attire, including methods of making, intermittently connect or disconnect with those of other cultures and previous eras.

My account is trans-disciplinary, mindful that different cultural views of time have existed and continue to do so in customs around the world. I draw from a range of sources including material culture studies, fashion and dress history, cultural anthropology, archaeology, ethnography, curatorship, and art history. I reconsider familiar Eurocentric methods of approach to the subject, such as progressive linear chronology, context, and periodization of style, to show their limitations and offer alternatives. Whilst my book favors an object-based approach, the contextual is not discounted. Attempts to integrate makers and users in more personal ways are also within the remit. For instance, I embrace Sampson's theoretical view of the transaction of making bespoke garments that has, in the past, disassociated makers from those who wear the garments they create. Offering an alternative to writing on consumption, she argues that the agency of makers, the material nature of the garments they make and also that of wearers are entangled. This creates a subtle matrix between these various constituents but also allows for each to be subjected to temporal analysis.[12]

The Eurocentric tenor of much writing on fashion and dress has, until recently, assumed an artificially polarized separation between Western and non-Western cultures. This separation has in the past created short comings in the understanding of economic and intersocial relations. A number of authors who have challenged such "center-to-periphery boundaries" are outlined by Jenss and Hofmann.[13] I take this discussion further in Chapter 4 by considering widespread transnational influences, adaptations, and exchanges that have taken place in fabrics and garments over centuries, and the commercial networks that were established from the time when China first opened up trading systems beyond its borders. With reference to global interactions and cultural exchange, I acknowledge the exceptional publication *Object Lives and Global Histories* (2021) Lemire et al. (eds). Their challenging discussions on interactions between settler colonialism, imperial culture, and the agency of Indigenous peoples suggested useful new terminology, appropriate to the framework of their studies. By following an atypical time line and by using more "capacious chronologies," best suited to the challenges of their subject matter, the authors opened my eyes to a much broader understanding of the subject of dress and demonstrated its usefulness to my own book.[14]

Lou Taylor's work has also been a strong influence on my thinking. For her, material culture studies place their focus on the smallest observable details, sometimes considered "trivial." These include stitching, repairing, or identifying out-of-sight items and other intangible factors. Here she asserts the need to draw on aspects of feeling, comfort, nostalgia, smell, or the sound of fabric in her own version of "the lived experience of dress."[15] These ancillary aspects or "trivia," in fact, form some of the essential "distinctions" in dress and can be called the unspoken experiential aspects of clothing which inform some of the chapters in my book. Her insights into the dress of the underclasses of our society has also influenced comments in my book which claim it is essential we study the entire spectrum of a culture's dress beyond the aesthetic treasures of the upper social classes.

My study joins what is a renewed interest being paid to all forms of materiality and its meanings in dress studies. I move beyond what have been described as the formal and technical characteristics of early studies of the material formerly associated with the contextual.[16] I use time to open up these ideas and methods and engage with further complexities. Material artifacts of attire and personal adornment (including fashion) are never static. Individually they partake of ingredients of the past, serve the needs of the present and cause speculations about the future. They exist as mutable entities whose changing manifestations take place along entangled historical pathways.

In summary, this book explores ways particular constructs and constituencies of time are fundamental to the dress of the gendered and class-based body. It uses the cultural relativities of time as research tools to explore how clothes, as embodied arrangements of material things, are infused with evidence of the mutable, in turn reinforcing the nature and impact of social mores. I show how the intentions behind wearing, social hierarchies, attitudes to the self, ways clothes are perceived and the messages conveyed, including the political, are changing constantly. As the questions I ask of dress are subject to the relativities of time they hopefuly point the way for others to follow. Clothes can be read both as a sign of an integrated, relational social context but also as contradictory, irregular, and highly unsettled. My book offers former unexplored ways to re think clothes and the wearing body. To study clothing though the lens of time and in a multitude of social, historical, and geographical circumstances, is to view all dress in a new light.

# ACKNOWLEDGMENTS

I have many friends, colleagues, and family members who I would like to thank for ongoing support and assistance with this project over many years. My special gratitude goes to editor Frances Arnold, Joanne B. Eicher (University of Minnesota), and Regina A. Root (William and Mary University) for initially seeing the potential in this project.

I acknowledge Karen Finch OBE, Founder of the Textile Conservation Centre, a lifelong friend and supporter whose enthusiastic understanding of the significance of textiles was inspirational. I also thank textile conservator Rinske Car and dress historian Jane Bridgeman, whose research interests have influenced me and who assisted with sections of this book. Other colleagues who contributed in various ways include Peter McNeil (University of Technology Sydney), Roger Leong, Glynis Jones, and many others from the Museum of Applied Arts and Sciences, New South Wales.

I extend grateful thanks to the following for research advice: anthropologist Kim Akerman; Boris Gasparyan, researcher at the Institute of Archaeology and Ethnography of the National Academy of Sciences of the Republic of Armenia; Jana Jones (Macquarie University); independent researchers Laura Jocic, Catriona Fisk, and Mary Scott; Rector Alexander Borodin; curator Susan North; dress and textile historian Hilary Davidson and anthropologist Olga Soffer (University of Illinois). I thank Alison Matthews David (Ryerson University) for photographic assistance, and information from the Chicago History Museum.

For technical, organizational and bibliographic help and more, I sincerely thank Jan Nargar, as well as Miranda and Kerry Heckenberg, Louise Mayhew, and Stephen Kirby, not forgetting ongoing assistance from Rebecca Hamilton.

The sustained support I received from my family, Richard, Nick, and Nikki, and special friend Carol Doyle cannot be measured.

I thank the University of Queensland for my position as Honorary Research Consultant over a number of years.

# 1
# ABOUT TIME

What does time have to do with dress? For a start, defining time is daunting, if not impossible. Cultures worldwide have calculated time quite differently over the years, from the ancient Sumerians' approach to twenty-first-century digital recording. How do these differences in understanding social time open challenging and unorthodox ways of looking at, as well as interpreting, the meanings of textiles, garments, and body modifications? The premise of my study is that if we use time as an interrogative tool, we discover fascinating and dynamic relativities present in all garments, and extensive new meanings about dress and associated embellishment. But the implications for the sartorial, in terms of time, are particularly extraordinary. These lie at the heart of all historical studies—chronology, sequencing, cause and effect, the short and long term. I propose that time is a previously unrecognized player in the narrative of all clothing.[1] It presents an adventure in thinking and seeing.

Dress has been part of the evolution of humankind but its trajectory is by no means linear or straightforward. Its make-up reveals extraordinary subtle conversations between past and present, whether short lived or the reverse. Studies of historical and modern dressing (fashion, everyday wear, and more) have been intensively concerned with the progressive timeline approach. I suggest new ways to think about dress in relation to the possible origins of making cloth and clothing, the complex particularities of dress over the years, and about cultural exchanges from ancient times.

There is no doubt that beliefs about time have driven, and continue to drive, all forms of clothing around the world and across the centuries. Its dimensions have had profound and complicating implications for the meanings of apparel as well as its gendered and classed nature, be it everyday garments, high fashion, or ritual dressing. All categories of clothing have their own histories and are entangled with temporal pathways in association with others. I am not talking of a single narrative but an array of loose ends, as clothed wearers participate in the ebb and flow of social, spiritual, cultural, and mercantile engagements.[2] As fashion historian Ellen Sampson suggests: "garments accrue agencies as they pass between the hands that made them. . . . They are always exerting the other's agency back onto them via a cycle of imprint . . . . Makers and wearers of clothes, people and garments are entangled."[3]

A central and problematic issue discussed in this book is what might be the date of a dress, a suit, or a pair of shoes. Alexandra Palmer's opinion is that many historical costumes do not fit into established chronological development or match fashion plates. The reason being their construction may have been outside high fashion circles, due to the nature of personal taste, or even the age of the wearer and more.[4] I expand on Palmer's important point by examining whether any garment can have a firm date. It is, in fact, a far more complex query than it might seem.

Equally dress of various kinds is widely said to signify a particular decade or era. This is a convenient form of shorthand to be further examined. (See Focus 3b) The problem is pinning down what exactly *is* 1920s or 1940s fashion, or that of any other decade? By understanding many factors related to the temporal, the reader will find any answer to a question about the date of a garment surprising.

All dress (including body decoration and accessories) is made up variously of temporal particularities and ingredients, materially, spiritually, emotionally, and symbolically. Fashion consists of a multitude of movable components in which "there is a symbiosis between the perceived, the conceived and the experienced."[5] Some cultural theorists argue convincingly that we need to realize time and space cannot be separated: they are compressed.[6] Others posit that fashion, defined by change in time, becomes a historical process that defines time itself.[7] There are alternative views that need to be considered. Agnès Rocamora, in a discussion of acceleration as a mark of contemporary society (particularly in relation to fashion and the media), has opened up discussion about the way time has been taken for granted, especially in studies of fashion. She urges the temporal, as an unspoken element underpinning fashion's workings, needs to be further interrogated.[8]

The present account takes up her call but chooses to emphasize the impact of time *as part of the social* by focusing on a wider range of dress and its representation than fashion alone. Time lies at the center of all clothing concerns, not just those of high-end dress. Every garment has its own pace and even accrued emotions, all have their own separate life itineraries plus individual elements with different histories. The uses of garments change, being variously treasured, memorialized, stored, or (when no longer needed) discarded. Research conducted by the supermarket chain Sainsbury's in 2017 claimed 680 million unwanted clothes were thrown out in the UK in that year. Many were given to Oxfam to be sold in their charity shops, but 235 million items ended up in landfill.[9] The piece suggests the extent of used clothing in the Western world is gradually matching, if not overtaking, that of new fashions.

We need to be aware of the particularities of dress and fashion and see how time was implicated in profound changes related to the "natural" time of seasons, secular as well as ecclesiastical time, rigid courtly time, marine time, rural and urban time, leisure time, modern industrial time, and postmodern time. Clothing that fades and deteriorates, secondhand wear, or the remains of garments, obviously occupy different registers of time. The popular twenty-first-century use of castoff clothing, rebadged as "vintage," or the wearing of clothes borrowed from a close friend or partner, such as jumpers and jeans, are examples. The ambiguity of very tight jeans as high-priced brands, deliberately aged and torn simply as a fashion statement, also show how complicated is the relationship between time, dress, and consumption.

Nor should we forget the artificial Western supposition—now fully dismissed by Welters and Lillethun with their rich examples in *Fashion History: A Global View* (2018)—that non-Western dress is developmentally static. In fact, no "traditional" clothing suspends time, although its pace of change is likely to differ from the volatile characteristics of European high fashion.

# Time on the Body

An account of ancient time and dress begins with markings on the skin, a partly decorated or incised body and not clothes *per se*. Adornment has been a primary means of social non-verbal communication with others, a key indicator of status and sexuality. Social anthropologists would record a prehistoric or traditional passage into adulthood likely demonstrated by specific body paint or tattooing. Different practices were later introduced on reaching a state of adulthood. A vestige of this continues, for instance, in Bariai (on the coast of West New Britain, Papua New Guinea) which has had complex and lengthy traditional procedures for dressing mothers and their first born for ceremony. According to social anthropologists, a first-born child is painted red on one side of the body and black on the other. The back of the child's waistband is decorated with red, green, and yellow crotons. These have large and dramatic variegated leaves, and considered to be important items. Around the child's neck are hung boar tusks (heirlooms) and strings of the most highly valued shell money, *vula misi*.[10] Traditional signs of age and status have been indicated clearly by means of markings and body supplements.

Customs like these have ancient origins. Ceremony around children and mothers can explain something of the laborious life of early humankind around 10,000 to 8,000 BCE when the transition from hunter- gather societies changed gradually to the settled but overcrowded village life of agriculture and herding.[11] Disease, brought on by co-habiting, increased child mortality and dress associated with religious practices—including burial rituals and skull cults— became more complex, initially in the Fertile Crescent of the Middle East.

Yet new methods applied by archaeologists have moved past cataloguing finds as such, rather regarding "things" as traces or itineraries. Joyce suggests that understanding of life with material things is now being understood as "a sense of material in constant motion" blurring the separations between bodies, places, and things.[12] So, I take from this a shift from a prior static conception of the body as a public, legible surface, to an archaeological understanding of "wear" on the body as an active shaping of embodiment, centered on lived experiences. Further chapters explore changes indicated here and the place of the body in more detail.

# Sewing and More

Tangled interwoven paths of body supplements, and their making over time, are found from prewritten history (for some historians a preferred term for prehistory) up to the present day. The following examples of sewing, needles, and types of looms are examples of the history of the long term, a revisionist method admired by Corfield in one of her *Monthly Blogs,* for its return to a range of new agendas, echoing her very broad embrace and theoretical interpretation of time across multiple societies.[13] She suggests history resembles an exploding galaxy—or, the sum of many exploding galaxies where key human inventions came about at very different times and places.

   My examples are intended to act as a form of conversation between apparently unrelated items. They open up the possibility of rethinking limitations in the individualized and straightforward developmental method found in conventional dress history, presenting a challenge to chronology, linearity, even the cyclical life of products. I recognize them as episodic moments, individual concepts, largely linked to Western, industrialized society. A reversal of conventional chronology is another method of assessing the history of clothing and ripe for interrogation, one that looks back in time from the present. Broadly my book is a way to underline many different scales and rhythms of time found in apparel, and how sensitivity to temporal issues can stimulate new questions about the origin of textiles and by extension clothing.

   Consider examples from the nineteenth century as well as others from the ancient past. Practically all classes of Victorian women stitched and mended garments one way or another, as women have done for centuries. In the seventeenth century, embroidered cabinets and caskets, of which few now survive, were boxes richly stitched on the outside as well as inside. They held ink and quills and hid treasured items.[14] Women who worked at sewing tables and out of needlework caskets were well versed in fine embroidery and a wide range of decorative and plain stitching, sometimes lace-making as well (Figure 1.1). If we look inside this finely carved and inlaid sewing box of a well-to-do Victorian woman, lined with velvet or quilted silk, we find it filled with mother-of-pearl spools, bodkins, crochet hooks, and needles. By contrast, working

**Figure 1.1** Needlework casket *c.* 1670s. British, embroidered in silk, metal thread, seed pearls etc. It contains glass bottles, ivory thread winders, a bodkin and other ivory embroidery tools. (Credit: Metropolitan Museum of Art, Public domain 39-13.4a-aaa.)

women had more mundane stitching and mending tasks and hence simpler containers.

Now look far back in time to primeval history. Archaeologists agree items for sewing have an exceptionally ancient history. Sewing needles seem to have been one of humankind's first tools and clearly one of its most enduring. Dependent on the task, they were likely used by men as well as women (Figure 1.2). What is claimed as the world's oldest threading needle is made of bone, 7.6 cm long and at least 50,000 years old. It was found in 2016, discovered in the ancient Denisova Cave in the Altai Mountains, Siberia, occupied at various times over 282,000 years by Homo sapiens, Neanderthals and Denisova hominins (an archaic subspecies of humans).[15] Yet at Sibudu, a Middle Stone Age rock shelter in KwaZulu-Natal, South Africa, ancient tools including needles have been found dating from 61,000 to 57,000 BCE or earlier. A bird-bone awl thought to date from 76,000 years BCE has been found in the same area too.[16] Awls could pierce holes and likely allowed thread to pass through tough skins.

Early needles were made out of slivers of animal or bird bone, sharpened to a point at one end, with an eye at the other. Bird bones used for needles could be from large species.[17] They were probably used to sew light skins together, later to make thread knots to construct nets, and for stitching more pliable woven cloth. If bone needles were used for sewing garments and other ornaments, it raises the question of how long it took for makers to shape these tools, grow raw

**Figure 1.2** Bone tools including a thin sewing needle and fish hooks. France, Upper Palaeolithic/Late Magdalenian period. (Credit: DEA / G. DAGLI ORTI/De Agostini via Getty Images.)

materials for thread, perhaps acquire and tan leather, form the thread and to put it through needles.

# Making Cloth

Fundamental to almost all cloth production for making garments are the activities of weaving, twining, plaiting, and spinning from grass and from other fibers such as flax, cotton, silk, and wool. Flax is an especially complicated fiber to produce. To make thread, it needs to be soaked and retted, the latter a way of breaking down the stems to extract the inner fibers. All cloth-making by hand is a lengthy, even arduous, process. So, what do we know of the origins of weaving cloth? To examine how time is relevant to the making of fabric, I discuss three examples of tools, other than needles. These are millennia apart but also concurrent, making them seem strangely haunting. I compare the great Jacquard loom, the individual backstrap and standard looms, and the first imprints of weaving found on hardened clay or mud.

There is no neat chronology or progressive narrative between ancient clay imprints and the Jacquard power loom, while the simple backstrap loom is still used all over Asia and Africa, as are industrial, mechanized Jacquard looms. This reinforces the argument that chronology is not the only way to study apparel. The mechanical loom is no more a sign of ingenuity than a backstrap loom and handwoven cloth. To construct a timeline of weaving technology is impossible, subjective, and probably unproductive. The point is that if we dismiss the concept of straightforward evolutionary progress, we are free to think more widely in terms of temporal irregularities.

The timber Jacquard power loom was invented in 1804–05 with earlier prototypes in the first half of the eighteenth century. It is a marvel of engineering in which the thread for patterns is controlled by punch cards. Most of these looms, of which there are numerous types, are huge (Figure 1.3). Each component of the Jacquard loom has its own micro history and time trajectory, namely the timber, the carding, the threads, and of course many fabric designs. Jacquard looms were first used to weave the most exacting of brocade patterns and the designs spread around the world. Their thread produced the finest, softest, and most intricate of women's woven shawls of wool but other textiles as well. Modern factory looms used for mass production of textiles (in China, say) still employ the old practice of threading wefts, usually through vertical warps.

**Figure 1.3** Industrial weaving shed with power-driven Jacquard looms and punch cards carrying the patterns on the side and on top, engraved print. Paris, *c.* 1880. (Credit: Universal History Archive/Getty Images.)

Although modern thread mixes are mostly artificial fibers, the principle is the same as the historic woven cloth of the ancient past.

The second example is the hand loom, which has ancient origins but is still in common use across Asia and Africa. Both silk and wool shawls—the latter made from the thick fleece of mountain goats tended by semi-nomadic people living at high altitude in the Himalayan "foothills"—were initially woven on these hand looms by artisans in Mongolia, Nepal, and the Kashmir region (Figure 1.4). The cashmere shawl industry had a varied and complex history (see Chapter 4 for a fuller discussion of cultural exchange) but flourished locally in the fifteenth century. The ornate patterns on shawls centered on a botanical motif, often the teardrop- or almond-shaped Buddhist *boteh* motif, spread by the East India Company, and traded across Europe.[18] These shawls were increasingly popular toward the end of the eighteenth century. Indian and other Asian versions of Kashmir (pashmina) shawls, were brought back to Europe as souvenirs at this time by French and British travelers and returning soldiers.[19]

Indian patterns were copied by European and British weavers (mainly in the town of Paisley, Renfrewshire, Scotland) in the nineteenth century. They translated them to the Jacquard loom, which meant similar garments could be

**Figure 1.4** Artisans weaving cashmere shawls, Kashmir region, 1900. (Credit: George Rinhart/Corbis via Getty Images.)

produced on a large scale. Their popularity was extensive, partly as they were admired by Josephine Bonaparte and later Queen Victoria, but this was surely due as well to their colorful patterns and aura of the exotic.

Towards the end of the twentieth century, restructuring of the world's main economies and speed of digital information transfer altered the commercial success and popularity of local production centers across the globe, blurring and threatening national boundaries. New connections between production and consumption meant that design and making could happen anywhere. Kaiser sees computerization and other mechanization not as centralization of style, but as new sources of design, arising and traveling along open and multiple routes, while fashion labor and design ideas have become transnational and circuitous.[20] Yet the fact is that in different ways, and at different speeds, the traveling nature of style ideas happened a great deal earlier than the twenty-first century.

The third example is amongst the first evidence we have of spun fibers used to weave fabric, allegedly the earliest known indications of this human practice. No woven textiles remain from prewritten history but impressions of Upper Paleolithic flax or other fiber threads, dated about 27,000 years BP, were discovered by Olga Soffer and other anthropologists at Dolní Věstonice, Moravia, Czech Republic.[21] They were perhaps unintentionally pressed into small pieces of wet clay pottery, or plaster, and hardened. Various weaves and even fabric joins were detected. As "negative impressions" of former textiles and fibers, the chemical traces or fossil casts are labeled pseudomorphs.[22] The term "fossil" is not normally used about fabric impressions, but these artifacts have a certain similarity to ammonite fossils and are immensely significant. They have been described as the first known signs of weaving cloth, but indications are the practice was happening much earlier.

In fact, more recently the first colored wild flax fibers, some dyed in blue, pink, and green, were taken from Upper Paleolithic layers of soil at Dzudzuana Cave, in the Caucasus, Georgia. The cave was inhabited intermittently during several periods between 32,000 to 26,000 years BP. Threads more than 34,000 years old, likely used for cloth, were discovered by archaeologist Ofer Bar-Yosef and team but identified only by using a microscope as they are invisible to the naked eye. They further indicate prehistoric hunter-gatherers made cords and threads, some likely for sewing garments.[23] The great Jacquard loom and the small, ancient imprints found in the fragility of clay or microscopic items, are fascinating to compare. Woven threads are present in both but one most likely originated from a piece of cloth now physically absent.

Ancient textiles raise many questions: when and why was cloth first woven, on precisely what kind of loom and by whom? How long did it take to spin early threads and dye them, and how much time did it take to process dress fabrics? Hand looms are extraordinary technical inventions that offer many different ways to keep the warp threads stable for the weft. We are uncertain how gender relations impacted in early times, so it remains unclear whether weaving was undertaken by women or men or both. Cloth is an innovation of substantial importance to the study of humankind and its clothing. Placing time at the heart of clothing research allow us to see the long-term history of tools in relation to mechanization and the short and particular histories of varieties of looms, such as backstrap looms, apparently first seen in Eastern Asia from about 3000 BCE, and even earlier. Looms of all kinds have been found worldwide. Adding depth to our understanding of the relativities of weaving, the basic techniques—once discovered—have never been allowed to die.

# Differences: The Complexity of Garments

Many, often uncoordinated disparities in style coexist in the complexity and different modalities of garments people wear. Forms of attire can be made up of dynamically different meanings, as Durham has shown about the polyvalency of a entirely different culture of Herero women's garments, with what she terms their "slippery overabundance of meaning," alive with possibilities.[24] The relativity of worn clothing and the vibrant meanings of a possible European woman's outfit is well demonstrated in a hypothetical urban example. We might look at a photograph of someone, say in a city, and comment on her clothing as personal "style," with some reference to the latest dictates of fashion, perhaps drawn from a magazine or TV. But how accurate is this?

If we look more carefully, we might see an office-working Western woman of middle age walking down the street at midday in, say, 2004. She may wear a very recently bought fashionable linen skirt, but a long-time favorite hand-made cotton blouse or shirt, a hand-knitted wool cardigan that originally belonged to her sister, a deliberately "retro" brooch, well-used shoes, earrings of semi-precious stones, handed down from a family member, and an optician's prescription glasses. Her handbag could have been bought on holiday and one of her stockings has a hole. She wears a digital Fitbit on her wrist with a time dial included. It is a watch but so much more. (See Focus 1a)

Each item in this composite outfit is a separate entity, having its own temporal road map and different rationale. All these garments are separate but tangled in an impermanent relationship. In their coming together, they project a woman's identity, status, and perhaps age at a specific moment in time. The next day, the combination and meanings might be different. A similar argument might be made for the street clothes of a male office worker, or clothing worn in urban centers of many Asian or African countries at a similar time.

Yet in some areas in Africa and the Pacific, for instance, it is the practice for local dress and conventions, especially for leisure at home, to still play their part concurrently with global styles. For example, in Fiji, men and women wear

Western dress to work in cities. On returning home or to a village from the city, women may change into a cotton blouse worn tucked into a *sulu* (skirt), while men wear *isulu vakatoga* (style imported from Tonga) their familiar, local clothing.[25] At the same time, types of dress worn by Indigenous peoples, those emerging post-missionary influence, can be composite clothes, a mix of local and European stylistic elements. This is expediency, partly driven by the separation of work time from leisure but it is also a strong gesture toward local but mutable identity, a desire not to lose contact with familiar wear of the past.

# Individuating Evidence

Individuality of dress is important to understand, especially in a time of mass production. For instance, if we look closely at the interior structure of a garment that has been much worn, such as a T-shirt or pair of jeans, perhaps shoes for rough walking in bush land, we can find individuating evidence such as wear and stains that are linked to habits and bodies of individual wearers. The individual imprint of any garment is important. Sykas, with years of experience looking at textiles and their methods, says very few garments that entered museum collections before his time of writing were free of previous alterations or changes made by different wearers.[26] None was pristine.

An example is a 1745–60 tight-bodied English Spitalfields silk *robe à l'anglaise* of a wealthy woman, now in the collection of the Art Gallery of South Australia, which shows both perspiration stains from use, and where it has been altered and adjusted. The garment's history does not match its material appearance.[27] Beyond its presumed date, it was worn as well in the 1870s and probably also in the 1930s. Even in the twenty-first century, every made-up garment is a little like a unique fingerprint, with its own biography and genealogy, as well as its own history of conception, use, status, and changing story of fabrication and wearing.[28] Much clothing, whether stylish outfits, copies or customary wear, if closely observed, has many marks of use, perhaps a lingering smell or darn, a patchwork of distinct elements all accrued over time. When garments are photographed the precise evidence of time may be erased, thus presenting a "magazine style" of dress history that belies the actual use of garments. Time is "woven" into all the material particulars of attire, as well as the disparate personal and collective memories of groups and individuals, their cultural specificities and associated mores.

Understanding the significance of time allows us to explore meanings in clothes which are not just worn but have individual complex after lives. Clothing is unlikely to retain its original social use forever. It can outlive the physical body. Some clothing, if left unworn—in a museum, say—loses its links with the body. It becomes an artifact or relic onto which new meanings can be attached. (See

Focus 5a) Unworn garments call into question issues of relative longevity and personal or collective value, selective preservation, and disposability. We should bear in mind historic garments, made of textiles or even leather, are complicated by their potential instability and their ephemeral nature, a fugitive quality of decay, even rarity, that enhances their significance. [29] Archaeological finds of body supplements of the ancient past are, on the whole, extremely rare and this gives them the perception of being of great value. (See Focus 1b and 2b)

The physical existence of clothes may be as independent or individuated temporal objects, but there is also a little understood, sometimes hidden life of clothes, beyond their obvious initial use or presence today. Why clothes are sometimes preserved or found buried collectively is not always clear. The latter is the case in the UK. So called "hoards" of weapons, body ornaments, coins, and occasionally textiles have been excavated, abiding by certain regional arrangements of items. The very large Galloway Hoard (two separate burials) was found on land in Dumfries and Galloway in 2014. It is not dated absolutely but regarded as a Viking Age collection from *c*. 900 CE.[30] By no means the earliest of its kind, it includes ornaments of silver and gold such as brooches, arm bands, a gold bird-shaped pin, an ingot, a pendant of rare metals, Byzantine textiles, and other artifacts.

But why were these things buried and what was the significance of each piece? Was it more than simply safe storage? Clothes are kept in the fabric of buildings to bring good fortune, perhaps unwanted but kept out of some superstitious fear that the past must not be forgotten. On the other hand, groups of garments, held collectively in museums, may be read less in terms of their integrated social context, rather as fortuitous even irregular objects, perhaps aesthetically displayed, and selected perhaps more for curatorial interest than their actual character warrants.

# Other Viewpoints

My book takes issue with a number of conservative mainstays of dress history methods, such as the contextual approach, period style, and the chronological account of the changing nature of fashion and dress. It does this by demonstrating how a close temporal analysis can open new avenues of thought. The work of Julia Kristeva is important as it engages with temporality as a feminist consideration, time's fluidity associated with "women's time," plus her concept of different kinds of time including periods, cycles, and the creative.

Central to this present study is the prime place accorded to material objects of clothing. My book is aware of the material "turn" in research which infused historical research some decades ago, challenging the postmodern preoccupation with theory-based knowledge. Here I acknowledge much prior work done by researchers such as Jules Prown and Lou Taylor, the latter instrumental over more recent years in championing object-based research. Taylor's preference has always been socially inclusive and supportive of the significance of detailed observation of actual garments. This was even when object-centred research in the early historiography of dress studies was put under pressure by cultural theory in the later twentieth century.

Prown believed material objects have different forms of value but "objects created in the past are the only historical occurrences that continue to exist in the present."[31] They allow us to encounter the past at first hand. This straightforward claim suggests some secure and stable continuity for objects. This is not my present view. Material objects are certainly a way to encounter the past and indeed the present, but dress and accessories as well as textiles do not unconditionally represent the past.

The argument here fits with larger ideas that can be drawn from clothing but is not categoric. One must focus closely on disparate material objects in their imprecision and wearing, seeing them differentially and mutable in their materiality as well as culturally. An Elizabethan gown of the royal household can be interpreted as a mixture of different sewing methods; moreover, the jewels, the shape of sleeves, and the lace-making of standing collars, all represent visual power, ownership of status, and the performance of wealth. Time, and hence the value of labor, is implicit in how fashions or dress are made, whether by hand or by machine, by men or women. The socio-economic meanings of clothes, fabrics, and other materials each have their own stories, but the tools with which they are made must also be included in a record of their material alterations over time.

Penelope Corfield is one scholar who believes in the integration between time and space, which she calls "time-space." But in discussing the new "temporal turn" of early twenty-first- century historical writing, she suggests the term encourages interaction of multiple dimensions and multiple layering. Periodization, she suggests is part of, not different from, a serious consideration of sequential chronology over the very long term. Here she favors the concept of the "inter-temporal." By this, she means allowing the interaction or discontinuity of multiple dimensions to throw light on the history of dress.[32] The method she endorses avoids pejorative concepts like "out-of-date" or "dated," which presuppose some ideal standard against which dress is measured.

She certainly favors history over the long term (what she calls through-time) or Braudel's term the *longue durée*. But she urges historians to accept short-term focus studies that can be located within these longer-term frameworks, thus accepting interconnections. Subjectivity, as opposed to object-based assessment, is part of this irregular interchange. While the issue of emotions is not her particular concern, her ideas are significant for understanding the association between fashion/dress, time and subjectivity.

An interesting new development in clothing studies is the issue of replicas and their value. (See Focus 8b) Relatively recently there has been a reassessment of the research benefits of precise recreation of historical garments, and a number of studies have been published. Although making alleged replica costumes for the stage has a history prior to the 1830s, encouraged by the work of antiquarian James Planché, this latest approach is far more accurate and has a clear rationale. It is a way of reconsidering dress by recognizing the processes of making, remaking, and reconstructing historic garments as a valid methodology, with quantifiable, academic outcomes. It shows that conservators and makers of replica garments benefit from each other and the results offer scholars new information about dressmaking, pattern-cutting, suitability of stitching, and—importantly—wearing.

Studying time, especially in relation to dress, unavoidably involves issues of power in Western cultures and those of India, Asia, South America, and Africa. Spatial issues, geography, and governance underpin uses of dress, not least in colonial trade exchanges and influences. In his important book *Time and the Other. How Anthropology Makes its Object* (2002), anthropologist Johannes Fabian is concerned with temporal aspects of ethnography and anthropology, especially intersubjective fieldwork. He claims those who study cultures beyond their own do so from a perspective outside and above.[33] He argues the conventional distancing of the beholder (the imperialist anthropologist) from the observed foreign cultures, (the subjects of ethnographic research) results in cultural relativism that relegates distant subjects to another time, one that is static and "primitive" which inevitably create a politics of us and them.

Kaiser takes this "divide" in a different direction but with some affinities. In *Fashion and Cultural Studies*, she points out one of the problems in modern Western approaches to fashion is thinking of time as a linear narrative concerning highly placed bourgeois women and men. It is a progressive one which arrives at a high point of fashion in major European centers like Paris, although this view started to lose traction toward the end of the twentieth century. But the divide has created shortcomings in the understanding of aesthetic values as well as economic and social relations, causing those "other" cultures outside the linear narrative to be considered fixed or fossilized.[34] Thus, dress of Western and other cultures has been artificially polarized. Kaiser urges us to explore fashion as a global phenomenon, using concepts of multiple routes of influence, with porous connections (not boundaries). These are not singular routes but ones that detour and cross over others, a particular view that has special meaning for this study dealing with dress worldwide.

The premise of my book is that dynamic temporal mutability is manifest in all categories of garments and accessories, what they are made of, as well as their various stylish particularities. Extensive new meanings and associations about dress can be discovered if we use time as an interrogative tool. The concept that modern society is about relationships and that society regards time in respect of different social registers concerned Norbert Elias, writing from the perspective of the sociology of knowledge.[35] His view can be extended to dress. Time is not intrinsic to human beings, or a quality of the external world. but is different for cultural groups, genders, historical periods, and geographical areas. It is subjective and therefore unfixed, played out in all forms of dress and etiquette in multiple ways. In addition, "clothes themselves have agency" and often affect the wearer personally through emotions and feelings about wearing beyond style.[36]

Garments, textile materials and adornment everywhere and across millennia are entities whose constituents are shaped by complexities of the temporal. In comparison with existing methods and conventions of clothing history, I place time at the center of the discussion. This allows the opportunity to ask new and provocative questions about wearing, making, stylistic longevity, and the short lived. If we grasp the significance of time in its complex relationship with clothing, textiles, and indeed the body, it opens up dress of all kinds to an entire spectrum of imaginative, metaphorical and historical understandings. Unstable (sometimes contradictory) connotations of garments and the socio-cultural dimensions of the temporal are at the heart of this text. As material objects, garments and ornamentation offer untold riches to those who are prepared to look at them with fresh eyes. It is possible to see them in the process of temporal change at every stage of their lives. My book will take the reader on a provocative journey of heightened looking and interpretation of clothes worldwide through the medium of time.

---

## Focus 1a
## WEARING TIME ON THE BODY

Humankind's methods of calculating and marking the passage of time are of great antiquity. Clearly ancient understandings of time had close associations with habitual rites and magical practices. But exactly when early humans began to specifically record time with ritual body embellishments such as painted marks, incisions, and supplements, including handheld devices, is still unknown. Largely mysterious and unexplained, there are clear indications it happened in very early times of mortuary practices, but also celebrated favorable hunting achievements and significant life moments such as the onset of puberty.

The prewritten history of all cultures had ways to calculate time. Many ancient religious and mystical practices were calculated by cosmology or movements of the sun, and early civilizations had their own versions of calendars to record these observations. For instance, the ancient Mayans had a complex knowledge of mathematics. They created a number of highly accurate calendar systems, centered on their fascination with the time cycles of life, both for seasonal ceremonial purposes, and calendars to date historical and mythical events. These ritual systems impacted on clothing and body ornamentation.

An enigmatic ivory female statuette, the "Venus" of Hohle Fels, is possibly the oldest representation of a female figure known in Western Europe. Provisionally dated between 40,000 and 35,000 BCE, it is likely to have had talismanic connotations.[37] There are deliberate and deep horizontal creases above the waist, perhaps indicating tight binding or some form of body covering. It is also possible that the marks point to ritual scarification of some kind that permanently altered the body. These lines may indicate fertility, a temporal stage in a woman's life cycle, or a spiritual totem. According to Elizabeth Wayland Barber, the Lespurge "Venus" dated to about 25,000 years ago is considered more recent; she suggests that the marks indicated on the rear, hanging from the waist, are the earliest known representation of spun threads.[38]

Body markings of some kind are found on representations in many cultures, in tandem with the wide spread use of calendars. According to Birmingham University archaeologists, the Mesolithic hunter gatherer society of Warren Field, at Crathes Castle, Scotland, was sophisticated enough to produce a complex formation of twelve henges (circular earthworks) that appear to track the phases of the moon by at least 10,000 BP. It precedes the earliest known calendar in Mesopotamia by 5,000 years. The pits aligned on the midwinter sunrise, pointing to an annual "astronomic correction." These earthwork markings increased the accuracy of seasonal indicators, predicting the best times of the year for food collecting, procreating, and successful hunting. Lead archaeologist Vince Gaffney says the Scottish find "illustrates one important step towards the formal construction of time and therefore history itself."[39] Calendars such as this are likely to have had cultural significance that was translated into early body markings linked to seasonal rituals and significant life stages.

Painted embellishments on the body are shown in ancient rock art sites of various dates. The rock art at Tassili n'Ajjer, at Tanzoumaitak, southeast Algeria, contains about 15,000 individual paintings of figures, some of which are clearly female and elaborately dressed. The dates are uncertain but possibly 10,000 years old and thought to have ritualistic meaning.[40] (Figure 1.5). A vestige of this practice of placing marks on parts of the body has remained in religious or familial signs in India and elsewhere, like the red bindi on the forehead of married Hindus, or the cross of ash placed on Christian foreheads during Ash Wednesday observances.

Tattoos seem to be of more recent origin than scarification or painting but this is speculative. Ötzi, the so-called Iceman, who lived about 3400 to 3100 BCE, is possibly the first relatively firmly dated remains of a human with tattoos. Egyptians also used tattoos and, amongst other things, amulets for good luck during pregnancy. Egyptologists interpret tattoos on the mummy of Amunet, priestess of the goddess Hathor, dated to the 11th

**Figure 1.5** Two human petrograph figures from Tassili n'Ajjer, Tanzoumaitak, southeastern Algeria, possibly early Neolithic period. Articles, perhaps of leather, hang from their waists and their hair is either braided or they wear close-fitted caps that are possibly knotted or netted. Their bodies are decorated with paint. (Credit: Getty, Unesco World Heritage List, 1982).

Dynasty (2134–1991 BCE) and discovered with others south of Deir el-Bahri, as fertility symbols or tokens of magic.[41] The bodywork consists of a series of dots and dashes in an elliptical pattern of rows that cover the abdomen in the suprapubic area. Almost like nets, they are likely to have indicated expanding protection of a pregnant body.

Examples of ritual marking have continued over the centuries but only vestiges remain. Acknowledging significant acts of divination, or even an expression of cosmological beliefs or particular human milestones, many cultures have longstanding reasons for marking with incisions, tattoos, painted body decoration and special accessories. In terms of life cycles, these have acknowledged the first menstrual period, arrival of the first born, puberty, marriage, and death. In the Pacific culture of Fiji, until the arrival of Europeans, girls approaching menarche, the central event heralding puberty, began the extensive process of being tattooed (*veiqia*). Small semi-circle shapes were also tattooed, often at the corner of their mouths, when women were eligible for marriage.[42]

Prior to the arrival of missionaries in Papua New Guinea, the women of the Omie tribe of Oro Province made ornamental mulberry-paper barkcloth based, it is said, on the story of Suja, the first female ancestor. Design symbols placed on their decorated bark skirts signified to a husband that his wife's first menstruation had ceased and indicated her fertility.[43] The same patterns were sometimes tattooed onto faces of young women after initiation.

Telling the time emerged in ways other than astronomy, cosmology, the recording of solar movements, and important life events marked on the body. A wide range of time-telling devices developed, such as water clocks, fire clocks, bell-ringing and sand-trickling, to sundials and watches, some hand held.[44] In the later fifteenth century, very well-to-do Westerners started to use portable timekeeping devices as personal accessories. Increasingly small fashionable clocks, some luxurious, exquisitely painted or enamelled, attached with a chain to clothes of men and women, were kept in a pocket or attached to another accessory. For instance, a small portable clock was fitted to the hilt of a dagger for Frances I of France in 1518, and one worn in a finger ring by Elizabeth I.

As part of suites of personal accessories, luxury watches that hung from chains attached to a woman's belt were called equipage and later chatelaines. Small independent pocket watches are known from the late sixteenth century (Figure 1.6). In a 1605 portrait by Robert Peake, Lady Arabella Stuart—formally dressed in black with an

**Figure 1.6** "Portrait of Lady Arabella Stuart," in which the sitter holds open her pocket watch. Painting attributed to Robert Peake, 1605. (Credit: National Galleries Of Scotland/ Getty Images.)

exquisite lace collar plus a ruff—demonstrates her tiny handheld pocket watch by opening it to view. Ornamental items like these were less precise timekeepers than larger ones which were easier to read and more suited to manual, agrarian and later office work.

More accurate modern timekeepers, especially for men, were part of the proliferation of personal watches; first used in the sixteenth century attached to waistcoats, they were especially evident from the second half of the eighteenth century. With industrial development, they became part of the changes to industrial practices and factory labour. The historian Styles, who analysed thefts and contents of pawnbrokers' establishments in London at this time, shows watch-ownership increased amongst tradesmen and labourers of the period.[45] His view is that it was no longer the gentry who monopolized watch-wearing. Watches, particularly those with silver cases, were portable assets, a signal of prestige even for the less wealthy and, to a lesser degree, concerned with time. They were also easy to pawn.

The precise origin of the wristwatch is disputed, but by the nineteenth century, modern time was being measured daily and hourly. The range of shapes and mechanical ingenuity were extraordinary. Wristwatches for women probably originated at the same time as the invention of the bracelet watch attributed to Patek Phillipe (Geneva). In 1806, Empress Josephine of France commissioned companion bracelets for her daughter-in-law from the Parisian jeweller Nitot, one a small watch and the other a calendar dial. These were fashionable items but also seen as femininely stylish.

By the later nineteenth century, in the life of the middle to upper classes in Europe, the precise categorization of garments for activities at certain times of day, required special clothes. To these must be added specific dress for occupations in hospitals, shops, and offices. Women, newly working in city occupations, found utilitarian wristwatches a necessity. Men in the navy and military required practical and accurate watches. Omega's military model of 1913 was manufactured just before the First World War, which hastened the importance of precise timekeeping. Switzerland became the premier makers of wristwatches and were behind many design innovations. In 1972, the Swiss Hamilton Watch Company announced the first digital watch–the Pulsar Time Computer. The extremely stylish smartwatch, fitted with multiple applications, like the water-resistant, gender-neutral Apple Watch, which first came to market in 2015, is the offspring of this invention.

By the late twentieth century, many wristwatches had again became items of luxury. Flashy sports watches, used as chronometers or stopwatches, grew increasingly large and became expensive accessories for both men and women. Advertised as scientifically engineered, some brand-name wristwatches incorporated multiple facilities, such as built-in heart and sleep monitors as well as ways to count swimming laps, identify swim strokes, and monitor calorie use.

In the twenty-first century, a wristwatch is not just a functional timekeeper. They are sleek examples of advanced computation and design. If not fakes, they are the ultimate highly priced, fashionable, and high-status device for those modern consumers who are keen to lead and self-monitor a healthy life. Indeed perhaps their least important feature today is showing time on the body.

From using notation on the human body to body supplements to mark religious and secular activities, timekeeping has been evident in societies worldwide, some since remote antiquity. It has signaled moments of devotion, times of change in agricultural production, and social practices of various kinds. In particular, it marked significant moments in the life cycle of human beings, especially the onset of fertility. But the nature of timekeeping has expanded radically in modern times. The handheld mobile phone is much more than a device to tell the time.

## Focus 1b
## DRESS, VALUE, AND TIME

This focus asks how time affects the value we place on clothing, whether a garment, a piece of jewelry, or associated accessory. I am interested in the value placed on dress by the owner or buyer (private or institutional) but more importantly how its past history, its vicissitudes, and the passage of time lends it particular values. As a "woman's best friend," fine diamonds do not lose their worth. The Koh-i-Noor, an exceptionally fine white diamond (105.6 carats), is in fact considered priceless. After many changes of ownership, it has been valued over at €1 billion, and is now the property of the British Crown. Today's European would place great value on receiving a high-quality pink Argyle diamond ring or earrings, especially given that production ceased as of 2021. Men would perhaps feel the value of purchasing a pair of handmade Italian shoes or a bespoke suit made in Savile Row, London. But worth is more than price. The term is implicitly subjective in terms of both culture and individuals—it is historically and socially relative. Can the question be answered in terms that lie beyond the monetary worth? One way to do this is by a consideration of time.

Value refers to something rare, of exceptional quality of design, fabrication, color, and finesse. These qualities can be found as much in historical dress as haute couture. A garment or jewelry worn by a famous movie star, like Marilyn Monroe, garners remarkable attention at auction. The celebrated cocktail dress for the 1955 film *The Seven Year Itch* was sold in 2011 for $4.6 million. Yet the value is derived from the wearer's fame not the gown itself. The aesthetic beauty of a garment such as this nineteenth century painting by Tissot (Figure 1.7) or one designed by a couturier like

**Figure 1.7** "La Ambitieuse," painted by James Tissot 1884. (Credit: Picturenow/Universal Images Group via Getty Images.)

Balenciaga can take one's breath away. The same can be said about the valuable ornaments decorating the lavish dress of the Indian Emperor Shah Jahan, the fifth Mughal emperor, in a rare portrait by his court painter, Bichitr *c*. 1630.[46] It shows the emperor in full-skirted gown of intense orange, strings of precious stones hung round his neck and threaded into his turban.

Any suggestion that surface attractiveness, perhaps jeweled ornamentation, is the true sign of value, discounts layers of significance associated over the years with a garment's history of making and wearing, as well as unusual features, imperfection, and signs of use. In fact, what we learn from traces of alteration, repairs, patching, reuse, stains, memories, and general wear and tear, even deterioration, all fit into an independent spectrum of values. There is also personal significance or a special link to a known historical event, or the highly personal or emotional issues embedded in a worn and comforting garment. Such personal values are discussed in a moving account written with great feeling by de Perthuis about the jumper worn by her dying partner.[47] (See Chapter 7).

An assessment of items destined for a public collection, including their potential importance to a museum and its community, is likely to be quite different from that of a wearer. Significance to an organization is measured against policy criteria which can include the historic, artistic, scientific, social, and spiritual qualities for present and future generations.[48] For a museum, worth does not lie necessarily in the monetary, such as fine-quality fabrics; in fact, the reverse can be true. Often the basis of evaluation is the previous ownership, the age of a garment, links to an historical event, a named designer or a known, highly skilled craftsperson, a photographer, even its being an especially rare or unusual example. It could be its provenance, a guarantee of its origins and "paternity." Take away the temporal story or lineage and you take away much of the value. But worth can also be linked to the cultural, even personal relevance of a garment, to the extent that mass-produced items can also have special significance or provenance.

One unusual example of value is a pair of inelegant, everyday woman's buckle shoes from around the 1720s in the London Museum.[49] The shoes have been altered roughly into a new style, their uppers perhaps cut from a much earlier and finer piece of high-class embroidery, probably a bodice dating to $c$. 1625. The repurposed fabric may have been saved by a lady's maid. In the process of alteration, the shoes are shown to be "descending down the social scale," as the remaking is crude, suggesting they are for a lower class of wearer.[50] Their significance lies in the fact they are a rare surviving example of footwear from two different dates and class of wearer, found in a single pair of shoes. Everyday items of this date are unusual but being from very different sources gives these items special value and significance. In fact, a growing number of dress historians are questioning what special importance might lie in mundane garments of all kinds.

Material objects of dress, as vehicles of their own stories, are an important research method. According to Riello, material culture studies are often made up of empirical and theoretical approaches, "a mix of the modalities and dynamics through which objects take on meaning."[51] Through their materiality, objects convey their own history and value, but material qualities are derived not only from the object itself but are also subject to changing temporal opinions and alteration of external circumstances. Prown's model for analysing material culture suggests we encounter the past as firsthand evidence through historical objects, despite distortions of survival. He categorically separates the intrinsic value of an object or textile, such as rarity of materials used, from attached values such as aesthetics, or the spiritual or cultural symbolism imputed to objects by original makers and users.[52] I query this on several levels. No fabric or other material element of a garment has values that remain unaltered over time or has precisely the same enduring significance. Where does value lie if a garment has been repaired, slightly altered, or even repeatedly laundered? Further interesting questions can be asked of the value of replicas. (See Focus 8b)

An ostensibly valueless garment is a male convict shirt of cotton (Figure 1.8), c. 1819–48, held in the Hyde Park Barracks, Sydney Living Museums.[53] A second, but partial, shirt also found in the Barracks was excavated from under the museum's floorboards.[54] Only three purportedly convict shirts have survived, despite the fact that the British government transported large numbers of convicts to its penal establishments in Australia. The other shirt, found in Tasmania, is now in the National Museum of Australia, Canberra. All three were made with slightly different fabric weaves, are dissimilar in cut, and have their own histories of wear.

There has been is a tendency to believe that all convict clothing was uniformly the same in Australia, engendering greater interest in the few surviving garments than deserved. Objects associated with convicts are crowd-pleasers and have a "thrill value" in that they evoke a sense of brutality and cruelty of convict life and the horrors of existence in a colony far from home. This harsh view of convict life may be misplaced. It has recently been challenged suggesting that a great many convicts could not be identified by dress. [55]

Cotton is a fabric that has different qualities and in colonial society it had "higher-" and "lower-class" connotations. Some Indian cottons in the eighteenth to

**Figure 1.8** Convict shirt, 1819–48. Hyde Park Barracks Archaeology Collection, Sydney Living Museums. (Credit: Alex Kershaw.)

early nineteenth centuries were considered to be of high status. In colonial Australia, fine cotton fabrics were imported from India, especially during the 1820s, and used in fashionable garments for genteel women. Perhaps the intention was to mirror the quality fabric used in stylish European garments. Working men and women also dressed in cotton but the characteristics were different. So-called slop clothing, convict, and other early workers' clothing, was made in great quantities in the colonies, but in the case of convicts was never uniform. The Barracks Museum shirt has been claimed the most important artifact in historical archaeology in Australia.[56] Whilst this accords it extraordinary value, such a statement is debatable.

Between 1819 (when they opened) and 1848, an estimated 50,000 male convicts passed through the Barracks' accommodation. Convicts were given regular issues of clothing, as were ex-convicts, servants, and government workers. Those in the Barracks were issued with government shirts each year but the two shirts recovered are of different quality and made from different blue-and white-striped fabric, likely woven in Bengal, India. [57] By this time, blue-and white-striped imported Indian calico was the standard cloth for sailors and workers' shirts in Britain and for Australian convicts and workers as well. It was durable and convenient for hand-stitching. The two shirts are not dated precisely. They might have been made in the Female Factory at Parramatta, as there are records of inmates making shirts out of striped cotton for convict men $c.1840$. The one illustrated is marked on its lower left front with the BO mark (Board of Ordnance) and a Broad Arrow. These stamps do not necessarily indicate convict use, however, and are found on other government clothing.

The best preserved of the three shirts was found in a wall cavity of the Commandant's cottage at the Convict Station in Granton, a rural locality northwest of Hobart. The shirt, dated $c. 1830$, still has an undeciphered mark ("BPC") on the shoulder. Such sequestering practices are not unusual. Since the Middle Ages in the British Isles, it was a deliberate habit to hide shoes, garments (less often shirts), and other items in floors and walls of buildings, probably for talismanic protection of the site and to ward off evil spirits.[58] The habit was adopted in Australia. This shirt may never have been worn as it has no signs of wear and contains a large amount of starch. That the garment was probably deliberately hidden as a favorable omen, gives it additional importance aside from rarity.

Clothing and textiles are subject to differential rates of change or decay, their relation to time volatile and their past histories dynamic. This connection between value and time remains significant in the modern garment marketplace. New attitudes towards these attributes have emerged in luxury high fashion in the twenty-first century. Brands are deliberately creating merchandise with strategically conceived add-on qualities in order to differentiate their products from mass produced global styles. Their worth lies particularly in marketing via personalization and associated experiences. This individual quality is also acquired from the slow nature of handcrafted products. Alluding to "artisanal" or supposed "traditional" methods of production have become a marketing strategy known as "co-creation of value."[59]

The examples discussed show the ambiguity of a commodity's value, and the complex, fluctuating worth of clothing and accessories over time. They certainly exemplify the volatility of how we determine significance, both in tandem with and beyond the monetary.

# 2
# DEEP TIME: THE ORIGINS OF DRESS

Little if anything remains of body supplements, as part of the social life of humankind before written history, except for minimal painted skin decoration and ornamentation. I refer to this period as "deep time." What finds there are from this immensely distant past, have been located at numerous and widespread, unrelated archaeological sites in Africa, China, Central Asia, Europe, North America, and elsewhere. New examples are being discovered all the time, but these are often degraded or partial remains which reveal no consistent development. Even so, small fiber fragments even deteriorated are rich in significance for archaeologists and cultural historians.[1] Sometimes it's the rarity of found items, their current remote location, or difficulties of excavation that seems to increase their significance. Reliance on formal chronological dating, common to historians of dress, is not a feasible method of understanding dress in these ancient periods.

Archaeologists understandably differ in points of evaluation and dating of body covering of the deep past. Serious writing on ancient clothing has been largely their province and, like methods in any discipline, it is work in progress. The frequent development of new techniques of assessing "finds" creates exciting debate in the discipline. For scholars in other specialties, like dress history, discoveries also open up many new avenues for consideration, of which some can be contentious. For this reason, in giving attention to clothing I will suggest new perspectives on early dress and body decoration, but will not focus in detail on conflicting opinions about dates.

The question is how can a serious study of time and the extreme past offer new insights into cloth, body coverings and embellishments of early humankind? Establishing a chronological time frame for ancient remains before recorded history is not feasible at present. Nor is it the aim of my book, or that of many researchers such as anthropologist Rosemary Joyce. As briefly noted in Chapter 1, she suggests archaeology should explore objects in terms of itineraries rather than just particular locations where something is found. This will result in a sense or trace of things as historicized practices. She says this takes the emphasis away from individual objects and explores assemblages of things, the wider succession of how meanings change over time. The archaeological indication consists of what was found, as well as what was not found.[2]

Dealing with such early evidence, my book takes a somewhat different format from conventional dress history and accepts it's impossible to fully comprehend the making and meanings of ancient dress. In the case of the extreme past, my questions will include issues such as why and how did humankind come to invent tools for making textiles and garments, when did a mentality and urge to decorate arise, and when did aesthetics begin to play a part in ritual clothing. Most of these prehistoric dancing figures at Roca dels Moros, near the Catalonian village of Cogul, seem to be wearing forms of decorated "skirts," and also have shaped hairstyles or headwear. Claimed as ritualistic, their date is unclear (Figure 2.1). Perhaps ritual behavior, and the urge for the aesthetic, appeared at much the same time?

It is something of a truism to suggest the passage of time universally transforms objects—and the materials of which they are made—into rare and treasured items. This perceived rarity is questionable. So, what is it that gives so little value to some ancient body embellishment (or remains), or alternatively causes it to become overvalued? Can any "moment" in its lengthy history be considered as the date it was first created, especially if or when it is conserved and thus preserved for posterity? The proposition here is that there is no "real" or

**Figure 2.1** Dancers of Cogul, cave painting from the Roca dels Moros, near the village of Cogul in Catalonia, Spain. Post-Palaeolithic but date disputed. (Credit: Fine Art Images/Heritage Images/Getty Images.)

stable original moment in the life of any type of body covering or decoration, least of all those of the deep past.

In 1991, the rare mummified remains of a man who probably died about 3300 BCE was found in a glacier in the Ötzal Alps. It is an extraordinary, very early find of a human being, together with a complement of well-preserved clothes. Specialists have gained from this ice mummy much about materials and techniques of making early clothing including accessories, and the ways items were worn and used. Material evidence prior to the discovery of Ötzi is limited, often consisting of small clues and inferences, or almost entirely lost. Yet body coverings and embellishment existed a great deal earlier than Ötzi's clothing and tattoos.

Unfortunately, only limited evidence can be found about ancient artifacts, from representations on cave walls to incomplete representations and ornaments. Much is now forgotten, lost, imagined, or digitally recreated, and we can only postulate theories of the remote material practices of making and wearing. A consideration of how garments, textiles, and adornment as dynamic entities, were shaped by the temporal, opens new avenues of research for dress historians. Strangely, footwear is one category of wear that seems to have survived more than other body supplements, as discussed in Focus 2a.

It is understandable that views about the development of very early clothing differ as widely as they do. Problems are exacerbated by the different levels of fragility in rock art and the destructible nature of hides and fur for garments which, in their own ways, decompose more easily than materials made of vegetable matter. Clearly researchers of ancient dress have limited evidence to work with, but we can still hypothesize about who wore body coverings, how they were made and used and about how institutions over or under value the remains of body supplements and tools belonging to people of the distant past. The results will astound. A tiny fragment of semi-fossilized white cloth, wrapped around the handle of a tool made from an antler, was discovered at a Neolithic site, Çayönüu, in southeastern Turkey in 1993. An extraordinary find, it is thought to be the first prehistoric example of woven cloth in the world (not an item of dress). It has been radiocarbon-dated to 7000 years BCE, probably woven from fibers gathered from flax plants. This piece of cloth may well be the momentous sign of early co-existence with sedentary village life, the early evidence of craft-making and the move to agriculture itself.[3]

# Chronology and Alternatives

Bearing in mind the inconclusive nature of the present subject matter, I consider a number of significant points about research into ancient dress in this chapter. First, I discuss the limitations of chronology, as the main temporal organizing system. Artifacts are found in widely situated, independent sites (at places scholars today consider geographically remote) and cover vast historical spans of time. For instance, bark sandals worn by Australian Aborigines could still be found in Australia in the mid-twentieth century. (See Focus 2a) Yet the fiber structure and twined sage-brush style of ancient sandals, located at the Fort Rock Cave in Oregon, and which have some similarities, are claimed to date between 10,200 to 9,100 years BP.[4] This suggests any immediate acceptance of straightforward historical development or comparison, the mainstay of orthodox clothing history, needs to be challenged. Archaeologist Gavin Lucas suggests it is a mistake to rely universally on progressive chronological interpretations of change as they simplify the past and limit the possibilities of interpretation.[5] There are alternatives that include non-linear dynamics. These do not abandon chronology as such but replace the linear view of time and historical processes with the idea of individual temporal rhythms. Other scholars are also embracing different forms of temporality outside standard time frames. Lemire et al. demonstrate the entangled nature of global histories, the value of atypical timelines and "more capacious chronologies" that allow new questions to be asked about Indigenous, imperial, and colonial trade.[6]

The revitalized emphasis on garments as material evidence in dress history (object-based studies) needs to be taken into consideration, even in work on the deep past where "objects" are limited. In this chapter I stress the mutable nature of the topic, warning against inappropriate overtheorizing and also a simplistic attitude to context. One useful point is clearly expressed by anthropologist Lynn Meskell, writing on Egyptian archaeology, who says "there are no a priori objects"; they require human interventions and perceptions to bring them into existence. She suggests instead of worrying about precise dates of human groups and artifact making, it may be more productive to think about ancient places and objects constantly moving through new systems of meaning. This enables a constant reconsideration of their significance. The afterlives of objects or images are as important as they are themselves, and dates of finds are regularly altered by new methods of evaluation.

A further point Meskell makes is that problems coalesce around difficulties of dating items, although methods of investigation are becoming more sophisticated. Serendipitous discoveries, some alongside disparate types of remains, make it almost impossible to find points of social or cultural connection. Temporal interactions between materials (items or objects) and materiality (engagement with the wider world) remain inconclusive.[7]

We must certainly review the afterlives of ancient garments and ornamentation. They may have been found in situ but could have been far from points of making, some perhaps traded or more recently held in current holding places such as museums. Orchestrated into displays individually or thematically, examples of ancient body supplements can say more our about current tastes and beliefs about the past than the supposed life of original artifacts. Indications of the earliest use of body wrappings and later textiles used in prewritten history are undergoing constant reassessment and must be regarded as signs of many pasts. This uncertainty contributes to the overall intentions of my book, which are to show how the focus on time opens up challenging new ideas about dress and fashion, and de-emphasizes a historically linear approach to these topics. What evidence of very early body covering exists, suggests body painting, skins, woven fabric—primarily wild flax—and beadwork emerged at different places and at different times as opposed to chronologically.

# How Old is the Past?

Few historians of dress have attempted to study the clothes of early humankind, perhaps because evidence is difficult to find. Most has been left for archaeologists to research. Archaeological discoveries to date have not provided any substantiated proof of how body supplements and modifications differentially evolved in deep time, or provided any comparative accounts other than in extremely broad terms. In any case, this search for origins and evolution may not be the most productive way to study clothing. So, where should any historical account of time and dress begin?

Anthropologist Tim Ingold suggests determining how to define how old the past may be, or asking the age of an ancient "preserved" item, is not the same as describing something that has "persisted" and still does persist, in some form or another.[8] This is a challenge to accepted chronology. But the concept is useful, as it allows consideration of items in the present to provide a view into the past, rather than as a progressive development from a hypothetical beginning. The advantages of looking for similarities in history from objects in the present is an important aspect of the study of time and dress. For instance, the wearing of strings of beads, one of the most common forms of ornamentation we know today, is little different from similar artifacts in use in extreme antiquity. As beads were used for trading, and not always for personal adornment, interesting questions arise about use of ostensibly similar artifacts.

Previously, studies about the beginning of clothes-wearing have been minimal and part of lengthier and popular chronologies of dress.[9] Something of an exception is François Boucher's ambitious and richly illustrated *20,000 Years of Fashion: The History of Costume and Personal Adornment* (1965). This is a book written over 50 years ago, almost entirely about European dress, especially fashion. Yet the sections on "Prehistoric Costume," followed by "Costume in the Ancient East," "Crete and its Costume" and a further section on dress in "The Mediterranean Countries" are helpful. These chapters put forward the important fact that very early dress is found at uneven stages of complexity, but also with surprising similarities. Boucher suggests temporal disparities of dress occurred between those living in advanced civilizations, for instance during the Bronze Age and those of the contemporary Stone Age in the north of Europe, indicating, as one would expect climate and geography set limits on the kinds of clothing made and worn.

It is archaeologists who have shown how problematic time is in respect of their discipline. More generally, what constitutes a definition of the "past" is under consideration by some and a number of revisionist ideas have been circulated. Stella Souvatzi (a specialist in Neolithic Greece and the theory of archaeology and anthropology) suggests, as do others, archaeology is not just about chronology *per se* or even the long term, positing the acceptance of many different rhythms of time in findings.[10] She argues that a strength of archaeology is its access to multiple scales of space at much the same time, so it allows the possibility of considering different rates of social relations and their interlinkages.[11]

For instance, the belief we can start at some fixed "beginning" of clothing is an unsatisfactory understanding of the temporal complexities of the topic. The idea of slowness of change (the opposite of fashion's constant novelty), and multiple temporalities that may exist concurrently in one area and also worldwide, are both helpful in any study of early clothing. Slow, temporal scales of life obviously existed in ancient times and clearly different interpretative frameworks can be applied to "slowness" as a feature of dress in the past.

We are unlikely to discover precisely when different stages of human social development brought about singular changes to body coverings. Speculation on different climates and geographical resources are of course crucial to assessing past remains of clothes and their meanings. It is still unclear when the earliest links between body coverings and environmental conditions became historically meaningful, although the climatic conditions of the Ice Ages, discussed later in the chapter, are regarded as crucial. One problem is that archaeologists may deal with multiple historical periods clustered in one area, or across quite disparate unrelated sites. In deep time, we are dealing with extraordinarily complex temporalities, as well as constantly shifting grounds of assessment. A special "find" to one researcher may not be so to others. The serendipity of archaeological discoveries and the paucity of precisely datable excavated artifacts is a major obstacle to begin understanding the time frame of early clothing let alone trying to determine the age of the past. Forensic archaeologists and anthropologists, now using techniques such as DNA and MRI testing and profiling to tackle these tricky questions, are achieving outstanding results.

# Finds

As presently understood, evidence of prehistoric ornamentation and body supplements, have been found at widespread locations from Africa, to Europe,

Asia and more. Current opinions seem to show the decorated body and later protective clothing emerged at different historical moments across a wide range of global sites and cultures and dating excavated remains of any prehistoric "find," in relation to body supplements, is complex and inexact. The introduction of new technologies in disparate places has regularly undermined supposedly firm dates, showing much dating is inherently unstable.

An archaeological "find" in dress terms has seldom acquired an incontrovertible certainty of date, or an absolute socio-cultural meaning. Nor can a single discovery, or a few examples, be deemed to represent an entire or even partial cultural picture of wearing. For instance, the meaning of a curious fragmentary mammoth ivory artifact, known as the "Venus" of Brassempouy, which has coarse decorative marks on her head—perhaps a hood?—is unclear. It is a good example of the difficulties of dating ancient artifacts, one suggestion being that it is 36,000–25,000 years BCE (Figure 2.2). A more general date has been ascribed to it, however.

Ingold asks the question what is the date of an artifact. Is it when its source materials were made or gathered (like shells); when and how the article was

**Figure 2.2** "Venus" of Brassempouy, a mammoth-ivory figurine with a design indicating hair or some form of head covering. Upper Palaeolithic period. (Credit: DEA / G. DAGLI ORTI/De Agostini via Getty Images.)

changed or used differently over time; what was the moment when it was completed, or when it was found? [12] Dealing with processes not the finite is important, so enquiries about "the first of" an artifact should be less concerned with origins and more about the mutability of material forms.

As so little is known of the circumstances of found items, they can be given disproportionate and subjective attention by both scholars and the public. According to Meskell: "The past's materiality assumes supra-human importance and meaning because it transcends our own individual lives and histories."[13] She is writing about ancient Egyptian artifacts which have particularly appealing appearances, but if we consider less striking ancient fragments of (say) European dress, this may be less convincing. Yet excavations of all ancient pieces of dress, and the sense of mystery surrounding finding the "rare," certainly stimulate interest. Why so? Perhaps we feel clothes embody the spirit of those who wore them, and by looking at surviving artifacts of the distant past we come close to understanding something of the reality of our human ancestry.

Belief systems of early humans developed gradually and different social groups imbued some items of ornamentation, and not others, with prestige and hierarchical significance. If we consider Kalahari Bushmen, San, Saan, or Basarwa peoples, generic terms for Indigenous hunter-gatherer groups, the various Khoesān-speaking Indigenous occupants of Southern Africa are made up of multiple clans and linguistic groups.[14] Subtle differences in practices of adornment, and material use on the body, across different and very small social groups like these, and their associated symbolism, makes us alert to the possibility of the extraordinarily complex problems of dating finds from small groups in the deep past.

It is inevitable any discussion of dress and time is likely to privilege or speculate about what we can call "the earliest" of any form of apparel. When archaeologists claim to discover the "oldest" known shirt or "oldest" shoe, it is always newsworthy. (See Focus 2a) Yet to claim the origins of any dress is inevitably problematic and the "oldest" may not remain so for long. When and why humans first began to cover and decorate their bodies is a tantalizing question and at present can't be answered.

# Technologies

Our knowledge of body ornamentation in ancient times is limited and the pace of developing early tools like needles for sewing and looms for woven products would have been laborious. Styles of needles did vary according to site. Could different designs or fabrics have needed slightly different tools and might independent groups have worn dissimilar clothing? Some substantial evidence has been found regarding the making of ancient textiles by Olga Soffer. She has done in-depth work on Upper Palaeolithic plant-based nets, basketry, and plain and twined woven items.[15] Her very detailed work suggests that humans of this time made and probably wore a great variety of fabrics, "including twined wear and non-heddle-loom-woven plain weaves."[16] She has also made deductions from pseudomorphs or impressions on clay, and undertaken close studies of tools such as spinning whorls. Her research shows impressions of wool or plant fiber (some woven), and even the chemical breakdown of textiles on artifacts may lead to possible confirmation of the geographical origins of fibers.

Puzzling issues include where and when did humans begin to twine or twist fibers of animal hair or plants into yarn, or into string to make nets? Who found out that to overlap fibrous threads—a warp and a weft—on a simple loom could make basic textiles? Or when were threads or cord intertwined and twisted over to make sprang, a kind of open mesh? These are some of the great mysteries of the deep past. Of great interest is the view of archaeologist Elizabeth W. J. Barber, who strongly suggests the textile industry is older than pottery-making and perhaps even agriculture.[17]

What is fascinating is that despite the rarity of actual clothing and cloth, archaeological evidence about the tools for making garments is far more common than items of dress, and sometimes much older than items of historic clothing itself. This provides a significant and challenging new way to approach early dress history, namely via the technologies of making itself. Dating of finds can be based on "use-wear" found on tools and by identifying different tools for uses on different materials and perhaps on forms of clothing worn.[18]

In 2004, at Neumark-Nord, in the foothills of the Harz Mountains (near Leipzig, Germany), at a middle Paleolithic site dated more than 100,000 years old, a sharp flint blade was discovered in sediment. Attached to it at the top was a tiny, concentrated organic black mass found to contain oak tannin. Archaeologist Dietrich Mania thinks it indicates that tannin was known to these people and likely used to treat leather, perhaps for clothing and footwear.[19] He suggests this find is perhaps the oldest example we have of intelligently planned human behavior that uses two different technological processes. While this is a startling proposition, it is possible that minute indicators of this kind can point to the reality of complex historical scenarios at very early periods.

There is another issue that can be canvassed, one that challenges progressive ideas about dress. For instance, in a French cave used by Neanderthals 51,000 years ago, archaeologists suggest that the special bone lissoir tools of deer ribs (which smooth, soften, and make leather impermeable and pliable) found there, were chosen deliberately by early humans for these purposes.[20] Researchers found the first large piece of a lissoir at a cave called Pech de l'Azé I (First Phase), a complex of Middle and Lower Palaeolithic sites located on a tributary of the Dordogne Valley in southwest France. These seem to be the oldest specialized tools used in Europe in a Neanderthal context. The design is in fact consistent with the tools used by specialist leather workers in the twenty-first century. The similarity with the skills and tools of modern humans may be due to a sign of abilities not generally attributed to Neanderthals, or simply that their design could not be improved.

# Ornamentation, Ritual, and Aesthetics

There are undoubtedly many reasons why people covered and adorned the naked body. These range from the basic needs of warmth and protection, to exchanges of valuables in the case of trade beads, and more ritualistic purposes. Decorating skin for ritual seems to have emerged extremely early as humans discovered ways to make paint with raw materials such as ochre, commonly used in association with burial rites. Many (if not most) clothed figures and early body decoration depicted in rock paintings remain, as yet, indecipherable in dress terms. Surprisingly little is known about tattoos and their meanings. Prehistoric tattoo tools of obsidian glass were used in the South Pacific, about 3,000 years ago.[21] But the first firm evidence of the practice is on the body of Ötzi is 3250 BCE. Ciphers like these have never been translated and their exact purposes remain unknown.

Hundreds of pigments in a range of colors—brown, red, yellow, purple, blue-black, and pink, and not all local—have been found in sediment at the Twin Rivers Cave in Zambia, southern Africa. Himmelfarb, in an article on body painting, claims that as early as 400,000 years ago, pigment pieces were ground to make a powder, indicating systematic processing over a long period.[22] The difficulties of grinding suggest it was the colors that mattered, and they were probably used for ritual body painting, perhaps prior to the use of full corporeal coverings. Symbolic body paint may have been linked to individual groups who shared understanding of their meanings. These symbolic signs may have been among the earliest indications of cognitive abilities between distinctive groups of humans who had developed the ability to interact. Answers to questions like these seem to suggest adornment as a mix of minimal evidence and speculation.

A significant question that arises out of my research is when and why did a sense of aesthetics emerge in the lives of early peoples? Beads, buttons, and other forms of accessories such as necklaces and pendants are extraordinarily ancient forms of body adornment found widely dispersed geographically across the world. Welters and Lillethun are keen to see early signs of a "fashion impulse" here but funerary and other symbolic motives cannot be ruled out. Also, a matter of concern is whether beads or other decorations can be called clothing *per se*, as many seem to have had value as cultural exchange. Gift-giving systems, a way to improve social and economic relationships, cannot be ruled out.

Perforated marine shells, Nassarius gibbosulus (indicating stringing), were found at Skhūl in Israel dating back perhaps 135,000 to 100,000 years ago and have also been discovered at Oued Djebbana in Algeria, dating to 100,000 to 90,000 years ago (the site was about 200km from the sea at the time).[23] Both sets of shells were probably selected deliberately. Transported back to the home site, they may have been used as trade goods; if perforated, they could be signs of personal status. Beads found at the Grotte des Pigeons, Taforalt (an ancient cave near Morocco), a site also some distance from the sea, are estimated to be between 91,500 to 73,400 years old. They have perforations and some have residues of red ochre. Some skeletons there have post mortem cuts and are covered with plentiful ochre, reinforcing the supposition this was a funerary site. But was color used sometimes for aesthetic purposes as well? A particularly unusual skull of a young man of status, unearthed from a grave in the Arene Candide Cave, near Finale Ligure, Italy, and dated to the Late Stone Age, has what looks like a large head covering made entirely of small shells (Figure 2.3). Could this covering have had a double purpose?

The same question might be asked about the following. At the prehistoric archaeological site at the town of Krapina in northern Croatia, also known as

**Figure 2.3** Skeleton of a prehistoric young man wearing a cap of shells and a shell necklace. Arene Candide Cave near Finale Ligure, Liguria, Italy. The site was used over long periods of time from the late Stone Age. (Credit: Gustavo Tomsich/CORBIS/Corbis via Getty Images.)

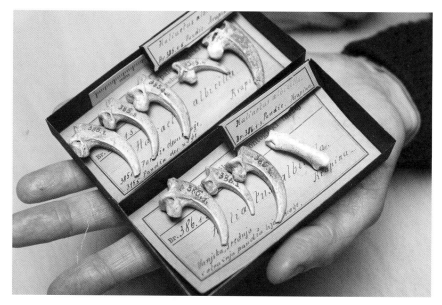

**Figure 2.4** Eight white-tailed eagle talons and a phalanx found at an archaeological site in Krapina in 2015. These Neolithic remains are now regarded as some of humankind's earliest known body supplements (jewelry). They are held in the Zagreb National Museum, Croatia. (Credit: STR/AFP via Getty Images.)

Hušnjakovo brdo (Croatian for "hill"), was located one of the largest and oldest collections of body supplements on record dated 130,000 years BP. In 2015, eight talons from the white-tailed eagle (Figure 2.4) were found here. They have no drilled holes but there are cut marks, made presumably when the talons were severed from the birds' legs; these have then been smoothed over and some burnished, perhaps tied or bound and then worn. Wing bones bearing large feathers were also cut through. Callaway, a scientist, and senior contributor to the magazine *Nature,* sees this as clear evidence that Neanderthals manipulated the claws for use as "jewelry," perhaps a necklace or pendant.[24] Ritual connections between body and ornaments certainly cannot be ruled out. In a number of geographically widespread sites, including those in Gibraltar, there is also evidence people decorated themselves with black feathers, most likely for ritual reasons. These were cut from raptor, eagle, falcon, and corvid bird remains. The preference for black and dark colored feathers has not yet been explained.

# Covering the Body—Clothing

Physical examples of body coverings (clothes) before the Pleistocene period (generally 2,000,000 to 10,000 years ago), have seemingly not survived.[25] As only later fragments of actual ancient clothing now exist, archaeologists have turned to rock art, carved figurines, associated tools, and pseudomorphs in order to develop an understanding of early dress and textiles. Representations of figures wearing some kind of body supplement are extremely rare and their meanings unclear. A small carved female figurine of mammoth ivory found in southwest Germany, the so-called "Venus" of Hohle Fels with inconclusive striations, perhaps indications of dress, was made at least 35,000 years ago.[26] (See Focus 1a) To date, this woman represents the oldest three-dimensional figure yet discovered. Her social function is not known.

The Ice Ages, which began 2.4 million years ago and lasted until 11,500 years ago, with interglacial periods in between, caused a major need for portable body coverings. Biologist David Reed claims humans were using some form of warm and simple body coverings (probably of fur), perhaps 170,000 years ago, long after body hair was lost, as they moved out of Africa to increasingly cold climates.[27] This information is based on temperature estimates in ice core studies, when Europe and other places experienced a period of increasingly cold weather. Significant evidence of assigning these dates is also drawn in part from the DNA of preserved body lice (Pediculus humanus humanus), which live on clothing, but not head or pubic lice from which they evolved.

Australian archaeologist Ian Gilligan, who has done extensive research on early body coverings and related tools, continues to argue for a two-stage thermal model in his recent book, explaining the origin of prehistoric human coverings and subscribing to the clothing lice theory.[28] Neanderthals were vigorous hunters of the mammoths, bears, and deer that shared their environment. At some point, they learned how to use hides to keep warm and dry. But these coverings were apparently inadequate for really cold extremes, although when the weather warmed, they were not needed. Evidence for this comes from the disappearance of hide-scraper tools in warm periods and their later reintroduction.

Gilligan hypothesizes there were two basic forms of early clothing. The first was draped loosely over the body and made of thick furry hides, which he calls "simple" but insufficient for total body warmth. The second form, which he terms "complex," appeared in the coldest stages of the last Ice Age. Modern humans were more precocious and behaviorally adaptive, and as they moved into the harsh areas of Alaska and the Arctic Circle, they required warmer clothing. They developed tools like hide-cutting blades, piercing awls, and needles for producing multi-layered, fitted and functional garments more able to survive the cold. These fitted clothes, consisting of numerous layers, enclosed the body and limbs, trapping in the warmth.

It is significant that, in lieu of any surviving clothes, Gilligan (as noted) based his theory partly on the indirect evidence of signs of "use-wear" on tools, which differed across clothing types. In his view, after the last Ice Age and in temperate or tropical areas, new tools were invented to weave textiles. These became the preferred option for clothes, as they allowed the air to circulate. His proposition is that it was the production of fiber for clothing that stimulated the change from hunter-gathering to agriculture.[29] Once complex clothing was established—he claims but does not prove convincingly—the decorative aspects of body ornamentation, such as painted symbols, beads, and shells, were transferred to clothes.

# Keeping Places: Museums

It is important to think critically when considering the place of ancient surviving items of body modifications, as these material objects of the past are treasured, perhaps even over-memorialized when displayed to the public. One question is whether ancient artifacts linked to dress have indeed been overvalued or given unsuitable status in museums and other collections? Significant issues have arisen when artifacts are removed from the place where they are found, and taken into the custody of museums and other kinds of collection.

Importance given to archaeological remains, and the sense of awe that surrounds some objects of the past, is partly a cultural decision and resides with those who prioritize items to collect and display to the public. So, we are perhaps on firmer ground, accounting for the afterlives of dress, when it enters an institutional keeping place. But the past is not neutral. Rather, it is valued in a variety of ways by the present, and partial objects can even enhance fascination with "finds" from the past.

There is of course a historiography of museum display which accounts for different ways objects are shown. To engage modern viewers, sensationalism is commonly used to display material artifacts of ancient times. How flawed is our understanding of the past if only serendipitous discoveries are those chosen for display? Ötzi is a fascinating example of how an ancient dressed body, discovered by accident, has been acclaimed, replicated, and now stands as an icon of a clothed person of the past—an archaeological celebrity.

In the twenty-first century, questions need to be asked about digitization and the past. Has the past now become the present? Do conservators using X-rays and MRI scans have special evidential powers via technology to expose a supposed original which seems to have transcended time? Does the scanning of objects like mummies—a kind of digital unwrapping—inadvertently invade the privacy that was accorded to the original? How can something be classified as unrepresentative, or falsely made to seem representative, when dealing with the remote past?

In terms of museum collections, another issue of concern is whether archaeological finds are even part of the history of dress. If they are located in a museum collection, it is likely they are sequestered in a section termed Anthropology or Ethnography. They are thus severed from the fluid networks that categorize the temporal history of dress and are subject to assessment characteristic of other methods of research. Whilst these likely open up fascinating new ways of consideration, it also places a disquieting barrier between "them and us" in methods by which body supplements and modifications are analysed.

Unlocking the nature of garments of early humans is extremely complex, not least because so little survives. It is only what is found that is possible to know. If there is no absolute "beginning," there can only be provisional accounts of early dress, and certainly not based on a timeline of archaeological evidence. In fact, Ingold challenges the core concept of an "archaeological record." He suggests archaeology and anthropology should replace the question of how old things are, with what he calls an ephemeral "pastness."[30] Here objects of the past are never "the original one" but are "deposited at successive moments" and tell their own different stories, while time itself moves forward in a different trajectory.

In the search for meanings, one suggestion I make in this book is that we might analyse garments, or trace clothing itineraries, back from the present to the past. Perhaps we would then be in a better position to ask more particular questions about when humankind began to consistently ornament their bodies with ochres, chalk, and charcoal, and make and wear bead neckwear and body coverings. While there is a tantalizing prospect of asking such a question, there is at present no likelihood of a clear answer.

## Focus 2a
# THE SIGNIFICANCE OF ANCIENT FOOTWEAR

This Focus section considers problems associated with dating and understanding particularly intriguing items of ancient footwear such as this shoe (Figure 2.5). Shoes and sandals of the distant past, many in poor condition and discovered in geographically isolated areas of the world, have been found in considerable numbers, especially in caves. Historians believe footwear from the deep past was of practical use but could also have had symbolic meanings. Assessing use and meanings of such ancient artifacts is problematic. Lacking associated footprints and other evidence, it is presently not possible to make links between a wearer's activities and any precise ritual practices. Even so, surviving foot coverings give potential insight into the lives of people before recorded history.

The item claimed as the world's earliest known leather shoe is a single, rare and quite mysterious shoe (not a pair) found in the Areni-1 Cave, in Armenia's Vayots Dzor province, which is close to the border with Iran and Turkey. Shaped for the right foot, it is made of a single piece of tanned cowhide with laces.[31] It has been radiocarbon-dated to 3630–3370 cal BC.[32] It was found upside down, filled with grass, beneath a broken

**Figure 2.5** An ancient single-skin leather moccasin-type shoe excavated by the Areni-1 Cave Consortium, Vayots Dzor Province, Armenia. Dated to *c*. 3630– 3370 cal BCE. Credit: Boris Gasparyan (DAVIT HAKOBYAN/AFP via Getty Images.)

ceramic vessel. Its significance seems greater than its proposed date.[33] To suggest this is the world's "oldest known" shoe is sadly fraught with problems. Being labeled "the first of" or "oldest" is often to attribute only short-lived fame to an artifact. Any study of dress and time needs to critically and carefully assess statements such as this. The "oldest" can probably never remain so. The archaeologist Boris Gasparyan and colleagues have discovered fragments of even earlier shoe segments and leather artifacts in Armenia, one of them dated to 4300 to 4000 cal BC.[34]

The Armenian cave site is complex and was divided into areas for habitation, working, and ritual respectively, including space for burial rites. Amongst other discoveries, the shoe survived because the cave's cold, dry climatic conditions were suited to preservation. It is a so-called "simple" shoe, of one piece of leather with no sole. It has some heel wear but no treads to indicate where it was worn. It was located near animal remains: the scapula of a red deer and two horns of an adult wild goat. A fish vertebra was on top of the pot. Three pots were found in the cave, each containing the skull of a person aged between eight and eighteen, two men one female. Exactly why a single shoe was in the cave, or what the real purpose was, has not been satisfactorily explained.

The Armenian shoe may have been soaked, then cut and fitted around a wearer's foot, using the latter as its last. It is stuffed with loose grass (normally for insulation) but here the purpose is unclear; perhaps it was functioning as a shoe tree? In the variable climate and context of the area where it was found, warmth might have been an issue, although even soft shoes kept out the cold to some extent. But if it were a ritual object, perhaps it was important to keep the shape of the shoe over time. Caves preserve items like leather reasonably well and given its location in a cave site, the position of the shoe and the vessel could indicate ritual purposes.

Not only does this early shoe excite because of its rarity, but the design has remarkable affinity with far more recent examples. It has similarities to moccasins, the soft leather shoes worn by Indigenous North Americans. The moccasin—or *makasin*—is a Powhatan word for shoe in the Algonquian language. These have continued to be made of a piece of leather and no heel and, over the years and with minor design modifications, are found all over the world. One example is the Irish *pampootie*, a traditional man's shoe, made from a single piece of untanned cowhide folded around the foot and stitched together.[35]

Some Aboriginal Indigenous people in the fairly recent past have been seen to place their feet inside a newly killed rabbit, which took the form of a wraparound skin forming a type of moccasin. All this suggests versions of the moccasin have been worn for thousands of years, over wide and diverse regions and probably independently invented. Modern high-class brands still make expensive loafers and shoes based on this original design.

Speculation about the symbolism of shoes both of the distant past and more recently allows us to explore questions of time in relation to ritual use and magic. A pair of empty shoes, and even one shoe, can call up deep-seated and powerful issues of remembrance and loss. Worn shoes tend to follow the unique physical shape of the wearer but also make other subtle, even emotional, connections with the owner or event. Grouped in large numbers, they are used as tokens of remembrance as well as folklore, magic and superstition.[36] Shoes with no wear or just scuff marks remain a mystery. Shoes and sandals can signal good luck, as well as loss, and also be socio-cultural keepsakes, like a baby's first shoe, or even a talisman when hanging outside temples as in Japan. They are the link between a tangible wearable object and intangible emotion, between the natural and the essence of the supernatural world.[37] The connection between the worldly and the spiritual may be central to many ancient shoes, as some have been included with other grave goods.

Anthropologists see the history of sandals as different from shoes, and for the most part they are dated earlier than surviving shoes. They are perhaps the oldest directly dated remains of human footwear found, and much earlier than the Armenian shoe. It is likely leather footwear with dried grass stuffing became necessary for warmth when the climate began to cool, but not necessary when the weather was warmer, although there are suggestions sandals were stuffed with grass in cold weather. Perhaps this form of footwear was protection for hunter gatherers traversing reasonably long distances across rough terrain, or guarding against desert heat or cold.

Ancient sandals survive in caves in the US in considerable numbers, but mostly in poor condition. These woven fiber sandals have been found, not all in pairs, at several archaic sites in southwest North America; several dozen have been recovered at the Fort Rock Cave site in southeast Oregon and in northern Nevada. Sandals for children as well as adults were excavated. Radiocarbon-dating shows the so called Fort Rock-style sandals can be roughly dated between 10,500 to 9200 cal BP.[38] They are made of shredded twined sagebrush bark (weft fibers twisted around warps), with a flat, close-twined sole that flips over to make the closed toe flap. Thongs on the sandal would have been wrapped around the ankle and then fastened securely. Fort Rock sandals disappear from the archaeological record of the Northern Great Basin about 9,300 years ago.[39]

Other styles of Neolithic fiber sandals show the varied nature of prehistoric footwear in sites around the world. The Arnold Research Cave in central Missouri has a long documented sequence of ancient shoe construction, beginning perhaps as early as 8300 cal BP. Much further afield, the burial site known as The Cave of the Warrior in the Judean Desert, which includes grave goods, has leather sandals stained with red ochre, dated to about 6,000 years ago.[40]

Scholars in Australia regard the making and wearing of shoes by First Nations peoples in ancient times as rare, and confined mainly to the west and northwest of the continent. Few examples remain and little is known of their uses. Oral history suggests they were used to walk over rocky ground, to help feet heal after injury, to guard against the heat of desert sand, and for sorcery. The various types include shoes of possum and kangaroo-rat skin, bark sandals, rabbit-skin moccasins, and *kadaitcha* shoes (used by sorcerers), with emu feather soles. The latter were in more widespread use than other shoes.[41]

A few Aboriginal sandals found in recent times seem similar in type to ancient North American footwear and appear to be part of the continuity of ancient conventions well into the twentieth century. Bark sandals of the Pintubi people from the Warburton Ranges, Gibson Desert, Western Australia, made from the *Crotalaria* bush, seem extraordinarily similar to Fort Rock-style sandals, and were still in use in the 1970s (Figure 2.6).[42]

Aside from the remains of footwear, ancient human footprints have been preserved at sites in some parts of the world, confirming the unique features of a wearer's foot placements and walking gait if not actual garments. In Australia, where remains of

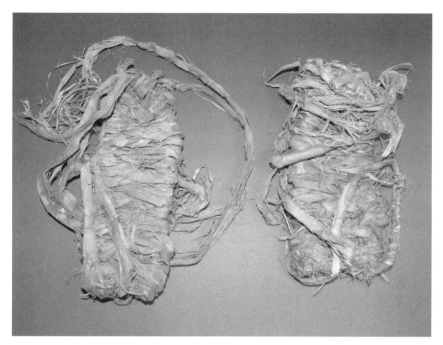

**Figure 2.6** Bark sandals made by Pintubi people from the Warburton Ranges, Gibson Desert, Western Australia. (Credit: Kim Akerman.)

footwear are negligible, about 450 extraordinary footprints were found in clay at Willandra Lakes World Heritage Area, dated to between 19,000–23,000 years ago, the largest number surviving from the Pleistocene era. There appear to be no shoe prints but there are signs of people walking in a line, and running, as well as children's prints.[43]

Footwear of the deep past has been excavated in geographically different regions around the world. Some shoes and sandals seem to have survived because they served some special—but unknown—purpose beyond the practical. Dating these garments with any degree of certainty is difficult, yet they contribute to our cultural understanding of how foot coverings were made over time. Although only individual footprints were discovered at Willandra, these marks contribute further to our understanding of the nature of human movement. Some shoe styles are practical while others have ritual significance, clearly so in the case of the Armenian example. Echoes of the original designs of early shoes and sandals have remained in some form or another until the present day. Although materially different, these designs have had lasting efficacy. Of perhaps greatest interest is that footwear has been used for ritual and magical purposes from prewritten history until the present. Speculation about early ritual meanings in particular, however, continues.

## Focus 2b
## MYSTERY! AN EGYPTIAN GARMENT

A particular kind of awe is felt in the presence of articles of ancient clothing, especially those of a civilization as fascinating as ancient Egypt. Time is an unsettling but important method of assessing garments; what is old today is older tomorrow, but it was also, at some point in time, a *new* piece of clothing. The so-called Tarkhan "dress" (Figure 2.7), now in the Petrie Museum of Egyptian Archaeology, University College, London, is an extremely enigmatic garment and its purpose remains somewhat unclear.[44] To an untrained eye, an ancient surviving handmade garment of decayed linen is a curiosity and of considerable rarity. Difficult to assess, it is claimed as the world's oldest woven cut-and-shaped garment, and generally considered to be a woman's garment.[45]

Found in an Egyptian tomb, the date of its making is slightly contentious. Opinion based on radiocarbon-dating in 2015 places it 95% likely to have been created between 3482 and 3102 BCE.[46] Any further testing would have had to be on a reasonably large

**Figure 2.7** Tarkan "dress." Egyptian, *c*. 3482–3102 BCE. (Credit: Petrie Museum of Egyptian Archaeology, University College, London.)

piece of the "dress" fabric, which would harm the fragile garment. That said, the date has been queried recently and may be earlier than thought. Describing the artifact as a "dress" may also be wide of the mark.

Relatively little is known of precisely how ancient Egyptians made and wore clothes. This garment is relatively small, with a V-neckline, and made from three pieces of hand-woven linen. One tubular piece originally formed the body (joined down one side with a fringe) and two pieces were used for sleeves. The lower part of the garment is missing; indeed, it was found in very poor condition, during an excavation over two seasons (1911 and 1913) by Egyptologist Flinders Petrie at the Tarkhan site, an Early Dynastic necropolis about 50km south of Cairo. He found it by chance in a 1st Dynasty *mastaba* (a rectangular tomb with sloping sides) amongst a pile of decayed linen rags and other artifacts, although the tomb had been ransacked in ancient times.

Considered of little worth, it was packed away with other finds and sent back to London for further analysis. Archaeologists seem at first to have dismissed the significance of the bundle but Petrie, who preserved all good evidence of artifacts, believed he could throw light on ancient Egyptian daily life. He felt the linens should be saved. The garment lay unidentified amongst other textiles the until 1977, when the bundle was sent for conservation.

The story of the casual treatment of a "soft" garment like this gives insight into the low esteem in which many historical textiles have previously been regarded, in comparison with artifacts of stone, pottery, or timber. It also shows how an artifact's reputation can change from being a rotting remnant to being declared the oldest surviving "complex" woven garment in the world. As previously noted, the date of the "dress" has only fairly recently been almost certainly confirmed. Yet even comparison with other associated artifacts from the Tarkhan site has not fully reassured archaeologists, who are still a little unsure of precisely when it was made. Fixation with the date of ancient clothing is interesting for it is a defining feature which may raise, or perhaps alter, conceptions of significance.

The Tarkhan garment raises a number of questions, not least being the status of the wearer. The cloth is a natural pale gray with an irregular stripe, which complements the neatly knife-pleated sleeves and bodice area. The pleats are horizontal on the shoulder and continue down the arm, yet look vertical. The missing part of the garment appears to have been cut off roughly, so we cannot tell whether it was a full-length or short garment originally. Its existing dimensions suggest it fitted a young teenager or a slim woman. It was originally found turned inside out.[47] There were creases at the elbows and under the armpits, which suggests it had been worn, or perhaps washed, but not turned the correct way around. Yet why was it found in a tomb?

Similar garments, but full length, depicted on relief stone slabs together with several other textile garments, have been found as offerings in tombs. Were they indicators of age, status, or rank, or for specific occasions? Were they worn by the elite or lower in rank? Petrie found two further complete garments of similar fabric elsewhere, but they were so excessively long and thin he felt they were expressly grave goods, but this is far from certain. The latter were part of a group of nine garments piled on top of a woman in her coffin.[48] A further question is, if these garments *had* been worn, what did they mean? Also why were they sometimes placed on top of corpses in coffins, and precisely how were they made? Were they mortuary goods?

They have been described variously as dresses, tunics, or shirts. As they are of great age and of unknown use, it is not surprising the terms are so varied, but it certainly alerts us to the temporal nature of dress terminology and its role in interpreting or misunderstanding the use of historic garments. And it is not certain how the pleating was accomplished. Some suggestions include its being woven in situ, perhaps dampened and rapidly dried, or the use of chemical fixtures or pleating boards.[49] It has been proposed that the weft is stubbed (irregular size), and the pleated effect could be due to "cramming and spacing" the warp.[50]

It is interesting that pleated garments are not all that rare and a number of similar examples were excavated between 1902–03 from a site about 69km south of Cairo. Now on display in the Museum of Fine Arts, Boston, they are full length and pleated, vertically on the lower part and the sleeves, but the pleats actually look horizontal as the sleeve turns over the shoulder. Other full-length examples are pleated horizontally. The purpose of this pleating is not clear and there are no suppositions at this stage. They would be too long for a woman even six feet tall, which adds further to their rather mysterious nature.[51]

The idea that they were made especially for burial purposes or shrouds has been discounted, as they show signs of wear. As noted, they, like other similar artifacts, do not evidence any particular social status, and similar dress has been painted on the walls of tombs. Troubling issues arise here in relation to the wearing of early Egyptian dress. Firstly, the garments' unusual sizes of garments, as well as signs of wear, present unresolved issues of being worn. Wear and tear give a symbolic aura of "the old" and encourages conjectures (sometimes erroneous), about use in ancient times, as well as a garment's survival. How do we assess these often isolated and deteriorated garments? Has archaeology, as a discipline, imposed its methods and expectations on what has been chosen for survival?

More fascinating is the suggestion that there were "two realities" in ancient Egypt.[52] The first was one of "action" delineating everyday "real" history, including wearing of actual clothes. The second, based on a theological principle, was "immutable ideological time," a religious canon governing representation. To simplify, this meant painted or carved clothing was governed by strict rules that did not match actual clothing. For instance, conventions for dress were applied to the fine, detailed depictions of body

**Figure 2.8** The scribe Menna and family fishing and fowling in the marshes of the Nile, Tomb of Menna, Luxor, Thebes, 18th Dynasty, New Kingdom, Egypt. (Credit: DeAgostini/ Getty Images.)

supplements that we see here (Figure 2.8). It was a form of stereotyping of the look of dressed people appropriate for certain kinds of mortuary representations.

Egyptian art and archaeology occupy a special iconic place in the imagination of the West. The public regard Egyptian artifacts almost with reverence.[53] Their apparently imprecise meanings seem to give them added value. One response to the relative scarcity of examples of early clothing, such as the Tarkhan "dress," is that little contextual information survives. This lack of substantiation engenders mystery, which further enhances the symbolic values of items and their representations. The viewer is free to speculate about origins and spurious meanings may be attached to them.

No historical garment remains exactly the same over time, nor does it have an original or enduring significance. In fact, can we ever say a garment is "original," especially if it has been repaired, altered, mended, or even washed and starched? Clothing and textiles are subject to differential rates of change or decay, their place in relation to time volatile and thus their pasts dynamic. The meaning of ancient clothes lies beyond simply their intrinsic value. They speak of historical times almost unimaginable to us, but at the same time they are sufficiently recognizable to be of our own time. These garments suggest the shifting and complex relationships that exist between time, value and the meaningful. (See also Focus 1b)

The values of historic garments fluctuate according to many cultural variables, which are perhaps associated with the materials from which they are made, and value can be overestimated. For example, the Tarkhan "dress" is made of fine linen rather than a roughly woven fabric. Yet the garment cannot necessarily be associated with a particular class of person. Another kind of value is linked to the item's use, which is even more curious. With sections missing and frayed, its aged and damaged appearance adds significantly to its mystery. Accidently found, forgotten for years, conserved, and then displayed on a museum stand, it seems to suggest a long and eventful history over time. It is a rare surviving article whose meaning, at the time of making and wearing, remains uncertain.

# 3
# CONTEXT: WHAT DOES IT MEAN?

"Context," "chronology," and "period style" are terms that have had long-term use in fashion and dress studies.[1] Time lies at the core of this terminology and, almost without question, influences the way fashion and dress is written about. In popular dress histories, these words are accepted almost without hesitation, although they are seldom applied to dressing outside the boundaries of Western Europe. So why do they need further analysis? I suggest they are obstacles to understanding the complexities and stylistic entanglements of dress of the past, through to clothes worn in global environments. They are deleterious ways of thinking about apparel, and also restrict more nuanced and multidimensional methods of assessment. Nor do they fit with requirements for cross-cultural histories which, it has been suggested, are not unitary histories at all and in fact require a "dislocated vision."[2]

Scholars of material culture are now accepting different valuations of temporality, outside standard understanding of time, and are "unsettling" well-worn Western time lines.[3] Archaeologists and anthropologists, currently engaged in revisionist thinking, are also open to wider questioning about the material past and looking for new, unbounded ways to interpret social and cultural networks and relationships.[4] In their major work on "object lives" and "global histories," Lemire et al. demonstrate how the nature of global trade in textiles and garments from the eighteenth century onward were networked, and use atypical timelines, in order that wider possibilities for issues can be studied. It is what Lemire terms these "more capacious chronologies" that allow new questions to be asked about trans-Atlantic trade, and the entanglements of ideas surrounding material objects across cultures.

If we apply these new ideas, we find relationships cut across any notion of "a context" as they demonstrate that multiple and irregular contextual differences apply to all components of clothing. More than this, different contexts apply to the same garments over time and worn by different individuals in different locations over their lifetime. Focus 3a offers further discussion on problems assigning fixed dates to surviving garments, and so increases the difficulties of using the term contextual.

Time is intrinsic to the story of all apparel. Temporal differences are applicable to every part of dress and body ornamentation, from those who conceive of clothing in the first instance, to making it and onward to its final dissemination and wearing. In this chapter, I consider why we need to rethink any terminology which limits understanding of dress and fashion, and to offer alternatives. Despite acknowledging that the terms highlighted at the start of this chapter have clear associations with the temporal, and that the use of "contextual" can be justified occasionally, I consider them frequently limiting and conventional.

## Complications of the Contextual

What is context and does it have any relevance for the study of dress including fashion? It is a complex and textually dense term that refers to the place of garments in association with big-picture social, political, and cultural concerns, at a specific period. The term "context" assumes fashion and/or dress can be understood at one particular time, as part of the larger socio-cultural and political environment when made and used. More generally, it may allude to a contained historical era and specific geographical location. Determining context needs to consider issues of class, gender, status, consumption, aesthetics, religious and other beliefs, technological developments, materials used, and personal taste. But the generalized term "context" used about clothing is almost deterministic. All aspects of dress are mutable, and all its components affected by differential temporal journeys, each related to a multitude of other, constantly changing elements. To suggest there is "a context" for any form of wearing is to limit our understanding of the temporal nature of dress.

In fact, in her essay "Context Stinks' in *New Literary History,* feminist Rita Felski spells out her views on its limitations. She suggests it is an endlessly contested but conventional concept. At the same time, she queries who could possibly take issue with it, as it is so entrenched. While Felski deals here with literary theory, visual art, and cultural studies, not dress *per se*, she has useful things to say about these limitations. It is, she says, shaped dogmatically by cultural symptoms of its own moment of origin, leaving no space to explore ways that objects (here dress and textiles) mutate over time or any potential for understanding trans-temporal movement.[5] I suggest that, in the case of clothing, "space" is in fact readily available. But we need to move beyond the conventional limitations she highlights and use the temporal to approach the issue in atypical ways.

The context of any garment or accessory needs to be reconsidered in relation to its many components. This applies to garments worn by men, children, or women, whatever their class or nationality. All over the world we find different combinations of dress that are visible signals of society's values and hierarchy;

clothes designed for work, for leisure, for ceremony, rites of passage, gender, age, as political statements or signs of hostility, of regimentation, and so on. In every example or material item of attire, there are numerous particularities that build up into histories of wearing that constitute new complexities in relation to context. So, clothes as worn can never be stable, for their parts have shifting characteristics as do the environments in which they are situated. Each change in social and cultural circumstances, tastes of wearers, age, and gender affects the need to reconsider what is actually meant by "context." As it stands, the term is a troubling generalization.

Useful examples to complicate our understanding of the contextual are the following body supplements which being accessories are both part of and separate from the body. Gloves have always been meaningful in terms of the society in which they have been and are worn, rich in relativities of contextual and emotional meanings as they travel between the hands that make them and those who wear them. Gloves have been both symbolic and practical garments since antiquity, replete with social, religious, and sexual meanings as well as indications of status. Gloves tell stories of class, etiquette, occupation, and protocol, some linked to individual garments, but also in relation to wider temporal, social, and cultural practices. So, there are general social practices of manual use or crafting and then personal, more changeable intimate ones with links to the symbolic. In addition, there have been makers of different kinds of gloves, the different materials of which the accessories have been made, the tools and stitching, as well as the social standing and age of users. There could be no single context here. During the Renaissance, a pair of gloves could be the sign of a worker, indicating utility, but a single glove was a favor given, a token of love.[6] The kissing of an elite gloved hand was a sign of service, while the shaking of a gloved hand a sign of greeting and then a legal contract.

And what of the gloved right hand raised in religious blessing or the place the wearer lays the gloved hand as a sign of appropriate etiquette? There is more information in a single glove than just the materials of which it might be made or daily protocol. If the glove were an official regal accessory, it was a metaphor for the power of a monarch. To then lend the glove to another would be to transfer to them royal authority in the monarch's temporary absence.[7] So, the role of the single glove, in terms of status and authority, would change as it was transferred to the hand of another. Besides this, gloves might signal those concerned with manual work (as noted), with sanitation, and also those who do everyday washing and cleaning. Fine stitched gloves wore out over time, so their use for one set of tasks could change to perform from that context to perform different work in the form of polishing silver or other less arduous cleaning.

Each change or transfer in the examples under discussion from maker to user to use is mediated and given new contextual life as the item moves from one stage of its life to another. Garments and accessories may take on new forms of relevance at any one time. Each item of attire undergoes changes of circumstance independently. Much the same can be said of motility as handheld bags for men, women, and children move from makers to users and uses.

Bags held by the hand are represented as far back as ancient Australian rock art in the Kimberley region. Their contents are unknown but over the years bags of different sizes and shapes, made of different materials and of varied types, have had complex and changing contextual meanings for each aspect of their forms, although these remain largely undeciphered. Bags are practical containers of an owner's personal taste and necessities linked to their current status and activities. They are also a key part of culturally appropriate dress in Western cultures, especially if used by women with matching gloves. For a European man to empty the contents of a woman's handbag is a violation. These articles depending on their historical circumstances have contexts of both privacy and fantasy linked to their various contents.[8]

Bags are used in cultures outside the West demonstrating subtle difference in cultural meaning and context. In Papua New Guinea, bilum bags, traditionally made with a needle using local twisted, looped, and knotted fibers, are made mostly by women but worn by both men and women. Men's bags are made of thicker bush rope. These bags are still made today in many different sizes and for a variety of reasons.[9] Women carry their babies in them on their backs, the weight falling on the mother's forehead. Men use them to store ritual items and

**Figure 3.1** Dani women wearing handmade noken bags of knotted wood or leaf fibers, with the weight carried on their foreheads. Obia Village, Central Highlands, West Papua. (Credit: Insights/Universal Images Group.)

other paraphernalia. The bags of men and those of women do not have the same social context. In the Central Highlands of West Papua, the bags are called "noken bags." This group of Dani or Ndani women from that area (Figure 3.1) wear them suspended from the forehead, in the characteristic manner of their neighbors in Papua New Guinea.

# An Extreme Example

One remarkable garment that can be contextually understood and fully topical to a particular moment in history is a very rare *gillet à sujet*, a French gentleman's waistcoat from about 1789–94 (Los Angeles County Museum) It is contextually, politically, and ideologically extraordinary (Figure 3.2). It is made of linen and silk in triangular shapes of red, white, and blue—Revolutionary colors. Worked in petit point (but deliberately resembling knitting), it is lined with fabric from a reused old green silk waistcoat. Green was the color of the livery of Louis XVI as well as the Revolutionary cockade.

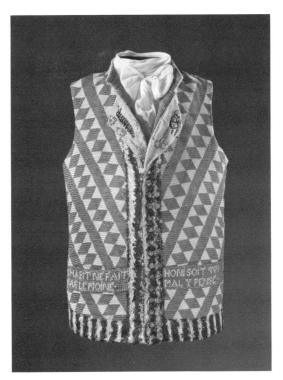

**Figure 3.2** Man's vest, 1789–94, France. Linen canvas with silk needlepoint, linen plain weave with silk supplementary-warp cut-pile trim and silk embroidery. (Credit: Los Angeles County Museum. License endorsed Art Resource, NY.)

According to Chrisman-Campbell, the item was intended to imitate knitting and the work of the "tricoteuses" (the women who knitted while attending public executions), paid supporters of the French Revolution.[10] The first three colors signified the desired union of the Crown and the people, but the green, she suggests, could cynically show either support for the Revolution or ironically a Counter-Revolutionary statement, depending on the political conviction of the wearer. Was he perhaps a turncoat? It is an outstanding and rich example of a contextual interpretation of a garment. Yet it is still inconclusive in that it may have been worn either by a Revolutionary sympathizer, or a Royalist, flaunting Revolutionary colors. Even so, seldom do we find such detailed and conventional a contextualization of a garment as here.

## Untidy Contexts

Context can also show that dress is not always integral to a social group but can be a statement of rebellion against the milieu in which it is worn. One obvious question is whether body modifications and supplements are aberrations and worn "out of context" in order to make a social statement of some kind? And what happens to "context" if the same garment is worn by someone else, perhaps for a different purpose or on a different occasion? This might cause disruption to current understandings of suitability and produce a challenge to accepted modes of wearing. Surely if a garment is altered, repaired, or reused, perhaps over long periods of time, it suggests multiple contexts.

Particularly salient is the problem of separating a succession of dates from first making, repairing and perhaps unwelcome later changes that may have taken place. If we consider the value of the "authentic" original as more significant than later accretions, the study of the context of surviving garments is made even more complex.[11] Context seems to imply limits or boundaries, yet material things are not finite but rather processes. We cannot determine how far "context" extends. Does it just fade away at a specified moment in time? For the most part, researchers have failed to rigorously investigate these possibilities.

Even if garments are stored away, wrapped up and out of view, they are never static. Daniel Miller argues that most of the material-culture studies he has worked with abjure stability. He gives the example of researching material qualities such as color, transparency, or sheen in eroticism. He suggests researchers should try to understand not what transparency is but what it means to individual peoples, the processes of becoming more or less transparent, and the consequences this has for them socially and culturally.[12] And sometimes there are no known social conditions to explain an individual's clothing. For instance, it is almost impossible to contextualize with confidence many surviving ancient garments, and tools for making them, as they are often found in isolation, and many have dates that are approximate, or far from certain.

If we stick with a single material object, determining context is dependent on dating clothes, not the other way around. Approximation can often be the only option. Few historic garments, even those acquired by museums, are ever free of alteration or repair. Changeability adds serious difficulties to precision dating of any clothes and makes contextualization difficult. An example of this is a woman's splendid princess-line eau de nil and gold-colored shot-silk gown made in Brisbane, Australia, by a well-regarded dressmaker and milliner Miss Margaret Scott.[13] It is tentatively dated to the late 1870s and thought to be an afternoon dress. But there is no certainty about its date, who wore it and on what occasion, although formal society "afternoon teas" were common in Australia at the time. How can we estimate the context of garments which have no precisely documented date, and can only be compared loosely to others that do? Colonial fashions are notoriously difficult to contextualise. Comparison with idealized fashion plates can be made but this is a very inexact method, especially in a colonial outpost or small provincial town. Dated photographs can occasionally be used, although they too can be inaccurately inscribed, unless they confirm the date of a wedding, birth or death. (See Focus 3a for discussion on dating and provenance.)

A further case of the limitations of a contextual reading of fashion is an eighteenth-century silk woman's gown, part of a collection held in Newstead House Museum in Brisbane, Queensland.[14] It belonged to a member of the quite influential landowning Hinckley family of Lichfield, Staffordshire, and was made in England prior to the emigration of the family to Australia. This robe à l'anglaise, which could be tied up (retroussée) to show its petticoat, is considered to date from c. 1780s. Time has not treated the gown kindly. It started out apparently as a mid-eighteenth-century sack-back,[15] before being remade as a more fitted garment and then reshaped extensively (perhaps in the mid-1800s) for a younger woman (Figure 3.3). It looks awkward in appearance. Handmade lace droops at the ends of the sleeves and at the neck, but the blue brocade silk satin fabric with silver patterning and brocaded floral motifs retain wonderful color.

The extensively researched catalogue by Catriona Fisk for the exhibition Connecting Threads, dealing with Newstead House and its contents, provides a very thoughtful account of the history of the dress, reading into its structural changes and wear. The interior is very much altered. It is both hand and machine stitched and may have been a family keepsake, but remains something of a mystery.[16] If it had been in a major collection, it may not have been considered suitable for display. Yet it is rich in meaning. How do we make sense of such a garment other than by a precise recording of the object as it stands? We cannot place it fully in its past social and economic contexts as it is so altered, and we don't know who wore it, nor even when or where.

**Figure 3.3** *Robe à l'anglaise, retroussé, c.* 1780s, made from an earlier gown and subsequently altered in the nineteenth century. Newstead House Brisbane (NID-52587). (Jenifer Garcia on behalf of The Board of Trustees of Newstead House, Brisbane, Textile Collection. Copyright holder of catalogue *Connecting Threads*, Catriona Fisk. Credit: Kevin Alexander.)

Having a life cycle like that of this gown, which extends into a history of display and visible signs of use for fancy dress in later years, clearly shows the inadequacy of a contextual analysis. The Newstead House gown has a history that covers its making, acquisition, wearing, original fabric composition, fastenings, any repair threads and remaking, how it may have been packed for the journey to Australia, or placed in a local museum, either stored away or at times worn or put on display. Its meanings are multiple, and its narrative more problematic than a gown of pristine quality.

Perhaps we should be asking different questions of context? Is it better explained if clothing and its correlates—power, social structure, gender, consumption, and ideology—are seen as enmeshed in dynamic networks, associations, and entanglements which show them endlessly mutating, rather than specific to a time and place? Perhaps context *should* be untidy? Although little discussed, these dynamic temporal relativities are manifest in all garments but also their composite parts. Accessories, fabric, thread, fastenings, and so on can have separate contexts. Each item or component part of dress has its own individual history, its own story. Thus, an outfit may have many contexts and many dates.

Commodities—in our case, clothes—are never stable but have individual narratives (biographies) embedded in a dense network of cultural relationships. I suggest that every garment and its parts, each accessory and bodily adornment, are separate but connected in relationships with each other. This confirms an amalgam of numerous disparate periodicities whose meaning is multi-contextual, contradictory, irregular, even highly unsettled and hence results in difficulties with the term "context." If you know little or nothing of the wearer or wearers, or circumstances of wearing, opinions have to be inferred from the "look" and comparisons with more securely documented items. We can never fully fix the precise moment or moments in which historical clothing such as the Newstead House gown was worn, either by one person or part of a cultural group or class. Dress is a visible correlation between how a particular social group is implicated in the temporal, and demonstrates it by material expressions of their social and religious lives. This is ostensibly contextual but it draws its information from the cellular levels of clothing, not just its external appearance.

# Chronology

The origin of the popular Western European chronological method to assess dress is hard to pinpoint, but can surely be traced back to The Enlightenment's idea of progress, and later notions of social evolution in the nineteenth century. The chronological method tends, like the contextual, to be a model for explaining fashions in this part of the world, and extends to its colonies and the United States. An historical time line is a continuing and firm but little considered convention. It offers sequential socio-temporal changes as the prime framework to understand fashion's evolution.

This is a weakness and inappropriate especially when discussing non-European dress. Johannes Fabian's claims (see Chapter One) regarding the conventional distancing of the beholder (the imperialist anthropologist) from observed subjects in foreign cultures, results in cultural relativism which relegates subjects to another time. If we move away from Western thinking, to consider ethnic or "tribal" clothing, in relation to chronology, we see further evidence that the habit of seeing customary dress as progressively linear, or even find it unchanging in terms of a time line is insupportable. Despite Welters and Lillethun's views that change is universal behavior and "the fashion impulse" is found among prehistoric people as it is anywhere else, the question is why has the chronological time-line method been so long lived and so pervasive?

The method is found frequently in twentieth-century texts. James Laver, for instance, believed women's fashions in particular followed one another in time, in the pursuit of novel ideas. Laver became Assistant Keeper in the Print Room at London's Victoria and Albert Museum in 1922, and worked there until his retirement in 1959. He was a prolific writer and defined fashion as the sum of all effects wrought on human activities by the passage of time and their work.[17] Ira Morris, author of a populist book about social mores in London after the Second World War, claimed "History shows that fashions evolve out of each, as do the events and opinions that shape them. . .Moreover their evolution follows a regular pattern."[18] Other sources, particularly in the popular press, categorize women's fashions in particular as cyclical, using the past as a resource to help the dressmaker in the supposed need for change.

It is "time" for more progressive dress historians to take a new position in regard to chronological accounts of their research. Like those in other disciplines, they would benefit from working against the grain. Certainly, the "material turn" is one example of new thinking that has gained traction. I suggest the global spread of style, and the unstable, networked ideas spreading across our highly digitized environment, constitute good reasons to approach the topic differently. The chronological account of fashion as linear and progressive promotes one stylistic invention replaced by another. As recently as 2017, the ICOM published its *Fashion Timeline of Silhouettes 1750s to 2000s* but there are many other examples and chapters of books that deal with discrete decades, one after the other.[19] Choice of dates are seldom rationalized. This approach sometimes takes the form of the biographical career of a designer, or it may study either a single decade or declare a seemingly arbitrary start date, and move steadily onward, building a decade by decades account from, say, 1830 to 1890.

It is not possible to support a serious account of fashion or dress between boundary dates like these. Whose fashions (male, female, rich or less than rich, young or old) can be discussed with certainty using these dates? How exactly is the dress of 1830 and 1890 different from, say, 1829 or 1889? James Laver's *Costume and Fashion,* first published in 1982, has many chapters arranged by century, for instance the seventeenth century and then half centuries (1850 to 1900 etc). From this, a notion of fashion as "period style" (see below) seems to have gained currency. Clearly, however, Laver was speaking about European clothing so we cannot apply his view universally across the globe, either in the past or the present.

In 2016, an exhibition at the National Portrait Gallery, London, called "*Vogue 100: A Century of Style*", celebrating fashion photography, was curated by Robin Muir. He defined the exhibition by decades, each one conveyed by separate rooms: 1920s, 1930s, 1940s, 1950s, 1960s, and so on. Here time and space were neatly but erroneously separated. An unusual recent example is an essay by Viveka Hansen, who uses reverse chronology to claim that women (1914–

1810) who were looking to remodel their fashions with new ideas, had little to go on except inspiration from images of past fashions. She suggests they looked back in time for ideas (a common practice for centuries), yet she still integrates the decade-by-decade method into her essay with seemingly arbitrary dates such as 1885–1890 etc.[20]

Archaeologists and anthropologists, by contrast, now frequently question the usefulness of a strictly linear and progressive form of chronology to frame their finds. There is a growing appreciation among them of different scales and rhythms of time, a sense that it should be conceptually refined to include multiple ideas of temporality and the uneven unfolding of social life. Specializing in the theory of archaeology and anthropology, Souvatzi suggests time for archaeologists is no longer just chronology, nor is there a single progressive evolutionary model of history. In step with a number of other scholars, she argues that history is instead "an interacting set of temporal processes" which combines the long, short and medium term.[21] Fixed notions of date, she says, should be replaced, or reconsidered in favor of accounts of these processes and social interaction which, when researching complex temporalities, may refer to age, class, gender, occupation, and so on.

Anthropologist Rosemary Joyce also questions orthodox ideas about time.[22] Discovered items, in her view, do not represent some static form of social whole; rather, the items flow through engagements and move along continuing but uneven itineraries. "Things" should be considered from the trace of their passages through time.[23] Tim Ingold, a social anthropologist, is supportive of progressive chronology but he too does not subscribe to a strict form of linearity. He claims pathways or trajectories along which practices unfold are not connections, nor do they describe relations between one thing and another. They are at once "itinerant, improvisatory and rhythmic."[24]

# Period Style

Popular dress history often associates historical linearity with the construction of clearly defined "periods." The latter are deterministic divisions, usually categorized by decades or centuries. The term "period style" is curious and needs careful analysis. There is also a form of style that is termed "of its period." Being dressed in "period costume" is slightly different from "period style," as the former is the best attempt by the present to construct individual costumes of a particular time in the past. "Period style" describes a broad selection of ingredients. These constitute a general attempt to generalize dress of a particular historical period, especially the fashions of the elite, and to understand its wearing.

The latter are made up of signs of dress or ornament from a chosen time frame, in a somewhat formulaic manner. For example, ornamental lace standing collars are a cypher that stands for elite Elizabethan women, wigs a sign of eighteenth-century men, waistcoats represent seventeenth- and eighteenth-century men's dress, hoops and bustles are a nod to eighteenth-century women, as crinolines are to those of the nineteenth century. Given subtle factors of class, gender, and age differences, the management of bodies and different timescales in making garments, we must regard "period style" as a generalization. (See Focus 3b) Periodization is not unique to fashion studies but in the case of fashion evades or overrides the importance of a multitude of subtle class factors and social, commercial, and emotional issues that affect clothing, and which shape personal tastes.

The concept of "period style" was first found in the work of eighteenth-century German scholar Johann Winckelmann, as a way of writing about classical art in general, rather than great artists and their works. This meant anonymous art could be compared with famous works of art on the basis of style. Winckelmann also claimed style had boundaries, envisaged in terms of the sequence of natural growth from birth to maturity and then decline, echoing his contemporary Gibbon's work, *The History of the Rise and Fall of the Roman Empire* (1776–88).

One particular costume historian who seems to have adopted the term, perhaps unwittingly from Winckelmann, was James Laver. The concept of period style was promoted vigorously in Laver's writings. In an early piece published in *Contemporary Essays* in 1933, called "The Triumph of Time," he muses prophetically on the way time seems to be accelerating and becoming the most dominant aspect of human existence—loyalties of locality (space) are being replaced by those of time. Laver's first book analysing dress, *Taste and Fashion,* was published in 1937. Laver felt, according to Carter, as much as we believe ourselves to be our own person, we are always embedded in the "time spirit" of our age.[25] In *Lectures on the Philosophy of History* (1822–30), the philosopher Georg Hegel used the phrase *der Geist seiner Zeit* (the spirit of his time), that is, "no man can surpass his own time, for the spirit of his time is also his own spirit." This may have influenced Laver's claim that dress is prime evidence of an era's *zeitgeist*, for he felt clothes were the most sensitive articles to rhythmic social changes of the "time spirit" in which everyone is embedded.

Warwick and Cavallaro refute the claim by some scholars, including Laver, that there have been inextricable and rational interconnections between all the separate visual arts, including fashion, which encapsulate a dominant metanarrative or spirit of the era.[26] They suggest the role of dress does not lie in grasping and embodying an ineffable "Spirit of the Age." The status of historical linearity is spurious, as fashion borrows novelty irrationally from the past. So, fashion is patently relative and impromptu and cannot be understood via linear continuity.

While I accept fashion and clothing are both under constant change, I refute the suggestion that fashion/dress is defined entirely by impromptu decisions of a wearer. Dressing is not something constructed arbitrarily, as its parts are almost always grounded in intentionality and in the desire to project identity. Even so, each garment, its origins and its components embody a specific life narrative and micro history. Yet development of this history is not seamless for gaps, lapses, and fragments of social knowledge are present in the history of all clothing. More than this, the term "impromptu" implies the act of freedom of choice and I would argue that for the poor and dispossessed, choice in what to wear is highly unlikely. For the most part, it is *lack of choice* that characterizes apparel that the destitute are able to wear.

There are particular characteristics of dress that alert us to a garment of a certain time such as the mini skirt, iconic of the 1960s. But the analysis of fashion strictly by decade seems to suggest there is only one form of iconic 1950s hat or 60s skirt. A single progressive evolution of the history of fashion or dress, set out as a sequence of defined periods, cannot be accepted as a given. Nor can we entertain anthropologist Alfred Kroeber's influential but flawed long-range "statistical" method of measuring Western women's dress, as he searched for some kind of ideal pattern, and where he suggested the dynamics of dress shapes behaved in repeatable ways like pendulums. As Carter says about all the women's fashions he analysed: "there is no hint of the context of wearing."[27]

In a global environment I suggest with others that there are now unstable networks and circuitous routes along which stylish ideas move. Given class, gender, and age differences, the management of bodies and different timescales in making garments, we must regard concepts such as "period style" as problematic. It is crucial to fully understand the multifarious ways material items are made, who makes them and where, who trades them and wears them. Moreover, there must be room for personal tastes or eccentric, even unusual, selections to challenge existing presumptions. The extent of much earlier and complex forms of cultural exchange of dress between Europe, North America, and Asia is discussed extensively in Chapter 4 and reinforces the need to reconsider conventional terminology that is overly prescriptive.

At the core of the problems plaguing context, chronology, and period style has been the assumption that dress of Western cultures was somehow set apart "from the rest." The problems have been exacerbated by thinking of time as linear and progressive. This has resulted in an incorrect presupposition, no longer accepted, that there was a "rise" of fashion, especially that of bourgeois and upper-class women, in major European centers like Paris from "a" beginning, which then advanced to the present and moved toward an even more advanced future.[28] The notional inner side of the Western cultural boundary seems erroneously to have been regarded by dress historians of greater significance than the outside, causing cultures beyond the linear narrative to be considered fixed or fossilised. This view has now been superseded by global developments in design and production but the earlier terminology is still in use. Another persistent problem is that the term "non-Western" itself still depends on being the opposite of "Western," unable to cut loose from the principal.

Certainly, there are associations between all three terms discussed in this chapter, and for instance period style can be part of how social context is determined and obviously has a relationship with chronology. But the vocabulary of dress and fashion should also regard these three separate terms as being unwelcome over generalizations. I maintain that in or out of context, new, more nuanced even pluralistic definitions of making and wearing should be part of greater fluidity of research into the future. This is a world in which there are many complex and competing fashion and dress systems, and these are not simply European. Current terms such as "context," "chronology," and "period style" do not sit productively with the novel and highly flexible arrangements of manufacturing and consumption constantly being plied across cultural boundaries in today's fast-moving, digitized global environment.

## Focus 3a
## THE PUZZLE OF DATES

Time plays tricks on museum curators of fashion. For them, the date of garments and their provenance (the origin or record of ownership) is highly significant but unfortunately many garments in public collections have inconclusive histories. To have a precisely dated time line of making, owning, or wearing a garment makes it easier for museums and researchers to formulate a narrative or provide a presumably accurate context for any garment. But problems exist in the time-line approach, as I show in Chapter 3.

Securing precise documentation and firm (or even *possible*) dates for a great many historic garments is extremely difficult, even unreliable. To illustrate this, I am using several examples of gowns from the collection of the Museum of Applied Arts and Sciences, Sydney, as they are typical of dating problems in many dress holdings worldwide. For example, this early nineteenth-century day gown of striped silk damask (Figure 3.4) worn by Elizabeth Marsden, wife of Reverend Samuel Marsden, is a garment with an uncertain history.[29] It is one of a relatively small number of surviving examples of early colonial dress in Australia, in this case part of a significant named collection.[30] The garments include a ball gown and a wedding dress, the latter thought to have been remade for the wedding of Elizabeth's daughter Ann in 1822.[31] There is another alleged wedding gown of white muslin, said to have belonged to the family, now in private hands.

Despite a handwritten note about their origin, the Marsden garments have proved difficult to date with precision. Colonial female garments from the first half of the

**Figure 3.4** Day dress thought to have been worn by Elizabeth Marsden, *c.* 1825–35. (Museum of Applied Arts and Sciences, Sydney. Credit: Sotha Bourn).

nineteenth century in Australia are particularly problematic in this regard. Far fewer surviving male garments have been acquired by museums and dating for them is equally, if not more, problematic. While fine male and female riding habits of the time frequently include the name of the tailor, most female dressmakers and shops began to label clothing only later in the century. In Australia, the distinctive labels of dressmakers first appear in quality garments in the 1870s.

As already mentioned, the day gown is thought to have been worn by Elizabeth Marsden, wife of the Reverend Samuel Marsden, senior Church of England chaplain in New South Wales (from 1810 until to his death in 1838). Samuel was well to do and prominent in the early colony's religious, social, judicial, and agricultural life. This was reflected in his family's quality of dress. His wife's gown, though, is something of a puzzle. It seems a rather striking garment for a chaplain's wife, especially as the Museum considers it to have been worn between 1825 and 1835.

Elizabeth was born in July 1772 and died in October 1835, meaning that if she *had* worn this dress, she would have been at least fifty-three, well into middle age. The dress stands as a warning not to make assumptions about dating and precise provenance of surviving clothing. It is also an excellent example of how complex it is to firmly accept the dates of historic garments, something on which dress and fashion historians continue to rely.

Numbers of treasured colonial garments were brought out by migrants from Britain to Australia and, especially in the early settlement years, they were emotional reminders of home.[32] For most women, mending and refurbishing existing garments was more feasible than purchasing new clothing. Sewing was class-specific and primarily plain needlework was expected of working-class women, whose dress has rarely survived. In rural areas these women would repair men's, women's, and children's clothes, do simple tailoring, and plait straw hats, as well as mend boots and shoes.

Fine sewing skills were also a sign of social standing and vital for women in any "respectable" family. There was a rule of etiquette that to maintain a sense of social acceptance, sewing clothes and undertaking related fine needlework activities was a key way for women to demonstrate their genteel status. Domestic items and clothing were maintained through various sewing practices, including mending and refurbishing by the "lady of the house." We know orders for fabric, trimmings, and other sewing materials were frequently dispatched to Britain but we cannot be sure just how closely colonial clothes aimed to follow overseas garments and fashion plates. Life in Australia was often less formal than in Britain and the etiquette observed was sometimes less strict than in the "mother country"—but not always. Christmas in the extreme heat of Australia was often the subject of engravings that compare the informality of the new country with the old (Figure 3.5). Indeed, Christmas Day in Australia was regarded as a newsworthy topic in British illustrated papers.

All these factors play into any assessment of the Marsden collection of garments, in particular the boldly striped silk damask day gown that is the subject of this Focus. The bodice of the Marsden gown is open down the front and fastens with brass hooks. This front-opening is unusual, perhaps suggesting it was altered from an earlier gown. Elizabeth suffered a stroke in 1811, whilst giving birth to her daughter Martha; she was left with one arm paralysed, and a front opening could have made the gown easier to put on. On the other hand, the dress could have belonged to Ann, or been handed down as a nursing dress, allowing her to breastfeed as well. Is it really a suitable dress for a woman so advanced in years, or is it a dress kept by her children or husband as a memento? Was the heat a factor in its wearing? It remains a mystery.

The full-skirted gown is well made. Its distinctive bishop sleeves, with their flat mancherons or decorative trimming, extend from the upper arm. The lower section of the sleeve is puffed. As with other Marsden garments, it is of good-quality fabric and finish, probably reflecting the family's social and financial position. It may be the work of a professional dressmaker, although Ann Marsden was known to have been a skilled seamstress and may have made the dress supposedly worn by her mother. As noted, repairs and renovations of colonial garments were common. Facing some scarcity of

**Figure 3.5** Christmas Day in Australia, published in the *Illustrated London News,* December 23, 1871, showing the leisurely life and informal clothes worn in the colony during holiday time. Engraving after a drawing by Nicholas Chevalier. (Credit: DEA / ICAS94 / Contributor.)

local fabrics, a home seamstress could have widened the bodice and waist of an existing dress or loosened pleats to accommodate a changing figure. The garment may have needed alteration to bring it in line with different tastes in Sydney or to refashion it for the climate.

Another altered garment of light figured silk, maker unknown, was supposedly worn by Ann on her marriage to Reverend Thomas Hassall at Parramatta in 1822. This garment also has a curious history. It is thought to have been the wedding dress worn by her mother Elizabeth in 1793, subsequently brought to Australia and remodeled. This simple, high-waisted empire-line gown has a low neck and long, ill-fitting sleeves with draped shoulder trim. The skirt is tubular and reaches the ankles. The lightweight fabric would have been stylish at a time when almost translucent fabrics were popular. Yet many years later, it was thought the expensive silk of the gown was appropriate enough to be extensively made over for her daughter, almost three decades after Elizabeth's own wedding.

There is one other significant dress in the Marsden collection. It is a cream-colored muslin gown with woven ribs and tambour-embroidery, believed to have been worn by Ann to a ball at Government House in 1822.[33] It has a lace border plus scallops at the hem and stylistically similar to her wedding dress. If it *is* a ball gown, the high-waisted style is rather out of date in comparison to formal European gowns. All these differences must be factored into any assessment of historic dress, particularly colonial garments where clients were far from the centers of European style.

So, the question to which period this garment belongs is demonstratively problematic for items in the Marsden collection. Those who work and deal with surviving clothes sometimes give garments approximate dates, whether high fashion or not. Dating to a particular decade such as the 1830s or 1890s, or a circa date, can be inaccurate, but necessary if garments are to be catalogued. But what exactly is a circa date? Some museums have a policy of taking it to mean five years from an estimated date either way, but it really means approximate or "more or less." Unfortunately, over time, approximations have easily been allowed to turn into fixed dates, and the circa conveniently dropped.

Dating is based on many comparative assumptions about style and provenance, but it does not account for age or taste and often fails to grasp that clothing is never static. A garment may have been altered at various times, perhaps used by other people, and the fabric and trimmings could have come from another source. Not all items belonging to an outfit were made and worn at the same time either, adding further complications to the idea of context.

Sometimes rather fractious debates occur about dates between theorists of fashion and object-based historians—the latter experts in empirical research. It has now become more usual to undertake modes of enquiry that draw on both conceptual and empirical scholarship. Some scholars are adept at arriving at dates on the basis of looking and comparing, plus using relevant documentation. Nevertheless, this is not always a fully reliable method either. Dating inevitably remains a tricky issue for all researchers, especially if concerned with the temporal life-histories of fashions, and bearing in mind the significant after-lives of clothes.

Accurate information about when a garment was made and the origin of its textiles, knowing when it was worn, repaired, and/or altered are still important to uncovering social and cultural meanings of clothes. If we wish to challenge methodologies, as is the case in this book, we need to bear in mind that the basic groundwork still needs to be done on so many surviving garments.

## Focus 3b
## WHAT ARE "1920S" FASHIONS?

Authors of popular as well as more academic accounts of fashion and dress have, for years, used over-simplified descriptive terms in their writing. Generalizations like "the

1920s" or "1950s" continue to define periods of dress, and with them come misrepresentations of the styles they discuss. While I suggest time is essential to understanding all garments, these expressions are ill defined and repetitious. My question is how can an arbitrary term for a decade seriously summarize the fashions or dress across any social and economic spectrum?

This Focus considers the limitations of the shorthand terminology of "the 1920s" and its companion, 20s "period style." Both refer to modern urban fashions and accessories, mostly for the younger woman in the decade after the First World War. They are fairly easily digested categories but belie a host of inconsistencies. Using these unconditional temporal boundaries ignores the complexities of style worn across age, gender, class, economic status, and geographical location. Although sometimes useful, terms like these should not be accepted unquestioningly.

After the Great War, women especially (but not entirely) were increasingly classified by generalized "Types." This was a practice that began in the late nineteenth century with descriptions of young women and their dress such as the "Gibson Girl," with her distinctive S-shaped pose, tailored shirts, and wide skirts.[34] Other categories of modernity included the "Modern Woman," the "Outdoor Type," the "Vamp," the "Business Girl" and later the "Flapper." Men were also categorized in a similar way. Terms like these were generic and in the 1920s a flapper was associated with certain kinds of young women keen to take up the affectations of modern life in clothing, and indulge in other unrestrictive behaviors.

But what about the dress of women working as house cleaners, or assistants in small shops and offices who may have aspired to look modern but could seldom match an up-to-date appearance? And not all younger women could or wanted to be characterized as "flappers." Describing something as "1920s" is largely insensitive to class and avoids discussion of the mundanity of everyday clothes for women on low incomes.[35] For them, the latest fashion was almost certainly more aspirational than actual.

Prior to the start of the Great Depression in 1929, there was a brief period of prosperity for some in Europe, the US, and beyond. It was a time when active young people, who could afford it, travelled widely, drove smart fast cars, listened to jazz, and visited speakeasies. Illustrations in many upper-end fashion and other magazines feature unrealistically thin and abstracted women striking exaggerated poses and wearing fashions that played a significant part in creating and perpetuating the flapper myth.

Accounts of dress in "20s style" are rapturous about women's fast-paced lives, the supposed freedoms of post-war life, and a new kind of public presence defined by the visual.[36] Days were supposed to be filled with hedonistic shopping, fun day trips, playing golf, seaside swimming, and at dancing the Charleston at night. The popular press was full of representations of uninhibited young women, said to be instantly recognizable by

**Figure 3.6** A vivacious flapper smoking. Sheet music cover, illustration by the French artist Roger de Valerio for "Valse de Rose-Marie," or "The Door of the Dreams" by Czech composer Rudolf Friml, Paris, *c*. 1925. (Credit: Paul Popper/Popperfoto via Getty Images.)

swinging knee-length skirts, shingled hair, a boyish Eton crop or Marcel waves, plus cloche hats (Figure 3.6). There was little sign of the more mature woman, except in some society magazines.

The French term *le style garçonne* described these svelte, sometimes risqué dressers.[37] Supposedly emancipated, they had waistlines reaching the hips, flattened chests, dressed in bright modernist shades, and openly wore cosmetics. Garments were loose fitting in glorious colors of gold, bois de rose, verdigris, lettuce and apple green, although occasionally some garments were black and beaded. Many were heavily sequined or embroidered. Sparkling with brilliants, some layered with fringes, these supposedly iconic garments have a fragility whose handwork has been much sought after by collectors.

The stereotype of the 1920s was that of cohorts of young women, all intent on trying to "keep up to date," for fashion was the aesthetic hall mark of modernism.[38] But in small towns, skirt-length was less extreme and tastes more conservative. The knee-length skirt was not worn by everyone. Aspects of style were relative to age, occasion, and status, and within these categories there were further variances. This vocabulary of urbane, cosmopolitan style was designed to set up new ideals of femininity, but only for some.

Modernist 1920s style was not confined to England and America, but young fashionable women such as these were common in Europe and certainly in Australia and many parts of Asia as well. Japan, in particular, had its own versions of daring young women called *mogas*. In Australia, though, modern ideals of beauty excluded Indigenous women, who were mocked by the media, which depicted them as anachronistic in up-to-date dress, imperfect and flawed.[39] A "flapper" was a young white or Asian woman, but not all ages and social classes dressed according to the typecast image so prevalent in flashy magazines.

So what did "up to date" mean? Various versions of being modern existed, challenging the popular notion of the concept being universal. Styles were to a large degree an imagined fabrication built around visually attractive and impossibly slender women depicted in stylistically abstract fashion illustrations and advertisements. The emancipated "flapper" is a debatable idea and could be somewhat pejorative when used as a description. In fact, at what age did someone cease to be a flapper? A glance at many photographs of the time shows extreme fashions were not worn by those with a fuller figure. It was largely a fiction.

The most iconic moment of modernity's legendary fashion period occurred when women's short skirts were at their most extreme and liberating. Yet this daring knee-length style was worn for a limited time only. But how short is short? Dates for this extreme style vary slightly, but 1924 to 1926 are commonly used. So "the 1920s" seems to stand for at most two or three years. These fitted with the date of the influential *Exposition Internationale des Arts Décoratifs et Industriels Modernes* held in Paris in 1925. This landmark exhibition prioritized newness and bold colors in the decorative arts, and gave rise to the term "Art Deco."

The new, popularized form of streamlined design showcased in the *Exposition* translated with ease into fashion and, of course, cosmetics. But even in the mid-20s, society woman could be seen in ankle-length gowns, especially in the evening, and somewhat below the knee in the day. More often than not, garments abbreviated to the knee had elegant hemlines that dipped either at the back or sides of an outfit. These were particularly characteristic of high fashion just before the Depression and beyond. The widely accepted concept of all "20s" fashions as streamlined with skirts at the knee and relaxed waistlines is not accurate.

The symbol of youthful independence, exuberance and convenience had much to do with the introduction of looser, elasticized corsetry that replaced the tightly constricted, boned styles of the previous century (Figure 3.7). Describing the changed body "Before" modern underwear and "After" were common advertising slogans for the new and up to date angular body shape, which replaced the exaggerated curves of the past. Many corset companies like Berlei and Warners were to achieve great success with customers, not only through orthodox paper-based advertising but via novel forms of entertainment

**Figure 3.7** An underwear model wearing a Campbell's corset, 1928. (Credit: Sasha/ Hulton Archive/Getty Images.)

such as theater revues, combining romantic stories, fashion parades, short plays, and dramatic stagecraft. Early film clips were also used to advertise underwear.

There is another side to the sleek modernist aesthetic. This was the romantic, historicist mode of dress, ignoring the dictates of the Paris *Exposition*, that all design references to the past be disregarded. Fashion columns during the 1920s speak about the revival of "bygone fashions," including the high-waisted Directoire style, references to the 1860s and 1870s, compressed waists, and a craze for an early Victorian phase with gathered skirts. Some were called "picture dresses" and matched with wide-brimmed hats that were festooned with ostrich feathers and worn concurrently with cloches. There was also the *robe de style*, with its links to the eighteenth century. It was the signature style of the couturier Jeanne Lanvin, and its very full skirt was kept away from the body with petticoats and even hoops.

Even more curious is the constantly reiterated and popular description of the period as "the roaring twenties." While use of a decade as an abbreviated term can sometimes be useful, in this case the nature of the decade is highly over simplified and the phrase repetitive. Mendes and de la Haye surprisingly use the term, saying that October 1929, with the collapse of the Wall Street Stock Exchange and the demise of many large-scale businesses, brought to an abrupt close "the roaring twenties."[40] There are many other examples, but what exactly does the term "roaring" mean? It continues to be used.

Representations of modern "up to date" dress was made widely available, encouraged by competing forms of representation from the sophisticated glossies like *Vogue* to graphics in more modest magazines, newspapers, the displays in shop windows, the cinema, popular fashion parades, and the theater. How women looked was played out to a large degree in stylish clothing, as many redefined themselves in this new more relaxed era and accepted new roles for themselves. But it was the sleek, stylized levels of advertising imagery in high-class magazines that were persuasive. It was not the images of the fuller figured women, in homemaker and trade magazines whose images looked more like unmediated family photographs.

The upper echelon of women's fashion of the decade vividly expressed the post-1918 mood for a limited time. Its familiar features became a high point in the middle of the 1920s. Even so, an analysis of advertising images shows this was to a degree something of a myth, created around certain cohorts of women.[41] As noted, knee-length skirts were not universal and the supposed unfettered behaviour and other freedoms for women were less an actuality than a desire. The impression of a cohesive decade with precise and definable indicators of style is incorrect. In terms of fashion, hairstyles, and accessories, women's dress of the 1920s cannot be called homogeneous. The desire, ideals, and temptations of an up-to-date appearance was widespread, but in reality modern fashions were not available to all.

# 4

# CULTURAL EXCHANGE: PAST AND PRESENT

In this chapter, I explore some of the extensive transnational influences affecting development in clothing and textile designs that took place from early historical times, via worldwide commercial networks. The circuitous nature of travel and resulting contacts between peoples and goods was behind the scaling-up of mercantile advantages. The movements of commodities and ideas at the center of these extensive journeys fostered trade as well as intercultural and intertemporal relationships between China, Eurasia, and later North America and many Pacific islands. The nature of goods traveling along the northern steppes of Eurasia altered when China opened its trade with the West. Luxury woven, printed and embroidered textiles—as well as spices, metals, and many other precious items—began to be exchanged along the ancient Silk Road Routes, linking China, India, the Middle East, Southeast Asia, and later Western Europe. These crucial commercial arteries connected key regions of the ancient world by traffic in valued material goods—textiles in particular—from the second century BCE until their decline at the end of the Ottoman Empire in 1453 CE. Time and its vicissitudes lie at the heart of these networks.

Constantinople was a center of silk-making. Its Byzantine silk was valued highly as a form of currency in Southeast Asia, and at the same time was used for making high-status dress. There was a route connecting North Russia with Byzantium as early as the ninth century CE and silk produced in the latter was regularly transported on Russian rivers to Scandinavia.[1] The temporal nature of, and varied cross-movements between, vastly different cultures, in respect of religious beliefs, scientific discoveries, and ideas, was to become increasingly apparent in the borrowing, adaptations, and interchanges of garment styles and textiles. But extending beyond the exchange of ideas were instances of the cultural assimilation of articles, or features of dress taken up by one culture but which belonged originally to another. This assimilation calls into question at what point, if any, the use of a general description such as "Indian," "Japanese," or "French" dress can be warranted. It also raises the question of appropriation discussed fully in Focus 4.1.

Important research by Lemire et al. has explored the extensive trading of goods between northern North America and the wider Atlantic world during the eighteenth and nineteenth centuries. This work shows in rich detail the production and circulation of different commodities, including clothing, as well as the transcultural assimilation and exchange of designs that flowed from contact between colonial and subject peoples. The authors give particular attention to the interaction between specific "lives" of the material culture of objects as they became entangled and interacted between settler colonialism, imperial culture, and the agency of Indigenous peoples.[2] This chapter considers a similar approach in terms of exchange between West and East, showing that it began much earlier in different ways, but gives similar attention to multifarious and sometimes hybrid or co-dependent material interrelationships.

As with the North American links between trade and design across widespread geographical areas, I discuss comparative borrowings and extensive transmutations and assimilations of design in both garments and textiles. Likewise, my discussion predates what is considered global trading. The status of Indian cloth in Southeast Asia was such that it could be traded for highly valued spices, and textiles were often used in place of currency or wages. Greater interest was shown in acquiring dress and body ornament than investing wealth in fixed property.[3] At the same time, a shift occurred. Despite the known interest in the valuable, exotic designs of the East, from the mid-sixteenth century designs for fashionable Western garments from Spain, northern Italy, and Germany were also spreading rapidly around the world, as practical printed tailoring manuals and pattern books became widely available.[4]

In the 1680s, the British East India Company tried to anticipate new fashions in Europe by obtaining samples of silk made in India and sending them to London and France for market-testing. If any found favor, they were then mass-produced in India and returned to Europe for sale.[5] The high esteem in which customers held expensive Indonesian patola—a glorious warp and weft *ikat*-patterned silk, and the most sought-after fabric in Southeast Asia—was long established.[6] Considered suited to the dress of nobility and for ceremony, and even said to have mystical powers, it actually originated in Patan in Gujarat, western India.[7] At the same time Indonesian traders purchased cheap woodblock cotton imitations of the fabric in India, selling it to far less affluent consumers in their own country. These cross-cultural influences in textiles and clothing created such diversity that to name a fabric made into a garment as "Indian," "Japanese," or "French" needs qualification.

## Patterns: Dress and Textiles

The Dutch East India Company revitalized the trade in silk and other high-end luxury fabrics from its inception in the Dutch Republic (The Netherlands) in 1602, opening up new and lucrative markets for Asian textiles of quality, such as carpets and shawls as well as other goods like furniture, metals, tea, and spices. It is not surprising that the Cape of Good Hope was an important anchoring point for trade ships, and European as well as Asian fabrics were bought and sold en route even before reaching final destinations. Fabrics had become so significant that when the Portuguese sailor Ferdinand Magellan, the first to sail around the world, landed in Timor in 1522, he persuaded the Timorese to trade Indian silk and cotton he had on board for food for his starving sailors.[8]

From the establishment of the Dutch East India Company until its decline and dissolution in the late eighteenth century, its trading activities constituted a period of great cultural interchange. For instance, an early eighteenth-century jacket (*baju*) that survives, made of fine Indian cotton, mordant printed and dyed batik, has a floral, chintz-like pattern originating from the Coromandel Coast (Tamil Nadu and Andhra Pradesh) but assembled in Indonesia.[9] *Baju* were traditional loose jackets worn by men and women but with gender differences in how they were cut. Those with chintzy flowers would likely have suited European tastes at the time. So, the textile design itself was intended for European customers, but its red background color more favored in the East Indies. Even so, the largest market for red Indian chintz fabric jackets, and widely adopted as local costume, was in the Dutch Friesland community at Hindeloopen, in the northern Netherlands. The garments there were called *kassakijntje*.[10] For dress, fabrics, and ornamentation, it was a time of constant transference of design ideas and tastes, of movements from place of printing to different locations for clothing manufacture, and to other places still for final marketing.

A further intercultural trade for ornamental cashmere shawls increased in the later 1700s, centered on Kashmir, where artisan weavers used the finest fiber of cashmere goats, far better than sheep's wool, in that it was softer and more insulating. High-value *Kani* shawls were produced on a handloom with small needles (*Kani*) carrying colored threads; these were, not woven but rather worked in an intricate tapestry-like pattern. Both Ladakh regional goats, who lived wild in the high areas of Tibet, and the domesticated animals in Mongolia produced wool for these finest-quality cashmere shawls, such as the pashmina wrap (See Chapter 1). These were originally intended for the elite, initially in Persia (Iran), and later worn by members of the Mughal empire in India. They soon became extremely popular in other parts of India and spread to Europe as an important part of the French East India Company's market. Their popularity was such that woolen shawls were designed in the West, to be made in Kashmir, and intended for the Western market.[11]

Some of the early motifs were based on a single flowering plant or tree complete with roots inspired by English herbals. These reached the Mughal court during the seventeenth century, again demonstrating extraordinary design relationships.[12] Shawls were also woven or embroidered with striking asymmetrical *boteh jehgeh*, teardrop- or almond-shaped symbols with curved tops.[13] This design probably originated in ancient Persia (Iran), although the absolute source is unclear. It has been an exceptionally long-lived and vibrant motif demonstrating cultural exchange of design over centuries between the Middle East, India, Europe, and the British Isles.

By the late eighteenth and nineteenth centuries, cashmere shawls became increasingly popular in Europe. The raw wool was imported from India into France (Reims) where it was spun into yarn before being exported to the Scottish town of Paisley, where it was finally woven into fabric. The design of these shawls was later called "Paisley" as well, and the company has used many widely inventive derivatives of the *boteh*. The brilliance of Paisley designs has become an almost universally recognizable style and is still used today, not only on shawls but often other clothes and soft furnishings. It is surprising that English-made Norwich shawls, also imitations of Indian shawls, did not have the significance of Paisley shawls. Yet from the end of the eighteenth century, these wonderful patterned and colored wraps successfully vied with Paisley, but took inspiration more directly from India.[14] By the 1960s, modified Paisley designs were popular worldwide but debased and mass-produced, gesturing to the psychedelic tastes of the time.

That said, Paisley motifs continue to be used, and have been revitalized for all classes of fabric, even by a high-end fashion stylist like Hermès. In 2019 a successful partnership was established between the Paisley Museum and the French luxury goods brand, boosting sales of scarves by rejuvenating Paisley patterns. These modern silk and cashmere scarves used designs from original 1830s pattern books, and were called "Paisley from Paisley."[15]

# Design and Cultural Exchange

The sixteenth century was a vibrant period of cross-fertilization of fashion ideas across Europe. Dress styles, especially for the upper classes, were frequently a mix of influences. Designs were drawn from historical elements and from geographically dispersed places. This sense of an unsettled but rich borrowing of fashion ideas, motifs, needlework techniques, and ornamentation can be seen in a comparison of the dress of two high-born women, one in England and the other in India.

The first example is a highly stylized Elizabethan portrait, by the English artist George Gower.[16] It depicts a fashionable lady of wealth painted about 1590, vividly demonstrating complex influences in her dress, in particular its range of borrowed designs, as well as foreign needlework techniques (Figure 4.1). The unknown lady wears an elaborate silk gown, richly adorned with gold chains, and her embroidered sleeves suggesting the influence of Indian textiles.[17] Her cuffs are embroidered in silk, with stylised pomegranate motifs (looking slightly

**Figure 4.1** "Portrait of a Lady," *c.* 1590, by British artist George Gower (*c.* 1540–96). Oil on wood panel, 78.1 x 64.7cm. South Australian Government Grant 1984. Art Gallery of South Australia, Adelaide.

like pineapples), then a rare fruit in England. The pomegranate design refers to both classical Greek myths and Christian symbols. It also echoes similar Ottoman motifs developed and popularized in the reign of Suleiman I, The Magnificent (who died in 1566). The pomegranate was also the heraldic device of the Spanish-born Catherine of Aragon, who married Henry VIII in 1509. The fruit patterns in Gower's painting are accompanied by other needlework designs, some picked out in gold. Common at the time on caps, shirts, sleeves, and here on cuffs was silk-thread embroidery termed "blackwork," or sometimes "Spanish work."[18] The false buttons were imported pearls from the tropics.[19] Fabrics were heavy, and the number of layers of clothing and elaborate stiff hair ornamentation created an extremely formalized appearance.

Clothing of the Indian elite at this time was extraordinarily lavish, and in its own way matched the richness of Elizabethan dress worn by the high-born sitter in Gower's portrait. The well-known, highly cultivated Indian noble woman Empress Nur Jahan, born in Persia, and the favorite wife of Emperor Jahangir, fourth Mughal emperor, lived at much the same period as the Gower sitter. She wore comparable embroidered garments, rare stones, and copious jewelry in order to present herself as a high-status member of society. Yet the cultures to which each belonged were vastly different and the dress of their respective social classes a powerful medium that set them apart from others.

This is reputed to be a portrait of Nur (Figure 4.2). Her clothing is ornamental and her garments of fine fabrics. She wears rings, bracelets, and necklaces, as well as a striking headdress. It is fascinating that Nur was just as attracted to the designs of English embroideries as many of the British stationed in the sub-

**Figure 4.2** Reputed portrait of the Mughal Empress Nur Jahan, consort of Emperor Jahangir. (Credit: Universal History Archive/Universal Images Group via Getty Images.)

continent were taken with the aesthetics of Indian handwork. These two examples show how ideas from distant parts of the world could be admired, taken up, and—like the Paisley design—become authentic aspects of two cultures.

Nur Jahan was a powerful, independently wealthy woman of considerable talents; she not only had an interest in fashionable dress design but was also attuned to the practices of her social position. Unlike the anonymous sitter in Gower's portrait, we know a fair bit about her. Her accomplishments, if they are to be believed, were extraordinary. She was politically astute, involved in matters of overseas trade (especially indigo dye), interested in poetry, a blender of perfumes, and a promoter of women's issues. She was a talented jeweler, textile, fashion, and garden designer and architect, as well as a skilled needlewoman, and said to have been interested in tiger-hunting and warfare as well.[20]

Her particular ambition was to reform society women's fashions for India's hot climate, long before the European Dress Reform movements of the later nineteenth century, whose members were mainly interested in simplified outfits for women. As part of her reforms, Nur introduced to the court lightweight gowns of muslin, embroidered with floral patterns (called *dodami*), replacing those of silk. She also recommended *dupattas* (shawls draped in many ways) and veils (*panchtoliya*) of cool cottons.[21] *Dupatta* shawls were called by different names across India, woven in wonderful colors, and often heavily ornamented with mirrors, beads, gold threads, sequins, block prints, and semi-precious stones. In this decorative sense, these features had similarities to formally ornate Elizabethan dress for public occasions. But the cool muslin and cotton for women's dress in India was the complete opposite of the stiff formality of the dress of the high-born in Elizabethan England.

# Temporality, Sources, and the Mutability of Design

The long-term significance of India, with its separate regional kingdoms, was highly influential in cross-cultural trade especially for fabrics, both luxurious and more commonplace. It continued to be a source of decorative skills, striking color schemes, and a vibrant approach to textile design. The silk trade plied between Europe, India, and across Asia, was driven by the various East India Companies in the seventeenth century. Further important commercial links with African ports on the west side of the Indian Ocean expanded, and the former neglected area of interest in these textiles has now emerged as a significant research field.[22]

The eastern half of Africa was closely connected with the Indian textile trade. The list of fabrics of all kinds, recorded as part of trade exchanges, includes an extraordinary list of weaves with evocative names including calicos, seersuckers, ginghams, sarasa, alliballies, humhums, jamdanies, and nainsooks.[23] In 1610, the French navigator François Pyrard de Laval observed "everyone from the Cape of Good Hope to China man and woman, is clothed from head to foot" in Indian textiles, showing the degree of trading networks and the extensive reach of India's talent and products.[24] Competition was fierce. That Indian clothing and textiles was exchanged so widely is a sign of unrestrained interchange in consumption and tastes, but also the unproblematic borrowing of designs, all signs of the role of time in the changing character of style.

Indians were willing to conform to the desires of foreign traders and obligingly copied designs from other cultures to service foreign sales as there were no reprisals. For instance, records show the Dutch East India Company regularly sent Indonesian textile patterns to India to be copied.[25] And it was not unusual for Indian textile artists to copy Javanese batik designs. In the late 1630s the Dutch set up a trade in Indian calico with Japan, especially for that market. Wealthy metropolitan Japanese imported these Indian calico textiles known generically as *sarasa*, a term borrowed from the Portuguese.[26] They were "resist dyed" and particularly popular from the early seventeenth to the mid-nineteenth centuries. Being expensive, these imported cotton fabrics were not used for garments until Japanese craftsmen began to make imitation Indian *sarasa* themselves.

The unconventional cotton fabrics, in vivid colors with striking designs, stood out in contrast to Japanese utilitarian blue indigo fabrics. Late eighteenth-century Japanese *sarasa* manuals, published in Edo (Tokyo) and Kyoto, included instructions for colors, encouraging Japanese textile printers to copy Indian designs. These beautiful, exotic chintz textiles rapidly became popular among the wealthy samurai and merchant classes, and later the locally produced cloth was made into an abundance of everyday summer *kimonos*.

Temporal interchanges of design were common almost everywhere before the twentieth century, from Asia to Europe, North America and Australia. For instance, Indian textiles as well as Chinese goods were widely available in Sydney reasonably soon after colonization. In 1820, a mantua-maker (dressmaker) in Upper Pitt Street in Sydney was advertising the newest fashions from India, as light, printed cottons were popular in the heat.[27] The earliest known fashionable garment in Australia is a high-waisted evening gown of delicate Indian muslin dating to *c.* 1805, and embroidered with sprigs and dots in gilded silver plate. The gown belonged to Anna King, wife of the third Governor of New South Wales.[28] Muslins were frequently imported directly from India at this early period but not of such fine quality or so delicately embroidered. It suggests the muslin may have been a special order or brought from Britain by Anna herself as a settler, and the gown then made in Sydney. Alternatively, it could have been a sign of status *not* to use common Indian muslins.

# Crosscurrents: East and West

In Europe during the seventeenth and eighteenth centuries, the stylish upper classes saw particular social advantages in wearing exotic clothes imported from India, Japan, or China, or those made to appear "orientalist," foreign or exotic. Why the well-to-do desired to wear these particularly "different" forms of dress, especially for informal wear, has attracted considerable research.[29] As trading relationships increased around the world from the early seventeenth century, one article of clothing that clearly illustrates this complex cross migration of materials, design ideas, techniques of making, use, and terminology was the Indian gown/nightgown or banyan of silk or cotton.[30] Popularly worn by men and women, it was a loose over-gown especially prestigious for men as a fashionably informal garment. Its nature and terminology over the years is confusing and it is difficult to say precisely what actual garments and visual representations were called at the time. The diverse history of these garments, their various forms of nomenclature and uses illustrate how liberal was cultural and temporal interchange, which was fostered particularly by trading organisations like the Dutch East India Company. Banyans have been extensively researched and show the complex temporal inweaving of sources and markets and the close economic relationships between Europe, Asia and northern North America.[31] The mix of trading itineraries and design reinterpretations of these garment types defies any clear time-line approach for stylish dress, and national attributions are clearly problematic.

These garments are first seen in the sixteenth century, but likely existed earlier as one-off garments for men and women, and are recorded in a variety of fabrics. Merchants connected to the Dutch East India Company soon began to export extensive supplies of them to the West. These loose gowns, initially made in India using silk or chintz, began to be popular by the seventeenth century. Some were quilted for warmth or fur lined. They had many names such as "morning" or "night gowns," "Persian gowns," "Indian gowns," "Japanese *kerimaone*," "*cambayon*," and even "Japan night gowns." The term "Indian" may have been due to the brilliant colors and rich designs of the chintzes often used in their making. The term *banyan* was added to the list of names and they began to be made in the Netherlands as *japonse rokken*. They gained fashionable status and popularity for men when King Charles II, who may have seen them when in exile in The Hague, wore them after his restoration to the English throne.[32]

Wide-sleeved and comfortable, they were a relaxing antidote to the complexity and pressure of being constantly in fashion, signaling a freedom from rigid court or official dress. The *banyan*—either voluminous or, later, more fitted—was for receiving private guests, conducting business, and leisurely reading in a library. Popular with wealthy European, American, Dutch, and English gentlemen, it fulfilled imagined needs for a life of leisure and tranquillity. Worn in the home as a

**Figure 4.3** Pierre Mignard's "Self portrait," making a silverpoint drawing, wearing a *banyan*, late seventeenth century. Louvre, Paris. (Credit: Leemage/Corbis via Getty Images.)

form of dressing gown, they were also a sign of a man's status, as well as his intellectual, scholarly, and philosophic qualities. Especially suited for portraits, they gave the sitter an aura of being studious. This mid-seventeenth-century self-portrait is by Pierre Mignard, a notable French painter, He is wearing one of these gowns and engaged in drawing, probably with a fine, silverpoint stylus (Figure 4.3). He wears a dark wig although these garments were sometimes companioned with a soft cap, even a turban over a shaven head, rather than a wig.

As *banyans* became widely popular in Europe, India established streamlined processes for ready-making the chintz examples by the end of the seventeenth century and into the eighteenth. Being of a simple pattern, an unskilled worker could cut the fabrics and pre-assemble them easily for the overseas market. Ready-made gowns were painted and dyed according to the garment's shape rather than yardage, and some were painted after assemblage. Gowns could be imported either fully ready-made, or partly so, and finished off in Europe. Orders of up to ninety garments at a time were spread amongst workshops. This was an exceptionally efficient process but was not entirely standardized in modern terms.[33]

Interestingly, a surviving version of the *banyan* dated 1820–40, of either moose or caribou hide, is based on the pattern of a cloth *banyan* that must have previously been imported to Hudson Bay.[34] In North America, nineteenth-century versions of *banyans* made from hide are of great interest as they were made by Indigenous women or British tailors but decorated only by Indigenous women using traditional materials like porcupine quills and paint. Peers suggests this is true hybridity and shows both the indigenizing of British skills and the transference of old Indigenous practices of making (such as their deep respect for animals) to new fashions intended for colonial men.[35]

A garment worn widely in Japan by men and women commoners, the T-shaped *kosode*, had design associations with the European/Indian loose gown and was in fact a predecessor to the *kimono*. Like the *banyan*, the *kimono* had a long and complex history and was subject to changes of style and meaning over time, the effects of cultural exchange continuing into the twenty-first century. Regarded as garments for women by the time of the Meiji Period from 1868, when Japan opened up to the West, they became more widely admired geographically. Popular as beautiful and healthy garments, they appealed to those with a taste for Japonisme and Aestheticism in France and Britain in the later years of the nineteenth century, especially as they did not require restrictive under garments.[36] In Japan, however, traditional *kimono*-wearing and its etiquette declined as the country moved into modern forms of consumption, and new attitudes towards *kimono* made of modern fabrics developed amongst the young, as well as provoking new concerns about cultural and national identity. (See Focus 4.2)

# Retaining Differences, Defining Differences

Temporal differences and the cultural exchange of clothing styles between settlers and First Nations peoples characterized much colonial dressing. In early contact history, there is evidence that in the Pacific Islands, some Europeans indiscriminately adopted aspects of local dress, sometimes including tattoos, while colonized people were initially coerced into adopting the dress of the alien newcomers. European uptake of local dress, for instance, was irregular and often in respect of some items only. In the late eighteenth century, Joseph Banks, traveling as official botanist on James Cook's first great voyage, viewed Tahiti favorably and took to wearing a local bark-cloth turban, perhaps to show his good opinion of the local people. Turbans of various fabrics and designs as previously noted were commonly worn for leisure in England, in association with the *banyan*. We can't assume what Banks meant by a turban, so the exact appearance of a local "turban" is difficult to determine.

In other Pacific Islands, caught up in the Protestant missionary drive to introduce Victorian modesty to island women, the latter were persuaded to wear billowing garments with round necks, no collar, and puffed sleeves. They were made of vivid cotton prints sourced from Manchester and traded in the Pacific by Indian-Fijians and Hawaiians. These dresses—or echoes of them—are still worn today and have become the clothing of choice, especially for special occasions. There are likely few ni-Vanuatu women (a citizen of Vanuatu) who do not own at least one and they are called "aelan dres."[37] Originally stemming from missionary influence, this dress became naturalized over time as "traditional," and at the time of independence in 1980 was adopted by women as their national dress.

Fabric and clothing are burdened with fluctuating meanings over time, relative to the age and status of the wearer but most importantly infused by influences on the culture to which they belong. With the strengthening of colonial control in many parts of the world, some changes of daily dress were written into legislation. Morality and religious practices of colonial rulers coerced subjects into wearing approved clothing that was quite different from the suitability to the culture over which they ruled. This was the case in Australia where government agencies, settlers, and later missionaries endeavored, not always successfully, to impose "orderly" European standards of cleanliness and clothing on Indigenous people.[38] The New South Wales government began the official habit of distributing blankets annually to Aborigines who regularly appeared in urban areas wearing no or few body supplements, and European farmers gave out "slop" clothing to those living on their farms.

Cultural exchange in terms of dress in India followed a distinct path as the impact of colonial rule hardened. The East India Company accepted Indigenous workers in their local Indian dress and many European officials at the turn of the nineteenth century also wore light, comfortable Indian clothing on public occasions,[39] particularly if they lived outside major cities. But in 1830, the Company, an increasingly bureaucratic organization, issued an official Ordinance banning the wearing of Indian dress on formal occasions.[40] With the commencement of the British Raj in 1858, rules about appearance were to impose further restrictions and employees were required to wear the hot, heavy, dark wool suits that were conventional in Britain. This was a clear demonstration of interference in cultural mores—a manifest sign of the power of the British in India.

# Mutability of Past and Present

Racial, religious, cultural, and geographical complexities, in which the temporal plays a part, are such that the fashioning of identity in the world of the twenty-first century is usually a conscious choice of combining multiple influences from both local populations and cultures elsewhere. Clothes worn together as ensembles can be of varied temporality, a mix of items, accessories, textiles, and ornaments selectively acquired. This has happened in Brazil, for example, but many other examples and anachronisms of dress exist as garments that have been adopted or recycled across cultures. The racial, religious, cultural, and geographical complexities in which the temporal plays a part, is such that the fashioning of Brazilian identity has been a conscious absorption of multiple influences from both its local Indigenous populations and cultures around the world. [41]

In what is a new phase of clothing, dress can be made up of numerous time frames where garments can be used selectively from wide-ranging sources; the modern alongside the second hand. In the two poverty stricken Congo capitals Kinshasa and Brazzaville, so-called *Sapeurs* (Société des Ambianceurs et Persons Élégantes (SAPE)) are a striking example of this almost theatrical incoherence (Figure 4.4). These style influencers acquire, alter and display miscellaneous high end brand labeled garments of all kinds to create a dramatized status of their own to redefine themselves.[42] Sierra Leone in West Africa has been a particularly fascinating example of this combination of strikingly different garments. Here, impoverished men and women in the capital, Freetown, self-consciously repurpose clothing from markets selling secondhand Western clothes, of multiple origin and designer rejects from the West. Customers mix these secondhand items plus flamboyant new African prints outrageously juxtaposed in order to represent themselves as deliberately out of sync with other fashion habits and aesthetic norms. The inventions in Freetown were made

**Figure 4.4** A group of *sapeurs* (Société des Ambianceurs et Persons Élégantes) in Kinshasa, Democratic Republic of the Congo, 2014. (Credit: Per-Anders Pettersson/ Contibutor.)

known through a 2011 series of TV documentaries hosted by UNICEF worker Jo Dunlop and called *Fashpack*.[43] These programs recorded the extraordinary talent of local Africans using style to show defiance against extreme poverty, social depravity, and the violence they experienced every day.

Dress around the world has been made up of material artifacts of great stylistic variety, used in different ways to project meanings about identity, status, cultural habits, and personal taste. As clothing is given different meanings by lived experiences, temporal engagements and design interactions between cultures, any suggestion that progressive time lines of style are possible is unsupportable. What we find over time are disjunctive relations in terms of worldwide cultural exchange of different forms of dress and ornamentation. Movements of ideas and commodities, as well as freedom of design trade-offs, have been characteristic of a great many cultures. To seek legal protection of any design or creative ideas concerned with body supplements and modifications has not succeeded to any serious degree, although copying ideas from a culture without permission (rather than borrowing or being inspired by it) has become highly controversial among First Nations peoples. Termed "cultural appropriation," this process usually refers to a violation of the rights of a minority culture and has moved into the area of illegal practice. While the legal question of copying ideas is problematic, so too is the definition of cultural ownership. Can a culture sequester its customary design motifs and declare ownership of them when defining any boundaries in a digitized, global world is so problematic? (See Focus 4a)

Clearly cultural assimilation is different and an important sign of merging aspects of one culture with that of another. Over time and across many vibrant cultures, artisan designers have metaphorically crossed cultural lines to advantageously borrow styles, fabrics, and methods from others without dispute. Examples of design in one culture have been consciously taken over by another, absorbed and altered in a form of creative hybridity. But the copying or appropriation of the designs, symbols, and aesthetic impulses of minority cultures without consent is quite different. It is seen as disrespectful and has now become highly politicized. Despite these clear differences, the very complexity of copyright for all designers needs careful consideration. This said, freedom of cultural exchange is a key element that has encouraged creativity over the centuries and is a topic that remains of considerable relevance to any study of dress and time.

## Focus 4a
# WHO SHOULD OWN THE PAST?

This Focus develops one aspect of extraordinary cultural exchanges of textile and clothing designs that took place from early times across Europe, Africa, and Asia. These included restless searches for new ideas to stimulate trade and commercial gain. Underlying these quests for ideas lie more philosophical questions about whether designs of any culture are free for others to use, or if they should be fiercely protected, especially those which have special meaning for them. Should a culture own their past, or is "the past" a moveable concept, a temporal relativity that is constantly being redefined?

Detailed work with items of material culture in northern North America in the eighteenth and early nineteenth centuries, demonstrates the singular advantages of hybridity in global trading relationships. In an essay, Laura Peers shows how some hybrid garments were part of financially advantageous cross-cultural arrangements during this time, although her examples are earlier than the ones I use here. She discusses easy exchange of skills between Indigenous women and British and French fur traders and tailors, to mutual benefit. Indigenous women, who learned tailoring from British tailors, imposed their older design motifs and aesthetics onto traditional hide coats, opening up new relationships and opportunities.[44] Here boundaries were not protected, but vibrant cultural relationships were enhanced.

Borrowing, reusing, reinterpreting, and even copying ideas from other cultures and eras, has been a long-standing artistic practice for European high fashion and textile designers. Even thirty to forty years ago, Europeans could take design motifs of all kinds from other social groups, usually without acknowledgement of sources. There had been no problem with nineteenth-century designers interpreting or copying Medieval embroidery, as the originals were deemed historical not contemporary. Creative work of "the past" was notionally free to be used without charges of plagiarism. In Australia even in the 1970s and 80s, the work of Sydney dress and textile designers Jenny Kee and Linda Jackson was obviously inspired by both Aboriginal and African designs. At that time, use of Indigenous sources was accepted without question.

This changed in the second half of the twentieth century and plagiarizing Indigenous creative ideas became an issue of political and legal concern.[45] This was partly because creativity has been problematic to define and Western law has found it difficult to grant copyright to ethnic groups rather than to individuals. In Australia, First Nations peoples are made up of numerous recognized cultural groups and defining design ownership is sensitive politically. This intended protection of Aboriginal creativity from copyists raises complex issues in respect of artistic works and production of souvenir products, all lucrative sources for unscrupulous agents. I am talking here about protecting cultural ideas from appropriation by outsiders, not cultural authentication which is how cultures have adopted and assimilated a design from another, different culture, intentionally making it part of their own.[46]

As European designers increasingly took design ideas from Indigenous peoples around the world, First Nations minorities began to seek ownership of their "traditional" designs and motifs. These former subject peoples became increasingly indignant over unacknowledged European use of these designs on wraps, T-shirts, skirts, and ponchos, considering it disrespectful, even discriminatory. They began to demand legal protection for their creativity.

In Australia the Copyright Act of 1968 and the Design Act of 2003, as well as various amendments, created a somewhat blurred definition of Indigenous creative work. Successive decisions by the courts purported to extend protection of the original Copyright Act but this has led nowhere. Collective rights could not be recognized and did not meet requirements for "originality."[47] Defining intellectual property rights has been—and remains—an important issue for all Indigenous designers, and affects many minority cultures around the world. On the other hand, it is significant that Indigenous people have also produced designs that reaffirmed their cultural identity, like the Kalabari people in southeastern Nigeria, who were able to reauthenticate their creative past, rather than see it used illegally and for profit.[48]

Generally speaking, copyright protection for Indigenous peoples in Australasia has proved difficult to implement. In fact, currently no laws domestic or international fully protect cultural design heritage. In New Zealand tattoos have become mainstream, but if a design is authentic to the Māori, with special cultural meanings for the person or group who wears them, the group has ownership of the designs. This is vague protection. Indian designer Nachiket Barve was highly successful in India's 2014 Fashion Week, held in New Delhi, his bold designs mixed Indian heritage and Māori "tribal" motifs unproblematically, using the national emblem of New Zealand, the fern frond design (Figure 4.5). Māori sports stars wear tā moko (tattoos on the body) with little respect for copyright laws.

Labels of authenticity have been created at various times in New Zealand, but a Māori trademark has not been a success. The Toi Iho Māori Made Mark was registered in 2002 to supposedly protect product authenticity for the use of the koru, (the spiral shape of an unfurling silver fern frond). Two other trademarks were created, acknowledging cross-cultural collaborations between Māori and non-Māori.[49] These were not enforced, however, and the New Zealand government disestablished the Toi Iho Māori Mark in 2009.

Another interesting example has been the company #Dsquaw, now Dsquared2, criticized for their collection of women's clothes at Milan Fashion Week 2015–16; the term "squaw" comes from the Algonquin word for a First Nations woman and is now considered derogatory. Canadian designers Dean and Dan Caten used "Indigenous"

**Figure 4.5** Model wearing a dress with a New Zealand Māori motif by Indian designer Nachiket Barve, at Wills Lifestyle India Fashion Week 2014, New Delhi. (Credit: Raajessh Kashyap/Hindustan Times via Getty Images.)

materials, "tribal-print" ponchos, tattoos, and coats trimmed with furs of animals which were considered to be of Indigenous significance.[50] What constituted the "past" for these designers was clearly ill considered, although Navajo textile motifs were accepted as the source. This photograph of a Navajo family outside their sod home shows age-old designs on body wrapping that inspires designers like these (Figure 4.6). The Canadian designers described their Indigenous theme as a "Captivating play on contrasts: an ode to America's native tribes meets the noble spirit of Old Europe," claiming the collection was partly inspired by Canadian/American Indian tribal wear, but neither "native" Canadian nor American artists were consulted. While the term "Old Europe" was acceptable, public outcries forced the designers to remove all references to #Dsquaw from their advertising.

The name "Navajo" and associated motifs have been used as inspiration by other clothing companies to sell its garments such as Urban Outfitters, a clothing business headquartered in Philadelphia.[51] This practice disregards the fact that Navajos are a

**Figure 4.6** Navajo family posed outside their home, wearing traditional blankets. Undated. (Credit: Bettmann / Contributor.)

people with their own political system and culture—not a brand. Their designs, which communicate clan association but also individual familial histories and identities, are sacred and not intended for use outside specific contexts of belief. While there are no proprietary rights to the cross, diamond, triangle, and zigzag patterns, it is unethical for a non-Native company to profit from "tribal" designs and names without the consent or collaboration of the community.

Tensions continue to exist worldwide between "owners'" of traditional creative work and laws enacted. In 2015 the Parisian designer Isabel Marant was criticised for using a blouse pattern in her haute couture collection that had allegedly been taken from the designs of the Indigenous Mixe people of Santa María Tlahuitoltepec, Oaxaca, Southern Mexico.[52] Another company associated with Marant, the Antik Brand, was also caught up in a copyright issue in relation to the Mixe.[53] The resulting legal case hinged on whether pattern designs and embroidery were outright copies or just inspiration. A non-binding decision of the Oaxaca Cultural Heritage Declaration confirmed the design *was* a symbol of Mixe cultural identity.[54] But Marant has continued to be inspired by the Mexican embroidery designs, here worn by herself and her daughter at the Paris opening of her 2016 collection (Figure 4.7).

**Figure 4.7** The designer Isabel Marant attends "Isabel Marant x Mytheresa" event at Paris Fashion Week, Fall/Winter 2016–17. She is wearing one of her own designs. (Credit: Victor Boyko/WireImage.)

The internet has added further complexities to issues of copyright of clothing design, unrelated to the creative work of Indigenous peoples. Canny Chinese women designers and entrepreneurs, engaged in dress marketing part time, are dodging the problem for they deal in fakes called *shanzhai*.[55] Some purchase original products and make sample versions, updating consumers on which parts they are modifying. They invite comment on social media. Potential customers offer personal opinions and may request alterations. If entrepreneurs copy ordinary ready-made clothes, they are not charged with infringement of copyright. But if the copied clothing is highly unusual and eye-catching, the police may curtail their activities.[56]

Ownership of copyright in clothing and design is increasingly difficult to define and protect. The appropriation of designs (in particular those of traditional cultures) has become highly politicized and contentious. The UN has deliberated on cultural appropriation since 1974 via its World Intellectual Property Organization, with a view to enshrine in law intellectual property rights for Indigenous peoples everywhere. But the difficulty is that contemporary clothing is increasingly locked into ever more rapid production of garments and textiles. Australian law has established some form of protection but has not been able to legislate strongly enough. The issue of minority cultures and their rights to claim ownership of their past heritage functions to a degree. But to answer the question of who owns the cultural past, is to enter an area of complexity to which at present no solution has been found.

## Focus 4b
## THE "KIMONO" CONTROVERSY

This Focus examines a vigorous dispute surrounding a French painting of a woman in traditional Japanese dress shown in an American art museum. The question of cultural exchange and ownership lies at the heart of this short essay. The picture is a well-known oil painting by Claude Monet called "La japonaise" (1876), which was shown in the "Looking East" exhibition at the Boston Museum of Fine Arts in 2015.[57] Monet's painting was originally displayed at the Second Impressionist Exhibition in Paris, exactly 100 years before. The painting is of the artist's wife disguised by a blond wig. She is wearing a sumptuous, very formal red embroidered Japanese *uchikake* (a warm coat-like garment) with padded hem, over a kimono, a form of double body supplement. The display of this picture raises important issues about how dress of the past can be challenged by a sense of ownership of its meanings in the present. It can also be caught up in cultural disagreements as a result of historical misunderstandings, undermining its value and perhaps the artist's original intentions. In the image below, a woman stands in front of the Monet painting (Figure 4.8). She is wearing a replica of the painted *uchikake*, calling into question the differences between an original garment, a painting of one, and a material copy.

    The garment pictured is normally worn over a kimono, the latter usually wrapped over from left over right, held closed by an *obi* waist band. The *uchikake* is a heavy garment, worn typically for special occasions like weddings or for theatrical performances. It trails along the ground and here the spread of its hem echoes the display of fans on the wall behind and on the floor. It is a painting that plays with European and Asian stereotypes of sexuality and aesthetic taste. One opinion is that its tone is performative, in that it appears to display wry insinuations of stereotypical European "Orientalism," the model wears a wig, and the garment may have been made for a male *kabuki* actor.[58] The sensual pose, suggestive look, and fan are in sharp contrast to the vulgar aggression of the *samurai* in the garment's design. At the original Impressionist Exhibition in Paris, Monet's painting attracted mixed opinions, but why did

**Figure 4.8** A visitor to the Boston Museum of Fine Arts in 2015 poses as wife Camille in front of Monet's painting "La Japonaise," wearing a replica of the painted *uchikake*. (Credit: John Blanding/The Boston Globe via Getty Images.)

it later become so controversial? When shown in Boston in 2015, it drew extremely outspoken comments and was regarded by many as highly contentious. [59]

Hand sewn, kimonos (literally things to wear) were garments worn by Japanese men and women for over 1,000 years. They were made of various fabrics, usually decorated with resist dyes and stencils, and came to consist of numerous layers of different colors, increasing their extraordinary aesthetic quality. Their colors were given poetic names.[60] The basic kimono form altered little for centuries, although cultural knowledge was required to understand its subtleties.[61] Over the years, it has been subject to a range of different interpretations—political, nationalist, aesthetic, and commercial—and the number of publications on the garment and its wearers seems to increase yearly.[62]

Japan first seriously encountered Western ideas when the American Commodore Matthew Perry arrived with his ships in 1853 and later formulated the first trade agreement with Japan in 1854. The Meiji emperor was restituted and the term kimono was adopted in the Meiji Period (1868–1912) as Japan opened up to the West and when cultural exchange began in earnest. At the time, Perry made unflattering comments about the kimono, saying all women in them looked the same. He maintained that they failed to show the wearer's social status and the dress appeared to him to be unchanging. This perceived lack of inventiveness has become a common European response about the clothing of "non-European" cultures. Used as a symbol to project a unified Japanese nation from the time it established relations with other countries, the kimono was to became a national symbol in Japan during the nineteenth century.

That said, the Meiji emperor was wearing Western-style clothing by 1872 and it was readily adopted by urban men in Japan as well. The empress was converted to Western dress by 1886, and the following year decreed all women be encouraged to adopt it. Many were not enthusiastic. By this time, kimonos had lost much of their subtle differences and nomenclature. At the same time, Europeans were impressed with the garment. The *kimono sada yacco*, named after the famous Japanese *geisha*, dancer, and actress, was produced for Western taste during the Belle Époque and sold widely in Paris department stores.[63] This was at much the same time that Monet was showing "La japonaise."

Monet's work was part of "Japonisme," the widespread fascination for all things Japanese in the 1870s and 1880s in France, Britain, the United States, and Australia. Appreciation extended to furniture, chinaware, screens, lacquer work, flower arrangements, and interior décor. Also termed "Aestheticism," the taste infused works of many British and French painters including Degas, Manet, and Whistler. In Monet's painting, there is an implicit sense that it references the eroticism of a *geisha* despite his wife being the subject. There is some suggestion Monet was offering his own critical comment about the Japanese craze. But his use of quite glaring colors is entirely different from the work of the aesthete Whistler with his subtle color harmonies.

In 2015 the Boston Museum, along with many art institutions, was keen to boost attendance and encourage ways to engage visitors by arranging enhanced encounters with works of art. They set up a program called "Kimono Wednesdays," endeavoring to give visitors the opportunity to think more deeply about Monet's painting. A lecture was advertised entitled "Monet. Flirting with the Exotic." Attendees on Wednesdays were encouraged to try on a heavy replica red *uchikake,* similar to the one in the painting, pose for photographs, and share them on social media. The aim was to experience what it would be like to wear the clothes of another time and culture. It would give visitors a tactile experience of kimonos, although ironically the garment they were encouraged to wear is not one. Even so, dressing up in the clothes of a culture and period in the past to which you do not belong, has become an activity considered by many as inappropriate, to lack respect, and to be embedded in issues of contemporary identity politics.[64]

When "La japonaise" was on loan to the Setagaya Art Museum in Tokyo, the Kyoto Municipal Museum, and the Nagoya/Boston Museum of Fine Arts, the program was a great success. This was partly why Boston adopted a similar series of events. But the temporal complexities of dress as painted and worn were evident in mixed public responses to the meanings of the exhibit in the US. Wearing of the ostensibly traditional kimono in public, by those who were not Japanese, was seriously frowned upon, and some Asian-American visitors regarded the activity as typecasting, racially inappropriate, and as exoticizing Asians. Others felt it mimicked Orientalizing colonial attitudes. On the other hand, many who self-identified as Japanese, living in the US, had only positive comments to make about the practice as a way of encouraging cultural understanding.

On the exhibition opening night, there was a small protest, and later three protesters confronted the museum with signs that read "Try on the kimono, learn what it's like to be a racist imperialist !!!today!!!" Some apparently organized a Facebook page, "Stand Against Yellow Face." As a result, trying on the replica garment was stopped, but it could be touched. Matthew Teitelbaum, the very recently appointed Director of the Museum, presented a panel discussion on "Kimono Wednesdays." In talking about the controversial program, he said he had been misguided and apologized for sensationalizing an important issue.

In the seventeenth century, the kimono had been worn daily both by men and women. Later it became a woman's preserve, and after the Second World War was regarded as a more formal and conservative garment. High-quality artist-designed kimonos began to be collected by museums and they became a symbol of Japan. But in some ways, labeling the garment as traditional seems to have diminished its relevance. Skills were being lost and silk, the ideal fabric for the kimono, was replaced by cheaper easy-care fabrics such as rayon and polyester. The *yukata* (Figure 4.9), a more informal, simpler garment, usually of cotton, became increasingly popular for summer wear. Its fabric could be Westernized, with European motifs tempting European as well as Japanese consumers. The belief that kimonos were essentially Japanese dissipated in the twentieth century.

In Japan, women had their own opinions about the Boston incident. Many were sad and puzzled that kimono-wearing generated such controversy and that people were denied the opportunity to wear what they felt was a significant garment. The Boston controversy was further complicated by the fact that the garment in question was *not* a kimono. The fact that the photograph showed a visitor who was not Japanese wearing a replica kimono seemed a bridge too far for many in the US.

At the core of this incident were numerous and disparate views about the use, if not misuse, of traditional garments by those beyond the culture of origin. The questionable authenticity of wearing this particular garment, which occupied different modalities of the temporal, highlighted issues of what might be considered appropriate forms of cultural exchange. The kimono is a sign of Japan, yet at the time, no Japanese apparently considered it offensive for others to wear the supposed replica. The garment

**Figure 4.9** Young women in floral summer *yukata* during a local festival in Yokkaichi City, Japan. (Credit: Dünzl/ullstein bild via Getty Images.)

was in fact paid for by the Japanese national broadcaster, NHK. Protests may have been misplaced as Monet's image is not a depiction of his Parisienne wife in fancy dress. It is more likely a theatricalized critique of Japonisme, not a reference to an authentic Japan. The image and surrounding controversy show that meanings behind use of a culture's past can be highly nuanced and may have less significance for some than for others.

# 5

# RITUALS: THE ROLE OF TIME

Dress is a significant indicator of the social life of humankind but, as I have shown, no clothing is straightforward, or developmentally progressive. In this chapter, I suggest that ritual dress has been made up of many extraordinary and uneven material elements and social interchanges between past and present. In terms of its symbolic components, it stands apart from expectations of the clothing of everyday life. Archaeologists have found representations, apparently showing ritual events with seemingly associated body supplements on cave walls, in unrelated geographical rock sites around the world, some believed to date at least as early as the Meseolithic era. In prewritten history, however, it is not possible to clarify when embellished participants started to become integral to ceremony and what a figure such as this one might mean (Figure 5.1).

**Figure 5.1** Rock painting of an apparently round-headed masked figure, with strips hanging from the waist, back and front, and likely body paint. Possibly early Neolithic Period. Tassili n'Ajjer, southeast Algeria. (Unesco World Heritage List, 1982), Algeria. (Credit: DeAgostini/Getty Images.)

In discussing ritual dress since ancient times, a progressive time-line approach to understanding early wear on the body is clearly inappropriate. It does not apply to what are obscure but evidently "special" forms of dress. In ancient representations, significance is to be found in the uneven and wider sense of if (and approximately when) changes occurred, not some form of neatly defined timetable. In far more recent history, the pace of change in ceremonial dress has continued to occur inconsistently, giving the impression that it has altered more slowly than items of everyday clothing. The sense in which it seems to change infrequently, if at all, needs careful consideration.

The topic of dress for ceremony is extensive and because of this I have selected examples where particularly pertinent interrelationships between dress and time exist. It is important to underline that dignified dress worn for socio-spiritual practices is not entirely disentangled from the secular display of power and status. All cultures use special body coverings and ornament to mark solemn occasions of both religious and secular significance, and demonstrate times when these occur. There are some garment shapes that have been worn worldwide and which have almost seemed to transcend time. But robes of investiture, formal ankle-length robes, cloaks, or mantles that have accrued practical and ritual value over extensive periods, do show certain distinct differences. Even so, the associated sense of worth and endurance in these garments has continued into contemporary examples infiltrating the dress of dignitaries around the world, such as judges and academics, even robes of post colonial leaders.

Before I consider instances of ceremonial use, it is important to clarify how I use the terms "ceremony" and "ritual." They are essentially synonymous, but I take the view that rituals imply frequent, regular enactments, being socio-spiritual narratives of great solemnity, but often smaller than a ceremony. In comparison, some ceremonies—such as the great seasonal processions of the Christian Church, or investitures and coronations—are more celebratory events, for larger numbers of attendees, and more ornamental in presentation. The magnificant Indian Durbars fit in here.

I concentrate primarily on Western European ceremonial dress, particularly garments connected with royalty and ecclesiastical robes worn on significant religious occasions, both inside and outside places of worship. For cultures within the scope of Western influence, ceremonial dress has been modeled on two particular design sources, that of classical Greece and Medieval Europe. But the "special" dress of societies beyond the European sphere do not necessarily follow this pattern to the same degree. Welters and Lillethun argue that categories of ecclesiastical and other ritual dress, which have evolved from late Roman times and persisted to the present, have shown little change.[1] They illustrate Armenian priests in 1717 wearing liturgical dress, which they claim has remained unchanged to the present day. Even here, the case regarding lack of change in ritual dress is somewhat overstated. There are two Armenian Churches—the

Apostolic and Orthodox—and although there have been many cultural similarities in dress components, the patterns, sizes, colors, and decorative motifs have varied. In this chapter, I suggest that it is in these subtle variations that significance lies.

# Early Evidence

The earliest signs so far of specific types of ritual activity amongst palaeolithic finds apparently made connections with "other" realms of gods and ancestors and were linked to propitiation and fertility. They were particularly associated with mortuary activities, where red ochre was highly prized. The Middle Stone Age Twin Rivers Cave in Zambia contains extremely large numbers of widely different colored iron oxide stones dating between 400,000–200,000 years old. British archaeologist Lawrence Barham excavated these stones, finding many were ground up for use as pigments; in his view, this was done expressly for body painting and associated cave walls.[2] Painting for ritual was of great significance and it was also Barham's opinion that people of the time had to have had some form of language to communicate repetitious activities associated with ceremonies, which were probably shamanistic. No material remains of body supplements or handheld objects have been found at these very earliest archaeological sites.

At some point, garments and handheld objects began to be more visibly entwined with ceremonies. Clothing clearly became integral to habitual events associated with the hunt, fertility, mortuary practices, spiritual propitiation, and more. It was also a sign of increasing interaction with material culture, such as necklaces, baskets, and other trade goods. Initially, the presence of animals in rock art seem to outweigh the depiction of humans or spiritual beings. Yet increasingly schematic figures, some with weaponry or other handheld objects, some with decorative halos, horns, or feather-like marks, began to appear, together with more human-like figures, although these are often unclear or faded. More than 13,000 mammoth-ivory beads were found on skeletons at the Russian site of Sungir, northeast of Moscow, and dated to the Mid-Upper Paleolithic period.[3] These seems very advanced for the time and accompany four burials rich with grave goods. There is the possibility these ornaments were also made for shamanistic reasons, making their use difficult to confirm.

# Religious Organizations

We know far more about the emergence of the great monotheistic religions of Islam, Judaism, and Christianity. They show the survival of some elements of ritual dress over long periods of time. In the case of Christianity, pictorial representations have assisted researchers in understanding the dates, the use of embellishments on the body, and the degree of replication that occurred in ecclesiastical garments.[4] Investiture robes had a common origin in Medieval Christianity and Medieval Islam. Islamic investitures are known from written sources and show robes of honor were personalized, sometimes as exchanges or substantial gifts from a ruler to a recipient. On occasion, this even consisted of transmission of the spiritual state of a ruler to the subject of exchange, enhancing the nature of rulership. Islamic investitures were inconsistent in nature, and are examined in detail elsewhere,[5] so here I will consider only rituals in the Christian and Russian Orthodox Churches.

Vestments of the Catholic and Anglican clergy had a measured pace of change and garments were largely modeled on high-status Roman dress. After the Roman Imperial Edit of Milan in 313 CE, which gave toleration to Christianity, relationships between vestments of the Christian church and the Roman state continued to be close. Conventions and garment types of the later Middle Ages remained remarkably similar until Vatican II (1962–5), which encouraged a more contemporary attitude to the design of vestments.

It is tempting to consider liturgical ceremonial dress as timeless, but any idea of vestments as unchanging is misleading. Through careful observation, it is clear the terms "traditional" and "unchanging" are not synonymous. Rather, modified developments *did* occur in some garments, which had formerly been considered to cling strictly to past conventions; importantly, their symbolic meanings changed as well. That traditions can be invented is now a more useful way to consider ceremonial developments in religious and coronation dress. Eicher, Evenson, and Lutz, with their combined and remarkable spread of knowledge of garments and textiles around the world, hold this view.[6] Lou Taylor's landmark object-based studies of "peasant life" in Europe also shows dress styles are never inherited intact from the past.[7]

The Roman Catholic cope is a significant example of long-term design and derives from the loose, everyday, outer secular clothing of Roman antiquity. This long semicircular capacious cope (*cappa serica*), is particularly associated with bishops (a Roman Catholic priest dispensing the Eucharist at Mass normally does not wear a cope). It is an ample and dignified processional garment and accompanied by a mitre.[8] Bishops' copes have, in the past, been made of priceless silk brocades—often of great richness of design—and heavily decorated with embroidery. In Britain during the Middle Ages, they were decorated with the technique of Opus Anglicanum (1100–1350). This embroidery is extraordinary, almost breathtaking in appearance. Workers used a silk or velvet ground embroidered with lustrous gold and silver thread. It was also stitched on orphreys, the ornamental borders of vestments found on chasubles and wide-sleeved dalmatics.

Ceremonial and liturgical dress are examples of how the term "traditional" for body supplements needs to be amended. These garments have differed over time in material terms, and changes have also been meaningful in strategic ways, serving political functions as well. They have been able to convey extra-lingual information and "communicate the unsaid and unsayable," especially to illiterate congregations and other public audiences.[9] It is possible that their degree of "sameness," plus small, mutable characteristics, have been used at times to both reassure and manipulate the populace, even to shape their beliefs. Worthy of respect, conventional in shape, but grandiose in fabric and ornamentation, ceremonial garments worn by kings, emperors, and bishops have reinforced their status and aided political and religious ambitions. It is useful to note the Marist Roman Catholic Bishop Jean-Baptiste Pompallier, who arrived in New Zealand in 1838 from France, had missionary intentions and his bright colored vestments were a good example of the potential strategic powers of liturgical robes.

At the first Mass he performed, he wore a splendid purple soutane (a form of cassock) and sash. At the signing of the Treaty of Waitangi, New Zealand's first and most significant agreement with local peoples in 1840, Pompallier sported an alluring dark purple robe, buttoned at the front, purple stockings, and a gold bishop's crozier. The splendor of his outfits had an emotional effect on the laity. For instance, they contrasted with many elderly Māori, sometimes draped in large mats of weft-twined flax overlaid with strips of dog-skin. Pompallier's garb was so impressive that many people agreed to convert.[10] He was said to have baptized 1,000 Māoris throughout New Zealand, and Wesleyan missionaries at the time criticized his colorful vestments (and the powerful formality of Catholic rituals) as unfair.[11]

Christian vestments of other faiths, such as those in the Greek and Russian Orthodox Churches, have certain similarities to those of Roman Catholics but there are some differences. The vestments of the Orthodox churches have many close links, but their nomenclature differs. The long cloak has survived over the years and is still worn today, as seen in this photograph of Russian Orthodox priests leaving the Assumption Cathedral, Vladimir, near Moscow in 2017 (Figure 5.2).[12] The *mandyas* or mantles which they wear are processional garments for bishops but can be worn by other priests during Mass. The headwear of gold fabric, seen on the extreme left of the group, indicates a high-ranking cleric. The color blue represents Mary, Mother of God. Underneath the mantle, Russian Orthodox priests wear a voluminous black, ankle-length garment called a *riassa* (*ryassa*).[13] It is a tradition in some parishes to touch the hem of the priest's vestment or *phelonion* (chasuble) as he passes by. The custom imitates the woman healed by touching the hem of Christ's robe. This is a form of ritual that reflects the power of "touch" also found in association with religious relics. (See Focus 5a)

**Figure 5.2** Russian Orthodox priests leaving the Assumption Cathedral, Vladimir, near Moscow, 2017. (Credit: Alison Matthews David.)

# The Head of State: Coronations

Coronation dress and regalia in Western Europe has ancient origins. The entanglement of age-old and more recent elements suggests time was almost compressed in categories of this regalia although its separate parts were made up of many microhistories, each with their own temporal narrative. Whilst early relations between church and state fluctuated between separation and integration, the Ancient Roman College of Pontiffs, the highest-ranking priests of the state's religion, was subsumed into the Imperial Office by Emperor Augustus. He was conferred with his Imperial title in 27 CE, but we know little of his investiture.[14]

The first Christian emperor, Constantine the Great, moved his capital from Rome to Byzantium in 306 CE. A suite of ritual conventions used by the Christian Church began in his capital Imperial Byzantium, and drew on precedents from classical Rome. The complex ceremonies and kings of the European Frankish tribes selectively followed Roman precedent in terms of dress. The history is highly complex, but added to previous investitures was a military presence. When exactly is unclear.[15] King Charles the Bald, fighting for his position in Europe, was crowned Holy Roman Emperor in 875 CE but was said to have miraculously received robes for himself and his ecclesiastical followers some time before, so the mix of regal and episcopal garments were brought together symbolically in a tradition where kings and bishops were thought "to reflect one another, as two visible aspects of a single, indivisible Christian reality."[16]

From then on in the West, there were three fundamental ingredients of ceremonial investitures for emperors and kings: the secular (royal), the religious, and the military.

By the end of the eighth century CE, records of coronations began to be kept and one of the two Patriarchal *Eucologia* in 795 CE contains extensive details of dress, behavior, and regalia that would confer royal status on Charlemagne the Holy Roman Emperor in 800 CE. [17] He was the first recognized emperor to rule from Europe since the fall of the Western Roman Empire, three centuries earlier. Charlemagne apparently wore a long alb, a dalmatic, and a stole crossed over the breast, gloves, and a red and gold semicircular mantle. But it is now certain he never wore the mantle. It was made later, in 1130–4, in the royal workshops in Palermo founded by Roger II, King of Sicily. The garment was embroidered by Byzantine workers in their own style and with a Kufi inscription.[18]

The precise detail of later investitures, whether in Italy or in Constantinople, became increasingly lavish. Common to most was an initial procession, the arrival at the declared site or church, the honor given by the military, the changing of clothes and footwear of various kinds, the covering with a *sagum* (a coarse cloak common to the military), entry with the Pope or Patriarch, a prayer said over a long *paludamentum*, a purple woolen cloak derived from a military garment, a gold diadem placed on the ruler's head, homage paid by senators, and gifts of gold coin to the military.

This ritual way of conducting coronations and their regalia was used with certain variations throughout Europe and Britain, and in revised form continued into the twentieth century, notably in Great Britain. The coronation of Her Majesty Queen Elizabeth II, Supreme Governor of the Anglican Church, and Head of the Armed Forces, was marked by the three historic and symbolic constituents, namely the ancient mix of secular, religious, and military practices.[19] Her coronation was conducted in 1953 by the Archbishop of Canterbury, who anointed her with oil and crowned her with one of the weighty St Edward the Confessor's crowns, copied for King Charles II in 1661. Over her dalmatic (a wide-sleeved, loose vestment open at the sides often worn by deacons and bishops) was a velvet mantle trimmed with ermine, a longtime heraldic symbol, and she was presented with a sword and golden spurs.[20] She was accompanied by her Yeomen of the Guard (the military component).[21]

**Figure 5.3** King Tupou VI of Tonga and his wife, Queen Nanasipauʻu Tukuʻaho, are crowned in Nuku'alofa, the capital of Tonga, in 2015. (Credit: Edwina Pickles/Fairfax Media/Getty Images.)

Of great interest is that Tonga, a Pacific nation that still has a king, remains closely allied to its colonial ruler. The British Western Pacific Territories (BWPT) was a colonial entity of the Pacific islands and the administration of Tonga was conducted by a representative of the British Crown which, until 2008, had veto power over its foreign policies and finances.[22] The nation continues to have a king, namely Tupou VI of Tonga, who was crowned formally alongside his queen in 2015 following the death of King Tupou V. (Figure 5.3). The ceremony was a pledge of allegiance to both Britain and ancient Tongan culture. The nobility who mourned the deceased king wore black undergarments, their bodies encased in capacious customary *ta'ovala* of plaited pandanus leaf. These striking body supplements were symbolic, intended to protect the *mana* of the wearer's inner person from vulnerability to supernatural forces. (See also Figure 6.9)[23]

Tonga retains official connections with the UK, and the coronation reflected this relationship. The style, materials of garments, and format of the ceremony to crown King Tupou was a simplified form of Queen Elizabeth II's coronation. For the event, the Tongan monarch wore a military-style jacket, a white wraparound lower garment, and a capacious crimson cloak trimmed with ermine, with wide cape collar. He had a tall gold crown designed for the occasion. It is an extraordinary example of a minimal version of the longstanding custom of lavish European cononations, based on dress worn since the Middle Ages, here translated into a modern island culture in the South Pacific. After the coronation, 150 Tongan nobles wearing white robes, with customary woven ta'ovala mats tied around their waists, celebrated the event at a social gathering in a significant mix of old and new.

Ceremonial garments and vestments have characteristics suggesting valued cultural concepts which reach back across the centuries. This has important religious, strategic, and political elements. Considered worthy of respect, grandiose ceremonial garments reinforce the political and religious ambitions, and power of rulers and heads of social organizations, kings, queens, emperors, and senators. Its symbolism in all cases is varied and complex.

# Inventing Ceremony

There have been occasions when coronation ceremonies have been invented, like those of Napoleon Bonaparte, who was certainly not of royal lineage. He manufactured his ancestry by means of two significant ceremonies, one as Emperor of the French (1804), partly signaling a temporal link with his supposed forebear, Emperor Augustus of ancient Rome, and the other as King of Italy (1805). So one could say he personally combined long held traditions in a curious and strategic mixture of the past and his personal ambitions to suit the present. The mixture was well reasoned, but there is no better example of a challenge to a chronological account of ceremonial dress history.

Napoleon, searching for a model for his two coronations, looked to earlier Imperial examples for ideas. He settled on the Imperial investiture of Charlemagne in 800 CE as his source, for Charlemagne had been crowned in Rome by Pope Leo III as Holy Roman Emperor. Napoleon used his artist friend Jean Isabey to design his dress, based on images of Charlemagne, although their accuracy is doubted. Napoleon was crowned in the cathedral of Notre-Dame de Paris with some of the regalia loaned to him by the Pope.[24] It consisted of an orb, a number of swords, a cross, St. Stephen's purse and other reliquaries, a bible, and the sceptre, the so-called "Saber" of Charlemagne.[25] The combination of ritual accoutrements indicated how a significant ceremony, one where past and present were conjoined, had all the meaningful associations that stemmed from the model of ancient Rome.

Napoleon trying to associate his appearance with Charlemagne, wore a long, loose, white satin embroidered garment (alb), although the Frankish Charlemagne had apparently been little interested in clothing. Napoleon's outer garment was a heavy mantle of crimson velvet, lined with ermine, a valuable white fur with black tippets that was reserved for European royalty from the fourteenth century, and in England it certainly became more widely worn as part of the official dress of peers of the realm and of aristocrats. Again supposedly referencing the robes of Charlemagne, the mantle was embroidered with images of the allegedly virtuous and diligent golden bee, a Christian symbol. Napoleon took the bee as his symbol, eschewing the traditional French fleur-de-lis, although Isabey mistook the cicada, symbol of Charlemagne, for a bee and suggested it to Napoleon who adopted it but incorrectly signaled his lineage in the process.

In 1804, with the Pope in attendance, he was anointed in Notre-Dame as noted above but—impatient and not inclined to wait for the pontiff—crowned himself with a replica of Charlemagne's crown, which was decorated with antique Roman cameos. Numerous religious attendees, courtiers, and the military were present. The senior officer and campaign official among the honored guests was Louis-Alexandre Berthier, later Vice-Constable of the Empire. The event was recorded by the painter Jacques-Louis David in a painting dated 1805–07, which depicted Napoleon crowning his wife, Josephine (Figure 5.4). In 1805, Napoleon had himself crowned as King of Italy (he was not, however, anointed) in the Duomo, Milan, with four crowns, one of which was the iron crown of Lombardy, again supposedly belonging to Charlemagne.

For both ceremonies Napoleon appropriated elements from vestments and other garments of the past. He did this in order to strengthen a new, contrived, Imperial future by inventing a tradition for himself, one reaching back to Rome. During the previous history of the Holy Roman Empire, all items of regalia enjoyed

**Figure 5.4** "Emperor Napoleon Crowning Empress Josephine in Notre-Dame de Paris," painting by Jacques-Louis David, 1805–07, Louvre Museum, Paris. (Credit: Exotica.im/Universal Images Group via Getty Images.)

great symbolic power and their reuse was particularly important whenever the legitimacy of the emperor was questioned. What is interesting is that Napoleon signed off on the ritual and robes of his ceremony in great detail. His coronations were strategically composed from materials drawn from a past he deemed worthy of his status, a curious self-made mixture of traditions that ended up as an artificial claim for his roles in the present. He was "wearing time" symbolically.

# Colonial Inventions

Off-shoots of English coronation ceremonies and conventions were imposed on Britain's various colonies in India and Oceania from the nineteenth century, some continuing after independence. Cloaks and draped garments, worn by European royalty, high-status citizens, the wealthy, or those in religious office, justices and celebrants at funerals, scholars, elders, and dignitaries, continued to play a significant part in ceremonial events. For special occasions, the supposed timelessness of certain garments was used for symbolic continuity and links to the past. There were also demonstrated differences, some responding to modern changes in governance. Interrelationships of style between past and present stressed symbolic continuity yet were open to modification.

The British Raj ruled India from 1858–1947, exercising authority over its subject peoples. In the later nineteenth century, the powers of the British colonial government in India were dramatically demonstrated by a number of formal Mughal court Durbars, or mass ceremonial and consultative meetings of rulers. These were organized by the Raj, honoring the coronations of three sequential British monarchs, Queen Victoria (Empress of India), King Edward VII, and King George V. The agendas set out for these occasions deliberately took over the procedures of local Durbars and in various ways imposed colonial administrative methods, traditions of dress and paraphernalia on Britain's subject peoples. The rituals of these Durbars, including the use of dress and garnering of respect for the British rulers, is discussed in detail by Julie Codell. She vividly outlines in detail the events that took place during the Durbars and the ways in which the magnificence of garments and accoutrements was deployed by the colonial power and matched by the Maharajahs.[26]

The events were held in the capital Delhi in 1877, 1903, and 1911. Combining the great history of Indian design with modern British organizing practices and enforced political superiority, they were official pageants of dignity, power, and prestige. The intention was to demonstrate a magnificence worthy of the ruling Empress of India, and later kings and consorts. Colonizer and colonized were to be brought together symbolically at the same time as loyalty was assured. The political aims were to cement the imperial place of colonial British monarchs in India, and materially demonstrate the significance of the ruling colonial government. India's spectacular rituals of the past were intended to be gradually subsumed into celebrations of the colonial rulers, in the hope that Indian rulers—and later, their people—would be fully persuaded to become British subjects.

Extraordinary demonstrations of this congruence were manifest in the pageants like pseudo-coronations that included immense staged processions, banquets, receptions, and garden parties. The outfitting of formal Durbars was highly elaborate. British officials were dressed in military uniforms and the maharajahs in their splendid Indian outfits and lavish jewelry. Noble families made careful wardrobe choices in order to project their role. At the first Durbar, gifts were exchanged of special clothes and brocades with the aim of not only transferring authority, but also demonstrating political continuity and hybridity between the nations. Time—past and present—was represented physically and ceremonially in the service of the political. But the mood of the ceremonies would change from ones of intended co-operation to those where rituals of the rulers were imposed on the ruled.

In 1877 the event was organized by Thomas Thornton, the first secretary to the East India Office, in order to formally proclaim Queen Victoria as Empress of India and to show her as Qaisar-i-Hind—the Urdu word *qaisar* derives from the Arabic approximation of the Latin *caesar*. The regalia of the hundreds of Indians who participated, gathered together the largest collection of jewels and unique Indian clothing traditions ever assembled in one place. In 1903 Lord Curzon of Kedlestone, Viceroy of India since 1858, organized the second Durbar with the theme of modernity and British power. He decided India should have a ceremony filled with pomp and pageantry to acknowledge the British coronation of Edward VII. It also celebrated the sepoys who fought for Britain in the Indian Mutiny of 1857. It was again held in Delhi and a contingent of notable people from Great Britain attended.

The British delegation of forty people brought forty-seven tons of dresses and uniforms for the festivities, but where the first Durbar was a coming-together of two great nations, by 1903 and 1911 it was the British who made sure the Indian maharajahs, nizams, and nawabs were subordinate to the colonial power in terms of spectacle and gift-giving. The gatherings continued to be symbolically staged events but ones at which the power of the colonizer triumphed.

## Post-colonial Ceremony

In post-colonial nations, the problem of creating new symbolic public dress for ceremonial occasions became imperative, especially for marking commencement of national independence. In Africa, as well as Asia and the Pacific, new leaders generally took their customs of clothing, particularly cloaks, into the modern world. but in their own ways. They chose to wear either dignified long gowns or self-decorated military uniforms. For instance, the monarchy of Libya ended in 1969 when military officers, led by Muammar Gaddafi, staged a *coup d'état* against King Idis I. As president, Gaddafi wore either a capacious open green and gold brocaded robe, with patterned stole and small pillbox hat (a diadem on some occasions), or else aggrandized military uniform with excessive braiding, exaggerated epaulettes, and the embellishment of numerous medals.

Like all clothing, the new artificial ceremonial dress was never firmly fixed in character but made up of multiple aspects, a tangled mixture of inherited elements plus current symbols. Although considered dignified, it never had the supposed timelessness of, say, Roman dress. By comparison, in his opening address on Ghana Independence Day in 1957, the first African country to gain independence, Dr. Kwame Nkrumah, the incoming president, stressed there was a new Africa in the world: "we are going to create our own African personality and identity."[27] But to demonstrate, he wore a self-designed voluminous toga-like garment that referenced the civic dress of the Romans while being composed of brilliantly colored strips of locally woven cloth that had been sewn together. Called kente (kenten) cloth, originally of silk, it was and is native to Akan groups in the Ashante region of Ghana, and was originally reserved for paramount chiefs.

A number of statues honoring Nkrumah were commissioned over his period of office. The statues were the target of militant opponents of Nkrumah and the center of the so called "monument wars."[28] In 1961, they were attacked by bombs. Nkrumah was one the main instigators of the Organization of African Unity in 1962, and a further statue of him was erected in 1963. Over three meters high and cast in bronze, it was based on the ancient Etruscan-Romano statue *L'Arringatore* ("The Orator") dedicated to Aulus Metellus, an Etruscan senator, in the declamatory pose of an orator, probably dated to the first millennium BCE. The orator wears a short toga exigua (narrow toga with an inscription on the hem) and high *calceus senatorious* boots. Here, the status value of the classical toga was translated into twentieth-century Africa, although the statue was toppled as soon as the leader was overthrown in a coup in 1966.

Ethiopia and Liberia were two African nations that managed to preserve their sovereignty from long-term colonization by a European power, although Ethiopia was occupied by Italy in 1936. Its history has therefore been different from other post-colonial countries, as has its formal dress. When Emperor Haile Selassie of Ethiopia was crowned in 1930, he wore an extraordinarily lavish and ornamented cloak with lengthy lappets and rich decoration, referencing a much earlier decorated cloak of Emperor Menelik II, and including a tall headdress. A 1931 photograph of the recently crowned emperor (Figure 5.5) shows a curious mix of pseudo-military details on cuffs and huge epaulettes, plus echoes of the ornate lappets on his original coronation robes. A strange topee-like helmet is placed on a nearby table. If there were references to a Western heritage, they were chosen selectively.

**Figure 5.5** Haile Selassie I of Ethiopia (Ras Tafari) photographed in c. 1931, a year after his coronation as emperor. (Credit: Imagno/Getty Images.)

Rituals which began in the deep past still echo in the format of many ceremonial practices. An ankle-length robe or cloak is part of an ancient tradition that has characterized dress for royal or imperial observances and religious ceremonies over time. Worn by persons of significance, these garments have— with variations along the way—acquired the ethos of dignity, authority, stability, and spirituality stretching back thousands of years. This sense of endurance and worthiness, projected in classical robes and cloaks, has continued into the formal clothing worn by dignitaries and religious leaders around the modern world. In countries like Australia and New Zealand, cloak-making and wearing retains its ancient mythical symbolism, yet at the same time it is enabled to speak to the present. (See Focus 5b)

## Focus 5a
## RELICS: REMAINS OF A PAST OR NOT?

How should we classify religious and other "relics" as they occupy a richly nuanced position in relation to time? Their implications are bound up with issues of posterity, memory, and the very nature of death itself. Relics are rare, incomplete items, perhaps a body part or a deteriorated fragment of a garment that belonged to someone of note, possibly a saint, royalty, or other deceased person of religious and cultural significance. Placed in a sanctuary, or carefully hidden in specially consecrated reliquaries, they raise a number of questions relating to value, memory, and emotion. Sanctified by both Western and Eastern religions, relics are deemed of inestimable value, yet seen only occasionally, if ever. Partially remembered histories, even those invented, are centered on these items. Here the mix of actual and sometimes the fictitious give them a ceremonial aura of great worth, yet they have little intrinsic value.

Preserving an alleged fragment of a significant person for posterity is integral to the very nature of a relic.[29] The tooth of the Buddha is one such symbolic object, yet there are a great many teeth relics in Asia, China, Japan, and Singapore. One is held in the Temple of the Sacred Tooth Relic in Kandy, Sri Lanka, in a closed casket and is never on public view. Other relics may be hair strands, perhaps part of a garment worn by a saint, a shirt or glove (a saint's clothing is a second-class relic according to Catholic doctrine). These items and even partial garments, supposedly used, worn, or touched by a notable person, enhance their value. That they tend to be incomplete is an emotional factor that augments their importance. It calls attention to the absence that originally constituted the whole and thus considered irreplaceable. Bodily remains, or other material fragments of a venerated historic saint or royal person, engage the general populace who, by proximity, are believed to receive some of their special powers.

Relics have quite different associations with a culture than curiosities. The term "curiosity," to which a relic is indirectly related, was generally used by European explorers traveling in places like the Pacific and Africa. They used it to describe souvenirs, such as the ancient skeletal remains of an Indigenous person, their ornamental handwork, and occasionally body supplements. Curiosities could be souvenirs, gifts, or exchanges of rarities as tokens of goodwill, but by the twentieth century these were regarded by many as politically problematic. Like relics, curiosities were linked to people of a "different" kind who lived in ways unlike the Europeans. Collectors might have sensed these items had some form of inherent power, different from their own which they coveted, or that the objects demonstrated the extent of the traveler's personal itineraries. They might even have been thought useful for scientific research. We know now that ownership of particular cultural items is questionable, especially if, as "curiosities," they are permanently held or on show in a museum far from where they originated. Some are now gradually being repatriated to their rightful cultural owners.[30]

I use two examples to illustrate the complex, often embellished, nature of relics and an additional item that does not at present fully qualify as a relic. The first is the unusual thirteenth-century linen shirt attributed to the crusader King Louis IX of France (canonized as St. Louis after his death in 1297).[31] His severely damaged tunic, with one sleeve missing, was first recorded in 1418, in the inventory of the Treasury of another French king, Charles VI. By 1480, it was in the Treasury inventories of the Sainte-Chapelle, Paris, and finally held in the Cathedral Treasury of Notre-Dame, Paris.[32] It came to be described as the shirt worn by Louis during his captivity in Egypt, where the focus of crusaders had shifted decisively after the fall of Jerusalem in 1187. However, the full provenance of this item is unknown, as is also the case for his cilice and hair shirt, kept at the church of St. Aspais in Melun. Garments like these are perceived reverentially by those who come after as items that cannot be disposed of. The French Revolution banned the collecting of relics and religious icons. Even so, the relics owned by St Louis, such as what is claimed to be Jesus's Crown of Thorns (many other items make this claim, however), were handed over to the Archbishop of Paris in 1804. They were later taken, as noted, to the Cathedral Treasury of Notre-Dame.

The second example is the well-known garment supposedly worn by King Charles I at his execution for treason in 1649. The beheading took place on a scaffold outside the Banqueting House on London's Whitehall. Souvenirs were collected by the public at the time. This long-sleeved garment (variously described as a waistcoat, vest, or shirt) is lightly stained and knitted in pale blue-green silk, a color occasionally called "watchet." Now in the Museum of London, the item is sometimes called a relic (Figure 5.6).[33] This history is debated. While the garment is *said* to have been worn by Charles—who for a time was the only person to be canonized by the Church of England since the English Reformation—the connection to the king is still a presumption. The stains on the garment, although subjected to analysis, cannot be identified precisely and no further testing is anticipated.[34] When purchased in 1925 for presentation to the Museum, an attached note of apparent authentication linked it to his beheading.

The execution took place on a cold morning and Charles is said to have requested extra covering, either for use over or under his shirt, to keep warm and prevent nervous shivering. After the beheading, Dr. Hobbs—Charles' personal physician, who had accompanied him—apparently preserved "the relic" and handed it down to his own relatives. There appear to have been no eyewitness representations of the actual execution, either painted or engraved, and proof that it was worn at the event is disputed.

Further items ostensibly linked to the execution or later exhumation of the king include the satin doublet, apparently with blood stains round the collar, held at Longleat in Somerset, fragments of cloth with spots of blood (perhaps handkerchiefs), strands of hair, and a shirt, acquired by Windsor Castle in 1911. Surely he cannot have worn all the shirts and the doublet? The Windsor shirt is in a display case in the Royal Library, labeled: "Shirt Worn by King Charles I at His Execution. Linen Shirt with Drawn Threadwork Borders. 17th Century." This kind of mislabeling is not unusual and the shirt is now believed to be a woman's smock, not a man's garment.

**Figure 5.6** The silk "vest" (undershirt) allegedly worn by King Charles I at his execution in 1649. Collection of the London Museum. From Memoirs Of The Martyr King by Allan Fea, published 1905. (Credit: Universal History Archive/Universal Images Group via Getty Images.)

The final example is Jackie Kennedy's blood-caked, vivid pink bouclé Chanel suit with navy-blue collar, worn when her husband was assassinated in 1963.[35] It is a complete outfit and not a relic as such, although the family were practicing Catholics (Figure 5.7). After the traumatic event, Jackie had the suit boxed and sent to her mother for safe-keeping. It was never cleaned and eventually sent to the National Archives. It is a souvenir of a momentous event but not considered a relic, although like a religious relic it is in closed storage with instructions not to be displayed until 2103.[36] As noted, a relic is a rare part of a body or garment that has some close link to an historic event or a revered religious person, accompanied by evidence of extreme self-sacrifice or an emotional or horrific death. Christian relics have a special association with time in that they are believed to offer solace or even cure ailments, the more dramatic or sensational the better. The Jackie suit seems not to qualify, based on some but not all of these criteria.

Prown claims historical objects have both intrinsic value in terms of their material nature but also more transient ones which are termed attached values.[37] The Jackie suit

**Figure 5.7** John F. Kennedy and wife Jackie arriving at Dallas Love Field (airport) in 1963. Jackie is wearing the vivid pink bouclé Chanel suit. (Credit: Bettmann / Contributor.)

seems to be more meaningful in terms of the second, its attached value. It also lacks the emotional powers believed to be a key part of a relic. Numerous photo representations of the event, ownership of the suit, its place at the heart of an historic moment in US history, and its current location of keeping, means it has a secure provenance. Lack of opportunity to closely inspect the outfit prevents first-hand assessment and seems to increase its mystery. Over time it may be cleaned or repaired, acquire supplementary narratives of use added layer by layer, and be embellished as it changes hands over time. Items such as this have many pasts, as do relics.

Institutional collections have, in the past, been keen to acquire relics and the habit is encouraged. In a drive to make the past relevant to modern visitors, to create an experience of history and increase attendances, museums like to display objects that trigger personal emotions. Illustrating dry historical facts about dress are less of a draw than an engaging narrative, especially one with dramatic associations. The intention in the twenty-first century has been to evoke history in this new, immersive manner, not just to illustrate the past. Affect and emotion, sometimes spurious, create an experiential engagement with an imagined past or stir feelings if clothing or body parts have supposedly "belonged" to a well-known person.[38]

Remains of an actual garment worn by an historic figure clearly have value that a souvenir or replica does not (See Focus 8b).[39] But relics are more than old clothes. Relics, whole or remnants thereof, occupy gaps in knowledge inviting a mysterious, almost ritualistic, narrative that engages emotions. If artifacts are partial or damaged, they provide a sense of mystique to a period of time or even events which may never have happened, or now so long past that facts have been misremembered or even reworked.

## Focus 5b
# FIRST NATIONS' CLOAKS: IDENTITY RECLAIMED

Full-length, capacious cloaks have had a long history connecting them to formal religious and secular ceremonies worldwide. Clearly, they are practical garments, but they have had other significant purposes and embody many meanings. Used by men as well as women, deliberately covering individual shapes of the body, cloaks have been signs of dignity and status. Worn from early times and for different reasons from Canada and the Americas to Europe, New Zealand, Australia, Africa, and the Pacific, they have carried particularly intense symbolic weight for First Nations peoples. Body supplements such as these were considered essential to material well-being and spiritual ritual prior to colonization, although few early cloaks seem to have survived.[40] This Focus concentrates on identity and the symbolic cloaks of Indigenous peoples in New Zealand, Australia, and Canada.

Aboriginal spirituality in Australia is a central defining feature of their culture and identity. This spirituality is communal and believed to have an inalienable connection to "country." While there is no word for "time" in any of their myriad languages, Indigenous people believe they live in the Dreaming, which is co-existent with the environment of the past and still exists today. This is time compressed. As Australia's First Nations peoples are not one but a multitude of different cultural groups, their possum- and kangaroo-skin cloaks have and show regional differences, their markings demonstrate connections between wearers and the spiritual realm.

Cloaks have transitioned in meaning over time. Traditional cloak-making and wearing in Australia was discouraged by the British. Instead, official government blankets were issued regularly from the early years of settlement, causing skills to die out. But from the later twentieth century, there has been a cloak-making revival. Cloaks are now formal public garments, rich with a clan's cultural beliefs.[41] This has coincided with increasingly politicized meanings. These garments are embedded in political attempts to gain racial recognition and land rites, and to honor the ancient past. Cloaks have become proud statements of identity.[42]

If we change geographical location, on Captain Cook's third voyage of discovery, in search of a passage through the Bering Strait, he sailed with two ships in need of repair into Nootka Sound, Vancouver Island in 1778, anchoring in Friendly Cove. This was the traditional territory of the northwest-coast First Nations people, the Mowachaht/Muchalaht. Canada recognizes three early peoples: the First Nations people, the Inuit, and the Métis (of mixed ancestry), all of whom have their own particular "regalia" and signs of identity.

Cook was welcomed and his ships given daily supplies of fish, as well as water, wood, oil, and furs, in exchange for metal, a material of great value. His expedition, which stayed a month, acquired basketry and twined cloaks of abstract design made by the local people using cedar bark and mountain-goat wool.[43] Some cloaks, rather like highly decorated blankets, were likely acquired from the Tlingit who lived off the Alaskan coast. The cloaks of the Chilkat (a Tlingit tribe), with highly stylized abstract designs, were coveted at nineteenth-century competitive potlatch ceremonies especially on the northwest coast of Canada and in the US. At these events, discussions were held and gifts of special quality and designs exchanged.[44]

These cloaks, sometimes called "robes," were three-part compositions showing different perspectives, worn by men of high status but sometimes hung flat on walls or used to cover the body when a dead chieftain lay in state. When the chieftain wore the garment, his crest's front covered his back, representing his lineage, history, wealth, and power, and its sides merged with his own. Art historian Jonaitis suggests "it is possible man and robe became a new hybridized being that shared a body, with the man's face in front and his crests' at the back."[45]

Australian Aboriginal men and women originally wore long, highly prized cloaks of fur or skin to protect wearers from the rain and in cold climates of the continent (Figure 5.8.) The cloaks were also used as coverings (rugs) in areas like Queensland, where the days are warm but the nights chilly. As repositories of cultural stories and indicators of personal identity and clan associations, information was included in ceremonial markings, demonstrating connections between the body, the land, and the spiritual realm. So, although being practical, cloaks were also symbolically marked and used in mortuary and other ceremonies. Small babies were given tiny cloaks at birth and these were continually enlarged over a lifetime, almost like a kind of biography.[46]

**Figure 5.8** Aboriginal woman wearing a long possum-skin cloak, *c*. 1870. (Credit: John Oxley Library, State Library of Queensland.)

Making was said to be a long physical, spiritual, and emotional journey, requiring patience and with support of ancestors, elders, and family. The cloaks were made of the fur of possums, kangaroos, wallabies, sugar-gliders, and quoll. The skins were pegged onto bark and then scraped clean of flesh with shells or grinding stones. Sharp kangaroo bones pierced holes in the skins, which were stitched together with kangaroo tendon fibers. The inner side, colored with ochre and fat, bore the complex signs of ownership, clan and group association, special landmarks and also social hierarchies related to the particular wearer.[47] They were reversible. Koori people from regions of Victoria and New South Wales—and in particular the Yorta Yorta people of southern New South Wales and northeastern Victoria—preferred possum skins for cloaks, whilst the Noongar people of southwest Western Australia liked kangaroo and wallaby. The latter garments, called *buka* or *boka*, were mainly the skins of two to three kangaroos sewn together.

Cloaks were normally (but not always) worn over one shoulder and under the other. They were fastened at the neck with a small piece of bone or wood. Wearing the cloak over one shoulder allowed for greater movement, which meant daily activities could be undertaken with ease. A baby could be carried in a pouch on the mother's back and, like the adult wearer of these cloaks, was believed to be "wrapped in country."

The first written records of Indigenous cloaks in New Zealand date from Captain Cook's initial visit in 1769–70. Initially of flax, Māori *kākahu* (a generic term for cloaks) were treasured and made by weft-twining shiny white, silk-like native flax, not woven on a loom. Before the eighteenth century, they had also been made from rat or dog fur and sealskins.[48] Each cloak had its own history. High-class cloaks differed from lower status ones by virtue of scarcity of required materials. Highly prized were those of *muka* (flax) stitched with rare bird feathers such as the *kahu kiwi* (soft brown kiwi feathers).

The Māori cloak, like those of the Chilkat, were believed to be an extension of a person and infused with the owner's *mana* (supernatural power). If the *mana* belonged to someone high born, the cloak could be exchanged on ceremonial occasions with another high-status Māori. It could not be touched or worn by someone of lesser status, however. [49] *Kahu kuri,* the most significant cloaks, were war cloaks for chiefs and warriors. They were made from the hide and hair of the *kuri*, a Pacific breed of dog.

Māori cloaks took on further temporal and transcultural meaning when worn by Europeans. For instance, the New Zealand flax cape, gifted to Captain James Cook on his first journey to New Zealand in 1768, was later passed to the botanist Sir Joseph Banks. This prestigious cape, called a *kaitaka*, was bordered with a decorative *taniko*.[50] It is worn by him in a portrait by Benjamin West dating to 1771–2 suggesting intercultural respect, well before the antagonisms that arose between Māori and nineteenth-century settlers.[51] The portrait depicts the important naturalist, explorer, and scientist proudly displaying artifacts after the triumphant return of Captain Cook's ship, the *Endeavour,* from the South Seas.

The *kahu huruhuru*, a cloak incorporating kiwi bird feathers, continues to be regarded as the most prestigious of all cloaks. Others incorporate the green and white feathers of the *kererū*, the New Zealand pigeon. The Māori cloak has recently gained increased political significance. In April 2018, Jacinda Ardern (the New Zealand Prime Minister) wore a prestigious type of Māori *korowai* cloak to a Commonwealth Heads of Government Meeting (CHOGM) dinner at Buckingham Palace. This type of garment is symbolic of power. Cloaks like this one are made of *muka* flax fiber with bird feathers fastened over the entire garment. It is also called a *kahu huruhuru*. Ardern showed respect for Māori people by wearing the cloak, a significant gesture of inclusivity noted by the world's media (Figure 5.9). Members of the British Royal Family themselves have generally worn a cloak on official visits to New Zealand.[52]

**Figure 5.9** Jacinda Ardern, Prime Minister of New Zealand, meeting Queen Elizabeth II at a CHOGM Dinner in London, 2018, wearing a symbolic three-quarter length *korowai* Māori cloak. (Credit: Victoria Jones–WPA Pool/Getty Images).

As cloak-making skills declined in New Zealand, various Māori groups began to revive authentic techniques of making cloaks in the 1950s.[53] They looked back in records for information and deliberately revived the expertise, seeing new potential in cloak-wearing. Much later in 1999, two Aboriginal artists found Indigenous cloaks deteriorating in the Museum of Melbourne.[54] They too initiated specific projects to revive old methods of creating cloaks. If they could not replicate old ways of making, they created new techniques to reclaim the past.[55] Thus, cloaks in the twenty-first century have traditional meanings but also partly acquired ones, as Indigenous people reinstate important links with their country and the past.

The public wearing of a long possum-skin cloak has become a formal statement of identity for Australia's Indigenous people on days of significance for them.[56] It is a sign of struggle for cultural recognition. One revival project, the Possum Skin Cloak Project, brought together Indigenous communities to create the thirty-seven cloaks worn by elders at the Opening Ceremony of the Commonwealth Games in Melbourne in 2006.[57] The designs on these cloaks tell the stories of ancient connection to country. Each cloak has the maker's totem, their clan markings, sites, and information of significance to their community.

Two years after the Games, at the opening of Parliament, the elder Ngambri-Ngunnawal, Matilda House, delivered the first "Welcome to Country" speech followed by the formal "National Apology to Australia's Indigenous People" by the then Prime Minister, the Hon. Kevin Rudd. She wore a possum-skin cloak created for her by Treanha Hamm, a Yarrawonga/ Mulwala woman.[58] A more recent political example is Clinton Prior, a Wajuk, Balardung, Kija, and Yulparitja man, who walked from Perth to Canberra to meet Prime Minister Malcolm Turnbull in 2017. He brought a message requesting the government grant Aborigines a formal Treaty, similar to the Māori Treaty of Waitangi in 1840. With a sense of the theatrical, he wore a capacious and glossy possum-skin cloak plus a crochet "beanie" cap of red, yellow, and black, the colors of the Aboriginal flag.[59]

One enduring question is why has the cloak, known from the archaic ancient past, been continuously chosen as an enduring model for ceremonial dress? For centuries it has been a practical garment but is also associated with dignity and respect while, as public or ceremonial dress, being perennially subject to social and political revisionism (see Chapter 5). These ceremonial garments are not unchanging. Rather, as garments of dignity they move through time at their own individual pace, but continue to suggest values which reach back across the centuries.

The capacious fur cloak demonstrates the links First Nations Indigenous peoples have had with their land, its resources, and elements of country that belonged to their ancestors and whose spiritual presence is believed to still reside in them. Creation is the work of ancestral beings or Dreamings and the earth is marked with the power of these ancestors. The living, clothed in ceremonial garments and body paint, symbolically reenact the deeds of their ancestors and are thus one with sacred sites and ancestral power.  Dreaming is time immemorial.[60] For Australian Indigenous peoples, the "then" remains one with the "now."

# 6
# THE WARDROBE STORY

What exactly is a wardrobe? It is a term that fluctuates widely in meaning. It can be a physical item of furniture, varied in design and size, a special room (closet) dedicated to storing personal collections of clothes, even a complex bureaucratic organization that at times was more than space for clothing. As a storage device, a wardrobe of one form or another is used by most cultures, excluding those who on ceremonial occasions use ephemeral flora as an element of their wear. Here body supplements are not necessarily intended for reuse. They may be flimsy, more temporary than Western fabrics and far less likely to need storage.[1] For those in Western cultures, a wardrobe is both a physical item where size and quantity of garments can be a status symbol. But it is far more than this. A wardrobe can be a highly personal and idealized concept, one that encourages aspirational dreams and desires.

Wardrobes are special containers or spaces that have housed an extraordinary range of diversified clothing over time, their contents selected by men and women, as well as by and on behalf of children.[2] They are not *just* pieces of furniture. Wardrobes, as well as the material artifacts they contain, including personal adornment, are never static. The clothing housed by them can be personal, corporate, or official. The contents of these receptacles depend on the circumstances of the wearer, their status, and occupations, and vary according to climate and cultural routines. Aspirations, tastes, and behavioral possibilities are marked out by different contents. The inventories and accounts of royal wardrobes testify to the most astonishing collections of all kinds of belongings. Yet a wardrobe can also be simply a collective term for a set of garments. For instance, it was used by suppliers of ready-made dress requirements for different classes of emigrants sailing to colonies like Australia and India, advising them to acquire complete emigration "wardrobes."[3]

Wardrobes physical and conceptual have a special relationship with time. They partake of ingredients of the past, serve the needs of the present, and invite speculation about the future. Wardrobes are mutable entities whose changing contents are manifestations of entangled historical pathways and defined by a multitude of social, historical, and geographical circumstances.

My focus is on Western wardrobes as well as those in India, South Asia, and Middle Eastern cultures. Physical storage places for wardrobes take a wide range of forms, from special rooms (the latter could be related only tangentially to clothing), trunks of timber or steel, chests for steamer travelers, baskets, armoires, linen presses, *almirahs* in India, suitcases and much more. Free-standing wardrobes have varied stylistically over the years, as can be seen in the heavily carved and capacious timber wardrobes of the seventeenth-century Dutch upper bourgeoisie, which continued to shape European tastes for highly ostentatious furniture in the nineteenth century (Figure 6.1). In turn, pieces like this were replaced by sleek modernist styles and eventually today's minimalist, built-in mirrored wardrobes.

For those who can afford them, wardrobes or wardrobe rooms contain a mix of clothing for everyday use or special occasions respectively. More than this, wardrobes are dynamic sartorial "narratives" of the status and tastes of wearers of both sexes, revealing their cultural identities, financial situations, and social and political proclivities. Their contents are personal but also public, from headwear to other body supplements, including hats, shoes, and other accessories. All have stories to tell in terms of class, age, race, gender, and personality, but also politics. To regard a wardrobe as merely the latest garments,

**Figure 6.1** Ornate white and gold wardrobe in the Royal Hall of the Seignior's apartment, ninth century, Sanluri Castle, Sardinia. (Credit: DEA/L. ROMANO / Contributor.)

following social ideals, is to limit understanding of their extensive sociocultural, biographical and temporal significance. They defy clear definition but are in many ways the keeping place of memories (see Chapter 7).

# Wardrobe Studies

A degree of attention has been paid to dress research into wardrobes, mainly by sociologists. These researchers use interviews to analyze taste and how current wearers interact with wardrobe contents. Interests in this research method have been developing in connection with contemporary consumption and economic attitudes to daily dressing, but there is little engagement with historical practices.[4] Some studies consider that wardrobes are not about "newness" of dress but rather everyday "ordinary" routines and continuity and that these signal individual biographies of wearing.[5] A degree of careful, object-based work on everyday dress, wardrobes, and the relation to the physical shape of wearers' bodies has also been undertaken, but while object-based study of dress is growing, much still remains to be done.[6] Changing relationships between wearers and wardrobes, as container and contents, have yet to be critically assessed in detail.

A highly illuminating exception to the examples above is *Opening Up the Wardrobe, A Methods Book* (2017), which offers readers a series of imaginative alternatives to the study of global clothing.[7] It contains a series of eclectic methods of approach undertaken by 50 contributors. They use different ways to explore both the material contents of wardrobes and ideas of self and clothing as lived experiences. The aim is to throw open the doors of the wardrobe literally and metaphorically.[8] The topics range from audits of specific wardrobes, interviews, diaries, memories, processes of decision-making, even sensory responses.[9] This book is not about wardrobes as fixed containers, or the industry of making clothes. Rather it looks at experiences of clothes in the context of "real lives," and the unpredictable dynamics of how everyday people engage with garments. The real aim of this text is to suggest imaginative approaches to research and new knowledge as a primary way to create a sustainable future for clothes.

This book takes a rather different approach. I show how time is a crucial method of inquiry into the changing use of wardrobes as material collectives and spatial structures, but also as entities that have political implications. This inevitably flows through to complex and shifting interactions between the social and financial status of owners, and their choice or obligations of wearing or not wearing garments of all kinds. Garments are dynamic entities, and move in and out of a wide range of wardrobe collectives. I suggest the temporal instability of dress and the particularities of clothes, both worn and unworn, are situated in variously networked arrangements, either in association with defined social practices of "wardrobe" use at the time or as challenges to them. For all kinds of reasons—statutory, financial, and social—these networks are not consistent. The reason is that choice and use of wardrobe contents is inseparable from wider temporal changes in official representations of high-born public figures, as well as more personal aims to fit with changing personal or group ideals.

Helpful research comes in the form of work by the sociologist Cwerner, whose main interest is to encourage attention to the web of physical spaces that affect clothing dynamics.[10] By this he means a focus on how the physical spaces of wardrobes, as well as their storage capabilities and procedures, impact on meanings, and affect the functions of their contents, especially those acquired to display specific fashioned identities in public. Ignoring any historical examples, he argues wardrobe contents are not straightforward forms of communication. While they are distinctive and apparently ordered, the spatial organizations of wardrobes are not systematic. They are "spatio-temporal" collectives, indicative of the rhythms and times that determine how we dress and undress. Items are moved in and out of wardrobes. Their mix is a sign of various personal attitudes to dressing and different uses that take place over time. In the author's view, wardrobes are like a pool of stored "identity tokens."[11] From these, hourly, daily or weekly selections are made, providing the different forms of self-presentation desired.

For Cwerner, the term "undressing" is as important as dressing, for it points to the private and almost invisible existence of clothes stored away and at rest.[12] It is the secret and unseen side of the wardrobe that provides a counterpoint to the obvious public aspect where clothes are on view. He suggests the two are a subtle and effectual cohort, shaping a wearer's ever-changing relationship with public presence and self-identity. The private spaces of intimacy, even secretive areas, can be disordered, storing both up-to-date items and relics of a sartorial past.[13] He claims between the public and private aspects of wardrobes there are manifold intertwining rhythms, routines and memories played out over time. But his work is limited historically and does not delve into the background of the public versus private rituals of dressing and undressing, particularly that of the nobility I discuss below.

# Public and Private Dressing

There is an unseen side to the act of formal dressing that escapes many texts on dress. For instance, it was the practice of royalty to dress in the limited presence of other nobility. The idea of a grand royal *levée* probably originated in France during the ninth century CE, and may have begun during the reign of the Emperor Charlemagne. Ironically, he appeared to have limited interest in garments beyond his native Frankish clothing but seems to have invited friends into his bedroom as he dressed. Here he settled disputes between the nobility and apparently also entertained a range of courtiers at the same time.[14] The practice, formalized at least by the mid-sixteenth century in the French royal court, continued almost until the Revolution.[15] The morning *levée* and evening *coucher* were not limited to France, either: by 1672, they were noted in England too, at the court of Charles II.[16]

We know the toilette or dressing of Marie Antoinette, wife of Louis XVI and queen of France from 1774 until the monarchy was abolished in 1792, was performed with detailed precision; each female member of the court had a formal role and duties to do with handling specific garments, cosmetics, and accessories. The ritual began at 11 a.m. The queen chose her clothes for the day, a bath was taken, hair dressed, the chemise, under-gown, and gown put on, and the cosmetics (such as rouge) applied, and so on.

Year earlier than the reign of Marie Antoinette, Hogarth—English painter and engraver—sharply satirized the custom in his "Marriage à la Mode," a series of paintings (and prints) from 1743–5 which suggested the practice extended beyond royalty. These mock a problematic "modern marriage" between a middle-class wife and a count, Scene Four showing "The Toilette of the Countess" (Figure 6.2.)[17] Here, rather than royalty, we see an alderman's

**Figure 6.2** The "Toilette of the Countess," Scene 4, "Marriage à la Mode," painted by William Hogarth, 1743–5. National Gallery, London. (Credit: Universal History Archive/UIG via Getty Images.)

daughter, who has been inappropriately elevated by marriage to a count, who is informally dressed, having her hair done at her bedroom "levée" (or rising) while hosting disparate classes of visitors and friends. It is a satire on royal practices in every way.

# A Living Wardrobe

As previously noted, the contents of wardrobes are living collectives of unsettled "things." Their contents fluctuate constantly between everyday items and dress for public and special events (day or night). They can be stylishly up to date, worn frequently, or remain unselected, perhaps preserved unworn or in disrepair. Clothes are constantly on the move. Garments are taken out of wardrobes for use with the weather in mind, and returned when it changes, particularly as the seasons alter. (See Focus 6b) They are taken perhaps to be cleaned and mended, then given to someone else, put back, or reused as rags. Wardrobes contain official garments and new clothes but also recycled ones, old garments, clothes used repeatedly for a time, or for specific purposes only. Some items are replaced, others stored for years and then discarded; some are well worn but valued emotionally, others not. They tell stories of use, recycling, revaluing, and repurposing.

One example of the changing nature of a high-class wardrobe is discussed in the diary of daily clothing kept between 1793 and 1839 by Lady Märta Helena Reenstierna. It is rich with insights. Märta, a member of the Swedish gentry, lived at Årsta Manor, on a large estate just south of Stockholm. Her diary has been expertly analyzed in great detail by Rasmussen, who has studied Märta's relationship with her wardrobe, including information on all kinds of items, from clothes and footwear to hats and accessories.[18]

This diary forms the widowed Märta's life history as depicted in garments both currently used, and older ones no longer worn. It tells the reader about her own and inherited garments, as well as fabric of different types, her age, and clothing consumption at the time. Märta was well off but economical; she reused previously worn garments and fabric, cared for clothes, made alterations, and stored things carefully. Rasmussen suggests the terms "old" and "new" in her case are relative, as existing garments and fabric were used to make new ones. Märta invested carefully in her clothes. This was not unusual in Sweden for her women of her social class, as clothes and fabric meant "wealth." Leftover fabric was valuable and could be exchanged for cash or even used to pay wages.[19] Fennetaux supports the central role accorded to reused clothing in eighteenth-century Britain, even for the elite, suggesting it was recycling of textiles and garments that was more significant than novelty in the scale of values.[20]

Märta's wardrobe, a cupboard, and other miscellaneous chests, constituted a show piece for visitors—almost a museum. They were invited to view it housed in the Grand Hall (one of her finest rooms). Visitors were asked to comment on its quality, so it was similar to viewing a collection of paintings or *objets d'art* as the owner was acutely aware of nuances of social status. On a February day in 1820, she made a note in her diary about her new headgear: below is an indication that a single garment was almost the equivalent of the family's statement of lineage. It also indicates the importance of re-using clothing at the time:

> Grönberg picked up . . . my old, many years old, red velvet Coéfure, which has now been remade. Modern and fine, with a white brim and white ribbons to tie under my chin like a negligée. It used to be my dear late mother's Mantille, after that my first daughter's little coat, then my son's vest, and now my showy Coéfure.[21]

A diary like this demonstrates how an item of wardrobe furniture and its clothing contents each have their own unique story to tell. To regard a wardrobe as merely the latest garments suited to a current social ideal is to limit understanding of the individual elements in their making and their extensive temporal and socio-cultural significance. The term "wardrobe" has created a false sense of dating coherence, for garments are far more than a fixed collection of items spelling out a specific moment in time. Each garment that contributes to a wardrobe might be acquired at widely different periods, and tell a quite different story about the wearer's tastes and, of course, finances.

# Organization: Royal Status and Control

Today, a wardrobe is largely evidence of personal choice and a sign of individuality. For some, it is formulated in reference to the prevailing idea of fashion in the media and celebrity outfits. This freedom was not always available, however. Almost nothing is known of wardrobes and contents in ancient European history, but as early as the rule of Emperor Marcus Aurelius (*r.* 161–80 CE), Imperial Romans certainly stored their highly valuable garments of state in the dedicated space of the Imperial wardrobe. Robes were one of the significant ways Romans represented their official Imperial power and regulated controls were exerted over wardrobe practices.

Marcus Aurelius was the last emperor of the *Pax Romana*, an age of relative peace and stability for the Empire. The official robes and jewelry of the emperor and his empress, Faustina, were administered by a special sub-treasury of the

Imperial finances called the Thesaurus. The garments were not personal property. In the case of Marcus Aurelius and his wife, they had additional wardrobes for their own clothing, separately financed and under their own personal administration. The luxurious so-called *serica* (silk) garments bought at great expense by Faustina seem to demonstrate there was no control over private luxury.[22]

Official authority for sumptuary regulation in early European "wardrobes" of royalty and the nobility was recorded from the time of Charlemagne.[23] Not until some degree of luxury was introduced to royal palaces and castles, however, were specific spaces set aside for jewelry, clothing, and accoutrements. At this time royalty across Europe, along with their households and retinues, lived life predominantly in the public domain, with all the clothing changes demanded of their station. The known contents of their wardrobes enhanced the impression of their nobility and that of their households.[24] Dress was largely symbolic, where social status, power, and display—including official alliances— was paramount. The head of state and higher members of the nobility had the largest wardrobes, and staff to attend to the complexity of daily and ceremonial wear.

In twelfth-century Britain, the King's Wardrobe was a large administrative and financial conglomerate where courtly garments, jewelry, armor, and accoutrements were officially stored and accounted for. It was an astonishing organization akin to a vast civil service, with financial and other keepers and controllers. It did not reside in one designated place, though. With direct control of the robes and treasures of the court as well, it was always on the move, accompanying the king as he traveled around his kingdom, and overseas too (when waging wars). The wardrobe's administrative staff ordered goods and arranged transport, as well as attending to the making and maintenance of clothing. The first mention of the *Magna Gardaroba* (Great Wardrobe) was in 1253 (during the reign of King Henry III), when it split off from the King's Wardrobe and changed its purview, accounting for apparel, liveries, and fabrics purchased, and the overseeing of dress for marriages and funerals.

Ironically this Great Wardrobe was only a segment of the primary King's Wardrobe and was itself later subdivided as well. The wars of King Edward I (who reigned 1272 to 1307) and his successors, boosted the Wardrobe's significance by making it the equivalent of a war treasury. It traveled with the campaigning king, receiving war funds from the Exchequer as well as from other royal sources, and paid soldiers' wages.[25] These official wardrobes were highly structured and integrated into the current needs of political power and the state. Changes in contents were under the control of officials but also when the seasons changed and for special occasions. None of Henry VIII's clothes survive, but we have evidence of his outfits drawn primarily from the great wardrobe accounts, wardrobe warrants, inventories, and paintings. The wardrobe of Queen Elizabeth

I was vast, and in her own lifetime she exhibited some of her embroidered gowns with other treasures in the Tower of London in order to amaze foreign visitors. Dress was a direct sign of status, power, and wealth.

Later, Louis XIV of France established the post of *Grand Maître de Garde-robe du Roi* in 1669, plus at least six lesser posts and three rooms on the ground floor of the central block of Versailles were set aside for garments.[26] The *Maître* organized clothing, oversaw the maintenance and the making of garments, kept accounts and controlled costs, as it had in Europe for centuries. The wardrobes of kings and other royal persons did not typically consist of items personally chosen as expressions of identity, although there were some exceptions. The nobility used their wardrobes for official business and these changed in response to endless shifts in national and international politics. The royal wardrobe was a calendar of the life and political changes of the ruler.

# Wardrobes: The Royal Calendar

For royalty in Europe, at least since the Middle Ages, to commission a "change" of one's wardrobe was to acquire annually an entirely new set of clothes. Charles II of England ordered between thirty and forty new suits, single garments or other sets of garments per year, although his tailors also undertook repairs and alterations.[27] The elegant Viennese-born Marie Antoinette was clearly extremely astute at using her dressed appearance as a strategic tool to advance her role at the French court. She had an extensive annual allowance for clothes, and ordered an extraordinary thirty-six gloriously elaborate, formal and semi-formal trimmed gowns of silk per year, plus more informal ones. Each season all were discarded and gala occasion dress was worn only once.[28] She spent an inordinate amount on her fashions annually, including for special occasions as seen in this outfit for court (Figure 6.3). Her costs were astounding.[29]

The lavishness of a royal wardrobe is demonstrated by the French Queen's *gazette des atours* (trappings). Whether or not these were a record of garments from which she chose each day, or account books, they were full of notations and fabric swatches. The book for 1782 shows seventy-eight samples (some may have vanished) of the newly fashionable range of subtle pastel colors, from pale gray to blues, stripes, tiny dots, and small sunbursts, the latter a great favorite.[30] The temporal whims and "conversations" about dress each day was like a royal bulletin.

Her personal whims affected not only her immediate staff but also the wider population, as was the case for the fortunes of silk-industry workers. Expectations of what she would wear were confounded when she abandoned the tight,

**Figure 6.3** "Queen Marie Antoinette with Globe," wearing lavish full court fashion, painted by Jean-Baptiste André Gautier-Dagoty in 1775. Versailles, France. (Credit: Leemage/ Corbis via Getty Images.)

uncomfortable, and vividly colored brocade g*rands habits de cours* with panniers and train (formal wear at Versailles), replacing them with informal, lightweight and gauzy white muslin *gaulles,* later termed *chemises à la reine,* with wide ribbon sashes. Her dressmaker, Rose Bertin, copied them from shifts worn by "creoles" and colonist's wives in the steamy Caribbean.[31] Compare this to the working poor of the time, who may have had only one or two sets of working clothes and perhaps another outfit for attending church.

The wardrobe of Marie Antoinette during her royal life in France played a crucial role during the *ancien régime* and its subsequent downfall. Her unpopular use of excessive and unseemly spending on fashion deeply affected the public perception of the monarchy as decadent. Toward the end of her reign, she thoughtlessly dedicated three rooms at the Palace of Versailles to her favorite clothes and accessories. The rooms were opened to public viewing. A frenzied destruction of almost this entire wardrobe during the height of the revolutionary period was a final defeat of her fascination with dress. This was a demonstration of a wardrobe under siege.

# Not Much Choice

It is interesting to compare the French queen's wardrobe—or perhaps that of the British royal family in the twenty-first century, even the wealthy upper classes—with Cwerner's idea of temporal dynamics that emphasizes choice, with what we know of the less fortunate. Impoverished people, for instance, cannot be left out of this discussion. The lives of the working poor, during the late eighteenth century for instance, were highly restricted and their finances would have meant they owned only a few items of dress. As noted above, some working-class men and women might have had special garments for festive days, but their clothing was otherwise limited.

It is now known that up and down the social scale in the eighteenth century, the lives of all garments were extended by passing them down to relatives, repairing damage, mending, remaking, and remodeling, as their real value lay in the fabric out of which they were made. Repairing was not just a necessity for the working poor.[32] This said, Taylor's remarkable research into a dumped collection of rural workers' rag clothing discovered in 2010, demonstrates in detail the sequential phases of the collection of used garments in Normandy as they deteriorated, including ways they were disposed of or remade for sale. The clothing ranged from rag waste and patched garments to upscaling for high-street designs but some were dumped in a warehouse and the worst-quality items manufactured into pulp for papermaking or textile mills.[33]

Discarded workers' clothes from the very early twentieth century show the degree to which rural clothing was patched, repaired, restitched, and patched again—evidence of the unstable nature of clothing collections. The term "wardrobe" seems inappropriate. We also know of improvised facilities at a much later date that served as storage for pioneer settler communities, such as those in Australia.[34] Then there are the bags and baskets of nomadic cultures and the minimal possessions of refugees. Nor should we forget scavengers searching for items in rubbish heaps, and those who make a small living from salvaging garment leftovers from clothing factories such as this Dhaka *jhoot godown* (warehouse) in 2018 (Figure 6.4).[35] There are also the decrepit items kept in plastic bags and trolleys of the destitute, and the disintegrating clothes of the homeless. These are an important social fact of life in most cities. Refugees are another category of the impoverished who may flee with wearing only a few things of their own; they may have no shoes or opportunities to clean themselves or their clothing.

In poor Indian villages, a wardrobe is likely to be a trunk but even here the sparse contents are integral to signaling respectability. Wearing cast-off saris is humiliating and marks out a woman's social position. The garment is a burden for it is regarded as being polluted with the pity of the previous owner and it would need to be washed over and over for associations with this former owner to be removed.[36]

**Figure 6.4** A *jhoot godown*, near Dhaka, where left-over waste from a clothing factory is deposited, 2018. (Credit: STORYPLUS.)

# Projecting Identity: Indian Women

Wardrobes are collections of old and new garments, all of which make up material memories and associated anecdotes. They are thus opportunities for owners who can afford it to reflect on identity, to pick and choose from a series of "looks" collected over time but also to engage the imagination and experiment with ephemeral aspirations. Indian saris are extraordinary garments in this respect and, like many clothes, evoke specific memories and embody stories associated with the garment. The book *The Sari* by Banerjee and Miller, explains just this and more, discussing in fascinating detail the wardrobes of women in India. These wardrobes, containing varied kinds of sari, are like a personal anthology, a changing collection of memories. They are "a multi-faceted, multilayered mirror which reflects back the full complexity of an individual's identity and history." [37]

Wardrobe contents encapsulate for Indian women the various personae they have adopted over the years, recall the people who have given them a sari, when they were worn, as well as what the woman hopes to become. As noted above, in villages, the wardrobe is probably a trunk, but in the urban homes of professionals, it is likely a substantial piece of furniture; it may be accompanied by other containers, including drawers within a dressing table. For village women, the sparse contents of their wardrobe trunk are integral to signaling their respectability and marking out their understanding of themselves. The numerous saris of women of the wealthy urban elite are significant for other reasons. They demonstrate a financial position that shows they can afford not to "repeat themselves" by wearing the same clothes.[38]

The sari might seem generic but it is a dynamic and changing garment. It can be worn in many different ways and have different meanings and qualities. *The Sari Series: An Anthology of Drape,* which can be viewed online, has over eighty extraordinarily beautiful examples of the subtlety of regional styles, showing each version's particular character and how they are differently draped.[39] Saris embody temporality in the performative acts of dressing. They also have an intimate relationship with wearers, as the owner moves through her life and discovers how best to inhabit these garments of ancient origin. They spell out a woman's own history, personality, her relationships, social position, and aesthetic tastes.

# Wardrobe Rooms

Many historical records and biographies, especially of the comfortably off, describe not just wardrobe furniture but descriptions of wardrobe rooms and how they were used. A wardrobe room is clearly not furniture. It can be a far larger space. In the mid-eighteenth century, Christinehof Castle in southern Sweden was the home of an aristocratic count and his wife. They each had an entire room for their wardrobes. Other family members used cupboards and chests of drawers. Clothing was stored flat or on pegs as the clothes hanger was not invented until about 1870. [40] The wardrobe of the great London diarist Samuel Pepys included activities beyond those associated with his appearance and clothed identity. Secretary to the Admiralty and Member of Parliament for a Norfolk constituency, Pepys includes, amongst his extraordinarily rich diary entries, details of clothing purchases and storage facilities in his city home.

Significantly in 1660, as his fortunes rose, he moved to a new home within the Navy Offices in Seething Lane. He felt he should change from storing his cloaks on nails in his chamber, to having a dedicated space in his new dwelling. On October 15, 1663, he notes "up to remove my chest and clothes upstairs to my new wardrobe that I may have all my things above where I lie." On August 25,1666, he records "my new closett, which pleases me mightily, and there I proceeded to put many things in order as far as I had time, and then set it in washing, and stood by myself a great while to see it washed." For Pepys, his wardrobe was not just a room in which to hang or store clothes but also an environment for illicit meetings, flirtations, hasty encounters with female friends, and even private dinners.

A very different example of a wardrobe room is the largest known still in existence. It is in the vast Purani Haveli or Old Palace in Hyderabad's Old City, although the structure of the palace has deteriorated. Hyderabad was one of the princely states in India between 1869 and 1911. The main palace is flanked by two wings, one of which included the vast wardrobe room of a former Nizam, the sixth ruler of Hyderabad state, Asaf Jah VI Mir Mahboob Ali Khan Siddiqi Bayafandi GCB GCSI (1866–1911). The phenomenally large wardrobe, lined with enduring Burmese teak, occupies two stories; the former walk-in wardrobe takes up both sides of a quarter of the 350m-long hall, which contains the oldest hand-wound elevator in India.[41]

Aware of his official position, the sixth Nizam is said to have never worn his clothes twice: they were given away after wear. Some claim he bought entire bales when getting his clothes tailored and had the unused fabric burnt to ensure there were no other outfits remotely like his. *Sherwanis*, shirts, coats, socks, shoes, headgear—he just could not have enough of them. The dress of the rich and influential in nineteenth-century India, like that sported by Nizam, was an interesting mix of the finest traditional British-style city clothes, plus recreational hunting gear. He wore customary Indian dress on occasion, too. There is no complete record of this famed collection and almost none of the garments still exist.[42] These almost empty rooms are only a spatial reminder of time past.

# Big Changes: A Digital Wardrobe

After the First World War, the term "wardrobe" for those of the middle to upper-middle classes in Europe, the UK and the US, continued to mean a set of stylish clothes, specified by dictates of the fashion industry, as well as storage facilities. While the role of women in the workplace expanded, middle-class women, especially those who made their own clothes, spent time planning their fashionable outfits for every season and event—walking in the park, matinees, traveling, lunches in town, evenings at the theater, and so on. Although the Second World War brought with it extreme challenges and shortages, home-sewers continued to consult paper-pattern volumes for ideas and later mused over the post-war plethora of fabric designs sold by department stores in yardage rolls.[43]

It was sometime after the middle of the twentieth century that the nature of the wardrobe and clothes-buying for men and women began to respond to the growing effects of digitization. There was a dissipation in the categories of prescribed social events throughout the day for the upper to middle classes, all of which required appropriate wear, and a similar shift away from the traditional dress "etiquette" that assumed clothes communicated their owner's identity and social place. An acceleration in access to stylish wear, and the nature and effect of the media on fashion, entirely altered the concept of forward-planning in dress. The impact of the digital on ways of selecting and purchasing clothing, especially in the form of online selling, increased the availability of fashions, their acquisition, and the effect on social meanings. Importantly, aspirations and choice were enhanced beyond measure by the new technology.

"Clock time" was gradually replaced, and the concept of duration superseded by the intense speeding-up of commerce that primarily valued the "immediate", a minute-by-minute flow of styles and fashion fragments. As Rocamora suggests, past and future collapsed into the present, made up "of a 'rapid succession of instants."[44] In a throwaway consumerist society, the wardrobe as furniture has become less important than the convenience of donating once-worn, flimsily made clothing to a goodwill or op shop.

Today, dress is reactive and mostly about possibilities and quick responses. Digital processes have speeded up fashion cycles, and live-streaming provides see-now-buy-now runway shows, not seasonally, but for weekly or fortnightly "retail drops." Apps like Metail at first had virtual "fitting rooms." Here the size and body shape of a customer was recreated so they could try on digital images of clothes wherever they wished, eliminating tedious shop fittings. The company's mission changed in 2021, however, when it became a virtual modeling agency and aimed to increase the selling capabilities of brands using compelling digital visualizations.

The notion of a unitary clothed "identity," expressed by clothes, has become fragmented, as has the space of wardrobes as items of furniture or dedicated rooms. The wondrous dreams of the wardrobes of the past, offering endless reshaped ideas and the limitless aesthetic possibilities of stylish dress, have been challenged. A shadow of unethical practices and waste hovers over them. This is the reality of environment degradation caused by countless low-cost garments being thrown away, perhaps seldom even worn.

The wardrobe as a concept has had to accommodate itself to the fast pace of modern fashion production, the nature of urban life, and the complications and benefits of a digital world. While dress generally is one of the world's greatest pollutants, as more clothing and apparel enters waterways and landfill, the physical wardrobe is on the brink of shattering. Claims to "sustainable fashion" are the catch-cry of designers, keen to appear ecologically aware. But what we have now are luxurious images of stunning design, the brilliant products of fashion's photographic advertising, as well as dramatic recurrence of catwalk spectaculars. What members of royal families, politicians, and media celebrities wear provides a relentless feed of "looks" on cellphones and other outlets. The public make instant assessments of what they see and comment accordingly, sometimes with lasting effects at the ballot box. But the wardrobe as furniture and container of ideals seems to be a concept too static for consumers. It has been replaced by the thirst for the striking, almost impossible-to-achieve visual effects of high-end style, bombarding the eye with the polished and imaginary aesthetics of the fashion photograph.

## Focus 6a
## A WIFE: WHAT IS SHE WORTH?

Trousseaux are collections of women's clothes and other items, set within the wider framework of socio-historical narratives of marriage and its finances. Previously I discussed dress and wardrobes being in a pronounced and dynamic relationship, much like a vocabulary from which selections are made and identity constructed, even revised. I suggested that while identity may be shaped by choice of dress, links between overall wardrobe contents and wearers are not stable; indeed, they are culturally unsettled. In this focus, I ask who provided the special wardrobe contents (trousseaux) in historic marriages between men and women.

Dowries and associated trousseaux have been part of the unsettled nature of meanings surrounding dress and wardrobes for women in cultures around the world. From ancient times, and across the world, a dowry has been an agreed financial arrangement that might include property (sometimes household goods) paid by a bride's family as a contribution to a daughter's suitor, at the time of her betrothal or wedding. It includes special clothing brought by a bride to her marriage, as part of a negotiated settlement at the time of a major life change. Some of the special articles of dress and household items used to be expressly made by the bride. Containers, even small items of furniture, were often crafted to store these items as an off shoot of a full wardrobe.

Assessing the value of a potential wife was significant as it was linked to children that might be a result, and thus maintenance of a family's lineage. The negotiation skills of both families were involved in calculating the worth of the dowry in money and goods, taking into account status, religion, caste and sub-caste, the groom's education, and physical attributes in some non-Western marriages, such as a bride's skin tone.[45]

A dowry was a legal and highly politicized exchange of wealth. It had symbolic meanings but materially demonstrated the prosperity and social position of the bride's family. If the marriage failed, the wife could receive a dower or share of her husband's estate, so a dowry notionally ensured a bride's security. Records were kept of the agreement, as lineage property and other belongings could revert to the bride if the marriage were dissolved. Claude Pelletier, the wife of a French merchant, François Arlais, sought entitlement in 1692 after separating from her husband. She petitioned for amounts from her designated lineage property to the amount of 800 *livres* from her dowry of 1,200 *livres*, as well as the value of her trousseau (consisting of a bed and its covers) plus nine *livres* for a dozen women's shirts.[46]

## The Trousseau

This term comes from the Old French word *trousse* or *trusse* (a bundle), and in Europe trousseaux augmented the special bridal outfit worn for the wedding ceremony itself.

Trousseaux were linked to dowries and were settlements and gifts to brides from their own families, consisting of a range of material goods as well as items of dress, including jewelry. They could be made up of many items beyond clothing, such as household linen, bed covers, curtains, and other valuables. Sometimes, a trousseau would be specifically compiled by a father on behalf of his daughter. For example, on her marriage to King Edward II of England in Boulogne in 1308, Philip IV of France gave his daughter Isabella a magnificent trousseau, including seven crowns, gold basins, brooches, circlets, a gown of crimson velvet, and one of red samite (heavy silk fabric).[47]

Generally, trousseaux were a selection of temporally disparate garments and objects, each with its own significance, value, and history of making. They were the appurtenances that a bride believed she would need for her life after her wedding, and she mostly chose or stitched the items herself. Trousseaux could include hand-embroidered garments, and also hand-stitched household linen. These were put aside in anticipation of gaining a suitable husband. This nineteenth-century woodcut of a girl shows her sewing something for her personal trousseau, an activity of great importance in the expectation of a satisfactory future marriage (Figure 6.5). As one might expect,

**Figure 6.5** Young woman sewing her trousseau/dowry, nineteenth-century woodcut. (Credit: Bildagentur-online/Universal Images Group via Getty Images.)

trousseaux were a small consideration in any union among the less financially fortunate, although even the very poor apparently scraped together a trousseau of sorts.

In Italy, during the first half of the fifteenth century, richly decorated timber Florentine marriage chests known as *cassoni* were collections associated with trousseaux and other bridal goods. They were commissioned by the groom or his family, on the occasion of a marriage; only rarely were they ordered by the bride's father. The primary function was to transport the bride's *donora,* her own collection of linens, clothes, and objects from her father's house to that of her husband, a sign of the severing of ties to her family. Highly colored and superbly hand-decorated Indian, and other, trousseau boxes, and larger trunks are still for sale on the internet, now probably used for different purposes.

## Royal Trousseaux

Historically, royal weddings have been political and highly significant arrangements via which alignments between nations were cemented and lineage possibilities were considered. The contents and amount of dowries for royal marriages were never prescribed or coherent. They always had some form of association with clothing and for royalty were often compiled by the Office of the Wardrobe. Trousseaux for royal brides in the fourteenth century could be vast collections of dazzlingly rich clothes, jewelry, silk cloth, and household items, often of gold, and might include religious vestments. When the Archduchess Josepha of Austria married the King of Naples in 1767, she brought with her a trousseau of ninety-nine dresses of rich silk with gold and silver lace.[48] At the time, this was considered unusually large. Yet Ribeiro shows that some trousseaux for the wealthy in the eighteenth century were surprisingly modest but still represented the most complete wardrobe any woman ever possessed. She cites Lady Frances Carteret who, in her 1748 trousseau, had only six dresses, one of which was her flounced white-satin wedding dress.[49]

Yet the place of a trousseau was of great strategic importance in some significant royal alliances. The trousseau compiled by one family might displease the other. One of the most curious examples of a royal bride and her trousseau at the change-over to marital status occurred when the Hapsburg Archduchess Marie Antoinette married the French Dauphin, Louis-Auguste, in 1770. They were married first by proxy in Vienna. The bride, aged fourteen, then traveled to France accompanied by a large retinue to meet the husband she had not yet seen in person. Her coach stopped on the bank of the Rhine and she crossed into a pavilion specially built on l'île des Épices, neither in France or Germany, for the ritual transfer or *remise* to take place.

At a moment of strategic importance, and surrounded by onlookers, she was stripped naked—even her stockings had to go. French courtiers remarked her clothes were "poorly" chosen, assuming she was wearing Austrian-made clothing rather than French dress.[50] She was required to discard garments acquired in Vienna and change into a *grand habit de cour* of gold cloth, newly made in France. This clothing was considered truly French, thus fully up to date and appropriate for her status.[51]

## A Modern Trousseau

The trousseau underwent significant changes in the early 20th century when, to save time, a complete personal trousseau could be purchased at a fixed price from West End stores in London. The *ideal* trousseau, however, was gathered from a number of shops and dressmakers. This image (Figure 6.6) shows a silk velvet negligee purchased in Paris for the Philadelphia wedding of Carolyn Baum and Modie Joseph Spiegel Jr in 1926. A matching silk crepe slip in poor condition also exists, indicative of the increased sexualization of underwear from the end of the nineteenth century. The garments in the photograph are in the Collection of the Chicago History Museum and include a "teddy" for Lena Samuels who married Howard Keagan in Chicago in 1928, and bra and panties made of silk satin and lace for another wedding trousseau in 1927.[52]

**Figure 6.6** Chicago trousseaux. Silk crepe teddy of Mrs Lena Kagan (1928), silk velvet negligee of Mrs Modie J Spiegel (1926), and bra and panties of Mrs Gardner H. Stern (1927). (Credit: Chicago History Museum/Getty Images).

By this date the intention of a trousseau was to show status but importantly also to reflect the *personality* of a bride, her taste and something of the tantalizing secrets that lay beneath her outer clothing. A trousseau was anticipation in material form of what a bride might need in her future life, and what social role she was expected to fulfill. A lifetime had to be considered and the garments needed to establish a new married identity.

## Beyond Europe and the US

The habit of gift-giving and exchanging goods on marriage still exists around the world, extending well beyond Europe and the US, to the Pacific Islands, Africa, China, India, parts of South America and more. Various forms of clothing and cloth are central to social exchanges where one stage of life is replaced by another. In Indigenous cultures, gift-giving at this time of life-change has been common; undergoing practices such as initiation ceremonies and body modification have also been widely practiced at the time of marriage.

In the Pacific Islands, woven cloth—sometimes beaten bark cloth—has played a key role in marriage negotiations. Islanders saw the considerable exchange value of calico and it became an accepted part of negotiating a bride price in the region.[53] In 1999, in the village of Ramvetlam, on the island of Ambrym, in the Vanuatu archipelago, Anna Eriksen recorded, in her analysis of their social practices, that at a wedding, the mother and father's sisters tied up the couple with calico and hung garlands over them for the entire ceremony.[54] Presents given by the bride's brothers included garden tools, saucepans, and calico, while relatives of the bride gave smaller pieces of calico. At weddings in Tonga, the bodies of the groom, bride, and relatives were oiled and then wrapped with mats and bark cloth as a cultural expression of protection against supernatural forces.[55] Designs on the bark cloth forged associations with the past and strengthened kinship relations different from the monetary negotiations of the dowry system.

Over the years, cultures around the world have used dress, body ornament, and textiles to mark momentous life events. Monetary value and the significance of materialism were at the heart of compiling early dowry practices. They were collectively a prediction, a safeguard, and an anticipation of a new future and new family. The value of the gift-exchange depended on the status and wealth of the parties, but would be of little import if it were a lower-class union. A dowry was a general bargaining price and the trousseau more self-selective, yet both were of strategic significance to the groom, as a wife was worth primarily what her family agreed to pay him and what he would agree to accept. The reason was that marriage was seldom a personal union, particularly in the case of royalty where alliances between nations were ceremonially cemented and lineage possibilities considered.

The gifting of money as well as household goods rather than lineage, still exists in many modern marriages of all kinds. High quality fabrics and garments continue to be central to most weddings and for both sexual partners especially in the form of the bride's gown and veil. The connection with 'cloth" remains. It is fascinating that this historic emphasis on clothing fabrication still demonstrates the commitment of a couple to a future life for themselves and their family.

## Focus 6b
## TIME TO CHANGE

To "change one's dress" is a common phrase used about Western clothes of both men and women. As I have previously suggested, a wardrobe is both a physical receptacle and a notional concept, being a range of garments affordable by a wearer of a particular class. To change into a different set of clothes is to move temporally from one form of dressing to another, within the parameters of the "wardrobe" as defined above. Use varies according to the weather, specific events, and related cultural routines. It is common to "change one's clothes" to go "out" of one's dwelling, for a debutante to "come out," or to select different clothes better suited to a new form of social engagement. This is not to deliberately discard old, worn-out garments, but perhaps move into clothes more appropriate to a rise in status or for a different activity.

For the well off, a wardrobe has been more than just a keeping place: it is a declaration of identity, as the contents of wardrobes depend on the circumstances of the wearer, their status, age, and occupation. There is an association between changes of dress, identity, and the unsettled nature of wardrobes, as well as an expanding and contracting relationship between what is taken out of a closet and worn, and what happens to clothes that are not worn.[56] With each change, perhaps informal to formal, new kinds of behavior are expected. But any discussion about wardrobes and changes of clothing should remember that for those struggling with poverty or homelessness, a "wardrobe" may be entirely different, simply a number of bags or suitcases in a supermarket trolley.

The degree to which members of a society change their dress varies widely. In the nineteenth-century, higher-class women of leisure changed multiple times in a day. The following are just a few categories of dress and etiquette advised by the book *Australian Etiquette*, published in 1885. For ladies it included morning dress, receiving calls, dress for courtship, dress for dinner and the theater, and for gentlemen city and evening dress, all clearly based on European prototypes.[57] The book includes rules on fashion and conduct, conversations, dress from breakfast to dinner, behavior for days at home, outdoor activities, formal and informal visits. These were practices left over from earlier rules of courtly society. Men *did* change their clothing but less often and fewer kinds were worn, but abiding by established sartorial mores was especially important for those with aspirations. Yet in a colonial society like Australia, attention to social niceties were reportedly either over exaggerated or neglected due to the mixed nature of social classes.

## Climate and the Seasons

I previously discussed how body covering, as we know it, probably originated with early humankind as the weather in Europe became colder. The relationship between clothing and the seasons has been profound, although marking the number of seasons has varied according to geography, cosmology, and social and religious practices. Although China officially uses the Gregorian calendar for commerce, it has a traditional lunisolar calendar with twenty-four solar terms, based on the sun's position and phases of the moon, identifying holidays and closely linked to farming and agriculture.

Around the world, people of all cultures, urban or agriculture based, continue to change their dress based on occupation and prevailing weather, and clothes are designed appropriately. In this image, a French mother and son wear winter clothes suited to the windy and icy conditions (Figure 6.7). Improved artificial heating and cooling in buildings has modified the need for many of these very obvious changes.

In the Middle Ages, European nobility dressed for the seasons as people do today. Differentiated largely by fabric and color, seasonal dress changes were almost the equivalent of a calendar, at a time when most working people could not read. Illustrations of different forms of seasonal dress are frequently represented in the wondrous illuminated prayer books intrinsic to the Christian calendar. Texts, such as Books of Hours, gleaming with gold decoration, indicate different types of clerical dress for liturgical seasons, the hours of the day, and if painted under patronage, the dress of higher classes. Over the Christian year, the clergy wore vestments of different colors, such as violet or purple for Lent and red for Palm Sunday. The working poor, as far as we can tell, remained in much the same drab clothes all year round, perhaps wearing an extra layer in the cold or special dress on feast days.

The famous *Très Riches Heures* of Jean de France, Duc de Berry, painted chiefly about 1415 by the Limbourg brothers, contains illuminated prayers for the canonical hours.[58] Amongst the illustrations are "The Labors of the Months," which shows agricultural employees at work. They are clearly dressed in dowdy garments made of rough fabrics. Their clothing contrasts with the highly colored, elaborate silk outfits of the duke, his family, friends, and personal retinue. In the January scene, the duke wears a *houppelande* (an expansive full-length garment with high neckline) of the most up-to-date fabric and gold ornamentation. His soft fur headdress is a

**Figure 6.7** "Walk in the Snow." A mother and son wear winter clothes for the windy and icy conditions. Illustration by E. A. Champlir in *Miroir des modes,* vol. 80, January 1920. (Credit: DEA /ICAS94 / Contributor.)

sign of winter, but in the warmer months wearing fur also indicated noble rank.[59] The April page (Figure 6.8) shows a high status betrothal taking place perhaps symbolic of a new season to come. The May page shows young male and female nobles out riding with musicians in livery enjoying the mild spring weather. Green garments are more prominent here suggesting the time of year.

Certain Indigenous people in Australia have had many named seasons, not just four. The Noo Angar people of southwest Western Australia recognize *maar-keyen bonar,* or six seasons lasting two months, but this has not been applicable to the whole continent. Local seasons were designated by amounts of available water and plant species for food, and importantly also for making body supplements. The weather affected dressing so in wet or cold times of year, skin cloaks were worn. Short bark or leaves for skirts were worn in warmer Arnhem Land, Bathurst and Melville Islands, and bark hats on Mornington Island.[60]

India has a highly complex climate; there are six climatic sub types with microclimates in many regions. It has conceded to the international scale of four

Figure 6.8 An April outing of the court of Jean, Duc de Berry, an illumination in *Les Très Riches Heures du Duc de Berry* (Book of Hours), *c.* 1413–16, Musée Condé, Chantilly, France. The duke is probably the person in a blue garment on the left-hand side. (Credit: DeAgostini/Getty Images.)

seasons: winter; summer; monsoon, especially in the south; and post-monsoon. A series of interviews with women and their dress in Banaras, Uttar Pradesh, between 1996–2003 showed it was common for these seasons to be marked by the choice of saris and ornaments: cotton in the summer, synthetic blends of silk and wool in the winter. Light pastel colors were worn for summer, and dark colors in the winter. Green for bangles or clothing celebrated the beginning of the southwest monsoon season of *shravan*, the fifth month of the civil Hindu calendar, and the month of abstinence (late July or early August). Women recorded making weekly and hourly changes of sari as well.[61]

## Courtly Dress

European courtly dress, represented in illuminated manuscripts, was echoed in the court and upper echelons of Japanese society where seasonal renewal, and specific activities for specific months of the year, were represented by different garments. Historically, Japan used a lunar calendar. The seasons are nowhere better illustrated than in the poetic and extraordinary private diary, the *Pillow Book* of Sei Shōnagon.[62] She was a lady-in-waiting at the hierarchical court of the empress-consort Teishi in the mid-Heian Period (794–1185 CE). Her diary contains charming anecdotes of the court: it is funny at times, salacious and petty at others. Her observations about people, the precise details of different court clothing, as well as poetic descriptions of changes in the weather, are absorbing.

Court members wore sumptuous silk *kimonos* of different colors and names in accordance with the time of year (and sometimes different days and colors within seasons). Garments could be made up of many layers of subtly changing colors. On New Year's Day, the first day of spring, and month number one, great care was given to personal make-up and clothing. The choice of colors for *kimonos* demonstrated the skilled art of *kasane no irome,* the layering of up to twelve silk garments (on occasions more) in personally coordinated combinations.[63] Court ladies indoors—clothed in cherry-blossom jackets worn draped loosely back from the shoulder, the robes a mix of wisteria and kerria-yellow japonica—would later signal the ending of the spring season.[64] Wearing the wrong color pattern for the season could be unfortunate for a lady's reputation and career.

In eighteenth-century France, court dress in public was extremely lavish and seasonal. Not so for the poorer classes. Marie Antoinette ordered thirty-six new gowns each summer and winter, plus additional light gowns from her *dame d'atours*, (one of her special attendants). She changed three times a day, selecting new garments each morning from swatches and notations in her *gazette des atours*[65] The *Mercure galante* (1672–4) seems to have been the first European magazine to publicly delineate fashion beyond the court as a response to season and weather—noting the fashion dates of Spring/Summer, Fall/ Winter as officially binding. This is a seasonal division still in use for some Paris haute couture showings.

## Life Changes

At its heart, European dress has responded to constant changes of social circumstances in daily life, and significant life milestones, by material modification to clothing and ornamentation. As noted earlier in this book, events such as birth, puberty, birthdays, leaving school, coming of age, marriage, childbirth, and the clothing associated with death are common and, to an extent, widely observed.

This differentiates Western dress from less frequent overt practices in early First Nations cultures. In addition to fashionable changes in adult clothing, Western dress for children (boys and girls) has altered as they moved through puberty to adulthood, assuming new forms of outfit, hairstyle, and etiquette. These changes have not been considered secret or sacred, but as modification to dress practices intrinsic to the age of the wearer. In India too, a young girl's reaching puberty was marked by the gift of her first sari. This practice has diminished somewhat but the school leaver "formal" in India, when the sari can be worn, has its equivalent in Western culture.[66]

An example of a life change linked to dress outside the Western sphere was that of the Indigenous Xam (Bushmen) in southern Africa. Recorded in the early twentieth century, at the time of marriage, the future Xam husband killed a steenbok (a small antelope). He prepared the animal's skin (a man's work) and sewed it into a skirt for his bride, a material manifestation of her womanhood. By hunting, the man had ritually respected and identified with the animal, and the relationship then flowed on to his future wife, via the clothing.[67] The entwining of identities between hunter, animal, and the clothing made for the bride, associated man and wife with the animal, and continued on to meaningful social relations in their married life.

Australia's numerous Indigenous cultures, each with their own language group, also marked stages of life linked to age, status, and gender. Before contact, Indigenous people were primarily unclothed, apart from adorning the body with earth-based pigments and ornaments like headbands, although men did wear elaborate feather headdresses for ceremonial occasions. The Arrernte of Central Australia are an Indigenous group that followed traditional habits. The main body supplement for men, given at puberty as part of initiation, was the hair belt and its pubic tassel, spun by the women to whom he was related. Young initiates had to earn the right to wear it and could keep the belt after various ordeals were undertaken.[68]

One of the most visually striking changes of dress in many cultures has been special clothes for mourning, although this habit has declined in the West. Types and colors of mourning dress have differed globally. In Japan, white was worn. In Victorian Britain, there were different degrees of mourning, starting with black, lightening to gray, mauve, and white. In Bariai, Papua New Guinea, widows have in the past worn black clothing, their bodies and hair covered with black soot. These women were considered "nothing" and even lost their names.[69]

Clothing and body supplements for funerals and other important cultural events in Tonga, have involved the wrapping of the bodies of participating persons in barkcloth (ngatu) of special quality and design. It is made from beating the inner bark of the paper mulberry tree. Ta'ovale are mats made from pandanus leaves or hibiscus bast fiber, and they too have been used and worn at funerals. In Figure 6.9, members of the royal family in Tonga greet the return of the body of the deceased King Tupou V in 2012 wrapped in ta'ovale. The designs and size of the huge wrappings are related to the members' place in the family and strengthen kinship ties. Wrapping is believed to be an act of empowerment that controls divine potency and protects the inner body from supernatural forces.[70]

**Figure 6.9** King Designate Tupou (2012) greets members of the Tonga royal family in *ta'ovala,* traditional mourning dress of fine, very large plaited wrappers of pandanus leaves. (Credit: TORSTEN BLACKWOOD/AFP via Getty Images.)

## Complexity of Change

In the modern world, many culturally established rules of dress for habitual diurnal activities for city-dwelling men and women have been much simplified in favor of dressing for work, sport, travel, and leisure. From early in the twentieth century, as more women worked outside the home, extensive formal categories of dress declined and others took their place. The nature of urban life, commercial occupations undertaken in clearly defined working weeks (until recently), and indoor climate controls have affected dress changes dramatically. These factors have reduced occasions when it is socially desirable, but not necessary, to alter one's clothes according to prescribed events. Changing dress is no longer tied to demands of class, local habits, and the marking of life stage achievements. "Time to change" is mostly associated with climatic imperatives more so than for social or occupational formalities. Even so, the future probably lies in trans-seasonal clothing.

# 7

# DRESS: TIME AND CULTURAL MEMORY

In her autobiography *A Backward Glance*, Edith Wharton recalls a very early childhood memory of how she first became aware of the importance of dress. She was out walking with her father on a bright midwinter day in New York, wearing a beautiful new bonnet. It was "of white satin, patterned with a pink and green plaid in raised velvet," and a veil of the finest white Shetland wool was drawn around it. As soon as she put on the beautiful bonnet, Wharton became conscious of herself as a subject of adornment. She dates from that hour the birth an awareness of "the conscious and feminine *me* in the little girl's vague soul."[1] In this chapter I deal with dress, time, the emotions, and memory. It builds on Wharton's first vivid memory of herself as a small child, at the moment she felt dress marked her birth as a woman.

To think productively about the significance of cultural memories and emotions generated by clothing over time, we must include the importance of embodiment. Clothes, the wearing body, and the social sense of self in time are implicitly linked. As Entwistle says, "the social world is a world of dressed bodies."[2] In her essay "Creases, Crumples and Folds," Sampson explains garments have a significant relationship with memory: "You are dressed in the things you have done today and the things you have done before. You are enveloped in material memories."[3] She gives the example of a crease or a fold as an archive of an act repeated over time. This is an important insight into any personal relationship with clothing, but the problem of suggesting a crease or fold as a material aspect of memory, is that a garment may then be worn by a different person, an original crease may be ironed out, flattened, augmented or other creases may occur during storage. In these examples, the relationship between memories and dress becomes demonstrably more convoluted.

Clothing has further complex interactions with memory and time. In Sampson's theoretical text dealing with making and using garments, she asks how is the agency of the maker(s) present for the current wearer of the clothes. She claims the maker is an essential aspect of the enduring bond between self and garment.[4] So, the self and the garment being used are intermingled, and the maker is always present in remembered form in the materials and manner in which it has been made. In a further essay Sampson argues that footwear, like any used garment, is a record of the experience of being worn as well as acts of touching. With touch and use, she suggests, we are entangled with these items and thus they retain material traces of the correlation.[5] Disparate relationships are set up in the experiences of making, wearing (and not wearing) of a garment. The latter is therefore an object in emotional flux.

All garments, including body ornamentation and the cloth or other materials from which they are made, are saturated with values of the past, which are potentially being reformed in the present. These in turn may engender other remembrances in the future. Clothes, and the materials from which they have been made, are historically rich deposits of memories. In the perceptive words of Stallybrass, "cloth *is* a kind of memory," a phrase which has become a classic insight into the fact that fabric has an emotional role to play in understanding dress. He suggests that in Renaissance England, cloth was a currency rather than gold in terms of exchange value.[6] In what he terms a "cloth" society, when fabric changes hands, it "binds people in networks of obligation." Cloth and clothing had the power to affect these networks and "to be permeated and transformed by maker and wearer alike." We have seen how some Asian cultures in the past have also valued cloth more than currency (Chapter 4), but it is not clear if this exchange included any personal and emotional obligations.

The sense of a social self, marked out by the wearing body in Western cultures, can apply to something more than endorsement of one's own embodiment. It can have a different application in the legal system which normally relies on outside memories of witnesses. Hauser, in her remarkable essay on forensic investigation of a single criminal's clothing, is a significant example of what meanings can be derived from a garment worn by one named person. Her essay "A Garment in the Dock" describes how a pair of jeans, worn by an accused person, was examined forensically, with attention to its fading, the wear marks of the accused, the size and style of the garment, the type of stitching used, even the color. She shows there was an indivisibility between "clothing and bodies that make and inhabit them." Yet in this case the "signatures" of the sewing methods of workers were utilized but their identities remained anonymous.[7] Even so, there were sufficient individualistic characteristics compared to other jeans to identify and bring about a criminal conviction.

To "remember" is a complicated feature of human nature and creates considerable uncertainty in terms of any causal link with a person. For instance, it is possible to look at an item of dress hanging in a wardrobe or displayed in a shop window but find, when worn, that one's initial impression of it has changed. Something similar can happen when clothes are used in an exhibition of fashion. The latter is a curated spectacle where the chosen garments cannot speak for themselves; neither can they project the original wearer's thoughts and memories of wearing to an unknown audience. These are mediated by the designer/ researcher, something decided *on behalf of* the exhibits. And the fashionable item of dress that is *not* chosen for display, and which does not suit the curator's rationale, is a garment that may or may not have a narrative or memory value appropriate for the circumstances of the exhibition. Moreover, when a dress is exhibited, its cultural memories are not necessarily considered to be information needed by viewers.

Representations can bring up many unpleasant memories and feelings linked to the experiences of wearing. At times of crisis, such as the death of a loved one, friends and family look to the very material garments of the deceased person for comfort and reassurance, and themselves dress ritually in ways that are reminders of the loss. A photograph is usually an attempt to hold fast to a particular fond memory of an event or a beloved person. In the nineteenth century, the photograph of the deceased provided a new tool of remembrance for mourners. Its memorial function could be very discomforting as bourgeois mourning practices of that time were elaborate and lengthy and photography, being a new invention of the time, was seemingly able to capture and prolong memories of sadness and loss in greater detail. In early portrait photographs, sitters are generally posed stiffly, their appearances unaccommodating in their formality. This was largely related to how the equipment of the new technology functioned. This image in a good example of double photographic memorializing of the time. Here a young girl in mourning dress, holds a photograph of her father, who has been killed during the Civil War. She stares fixedly at the camera/viewer, her highly intense pose pointing to the fragility of life and futility of war (Figure 7.1).

In exploring the nature of memory through representations, the past and the present are absorbed into one—a present that is one with the past. Can time therefore be inside time? There are many examples in European works of art where the artist has looked to the past for historical inspiration both in the dress of sitters and in painterly technique. It was particularly prevalent in the work of mid to late eighteenth-century society portrait painters like Gainsborough, Reynolds, and others. Here, time was selectively remembered rather than absorbed by the present. Many portraits painted by these artists paid subtle homage to seventeenth-century paintings by artists like Rubens and Van Dyke. Something similar happened at the end of the nineteenth century, when the eyes of artists turned back to the previous century for inspiration. It seems that in both cases, dress of the past and the present were related imaginatively, showing nostalgia for the lives and dress habits of wealthy patrons of an earlier society that was selectively conjoined with the present. By using the remembered clothing of the historic past, artists were able to achieve a grand sense of the timeless in their works but also a yearning for times lost.[8] (See Focus 7b.)

**Figure 7.1** Photograph of a young girl in black mourning dress, mid-nineteenth century. She is holding a framed photo of her father, who had been killed during the American Civil War, 1861–5. Liljenquist Family Collection, exhibited 2011, Library of Congress, Washington. (Credit: Library of Congress/Tribune News Service via Getty Images.)

# Values: A Range of Emotions

Emotions of various kinds play their part in how garments are valued. Dress conjures up particular reminders that are cherished, pleasurable, and valued, as well as memories of those that are not. An article of dress, regarded as aesthetically attractive by one person, might not appeal to everyone. The range of emotions is wide—happiness, sadness, fear, disdain, amusement, or even embarrassment. Clothing imparts intense memories of joy and other moments of great human significance such as grief. Some are engendered by encountering social difference, rarity, and (not forgetting) quality of workmanship.

That only some dress, and not all, has emotional value for Western cultures is because the concept of "worth" varies. Societies outside the West may have priorities that are quite different. In India, for instance, a customary method of recalling the past was by wearing fabrics on which symbolic motifs were replicated, while memories were also kept alive by other related activities such as dance and music. This is evident in the work of women in Hodka village, Gujarat (Figure 7.2). Here, women are creating memory values of their past culture by embroidering age-old geometric and floral patterns on cloth in vivid colors of yellow, green, and red. It is called *pakko* work, and the required embroidery skills and memories are passed from mothers to daughters. The latter also use this embroidered cloth to build up garments and quilts for their dowries (see Focus 6a).[9] These fabrics are partly a sign of cultural lineage but have now become a form of contrived sentiment. Unfortunately, the making of memories is artificially encouraged in order to stir the emotions of other cultures and to encourage the support of sales in India's tourist industry.

Fennetaux et al. discuss the value of remembering in the European eighteenth century, a period claimed as one of re-evaluation of objects, not an automatic desire for consumerist novelties. The authors explain how, compared to the present day, rather different temporal values existed between old and new objects, including dress. The increase of collecting "old things," such as worn fabric and dress no longer in use, was often more about memorial value and

**Figure 7.2** Two women embroider *pakko* textiles with customary motifs. They sit in front of their traditional circular house of mud brick in Harijan Vaas, Hodka Village, Gujarat, India. This activity is also set up to supply the nearby tourist market. (Credit: Gideon Mendel/In Pictures/Corbis via Getty Images.)

intimacy, not simply economics or parsimony. Certainly, it was economical to remake garments with existing textiles, but more importantly the fabric had the power to engage with memory and love, drawing together old and new.[10] A somewhat different view of the value of fabric is put forward in research by Dowdell, who is more emphatic that for all classes at the time there were pragmatic and economic reasons why the life of garments was considerably extended by alteration, repair, patching, and reuse. This included adjusting them in line with changes in fashion, until they reached the end of their usable life and were in rags.[11] Whatever the case, information found in historic wills and other written sources, examined by Stallybrass, still shows both textile scraps and garments were considered genealogical reminders, heirlooms or emotional tokens, as their closeness to the body of the wearer held intensely meaningful associations.[12]

According to Stallybrass, garments that are no longer in use have the ability to recall the specific body shapes of those who wore them. He suggests "clothes receive the human imprint," as well as the odor of those who wore them.[13] The

**Figure 7.3** Famed image of Marilyn Monroe's physical vibrancy in the golden dress from *Gentlemen Prefer Blondes* (1953). (Credit: Frank Povolny/Twentieth Century Fox/Sunset Boulevard/Corbis via Getty Images.)

garment of someone deceased can be a potent sign of the inevitable ending of life. A comment by the philosopher Karen Hanson suggests there is an uncanny quality about empty clothes, which may refer to the intense fact of our own embodiment and "at once murmur the truth of our real mortality."[14] Emptied of the cultural meanings associated with the living, and with memories dissipated, an unworn garment becomes available as an artifact onto which other emotions may be attached.

Yet any personal or public afterlife of an item creates a possible new layer of memory for wearers and observers. Clothes did not make Marilyn Monroe *the* woman of the silver screen. It was she (her body) who made the clothes. This was obvious when she moved, or when photographed as here, but faded once she had died (Figure 7.3). "The quality Marilyn brought to an image, a garment, a movie, a party, was something that could not be explained as anything other than lightning in a bottle."[15] I suggest that Marilyn's clothing lacked the sensational emotional essence for which she was known precisely when separated from her body, although the commercial value of her garments has only risen over the years.[16]

# Acts of Remembering

Different types of memories of clothes depend on personal circumstances, cultural mores, relationships, and more. Threads and fabrics are connected with a multitude of relative values beyond their physicality. Examples of the relationships with the temporal reach beyond actual garments and many memories of dress are linked to special events and milestones in life, prompting recollections of these pleasures. The fabrics from which clothes are made also have life stories that change, perhaps gaining and incorporating previous histories: "at each move of the object, its social relations will change."[17]

Some aspects are post-traumatic recollections, associated with the uniforms of war and loss of life. Remains of uniforms, with scars of action, and the medals granted to members of the armed forces who have been lost in battle are intense memorials both to relatives and the unit to which the person belonged. In this case the remembrance and futility of war are both private and public. Other kinds of remembering are those engendered by particular fragrances or individual items of dress that stand for a moment of insight into a person's past, such as Edith Wharton's recollections of her first winter bonnet.

Fragrances are some of the most powerful triggers of memory. The Christian Church has used incense smoking out of thuribles as they swing on chains at significant moments for centuries and for precisely this reason. Perfumes, made of musk, fragrant oils, and sweet spices infusing articles of dress and accessories of all kinds—shoes, gloves, earrings, bracelets, rings—were in use by all classes in Europe, especially from the second half of the sixteenth century.[18] It was as if the emotion of remembrance that was infused in a garment or lingering in rooms or household linens, would last in perpetuity. Perfume was a form of unspoken communication, and scented accessories like gloves could be exchanged as gifts and tokens between friends or suitors, signaling emotions of love, fidelity, and piety.

In the sixteenth century, perfumes were made in households; today, they are products of immense value to couture houses. The fashion designer Jean Paul Gaultier has always acknowledged the artistic influence of his grandmother, Marie Garrabe, a beautician and faith healer. He has explained how his creativity was stimulated by the fragrance of her face powder and nail polish. His perfume "Classique," with its signature bottle shaped like the torso of a woman, swirling beautifully with a rose at its heart, captured his own memories of his glamorous grandmother.[19]

In an unusual experiment, museum professional Katia Johansen recorded her collaboration with a professional perfumer to recreate a series of historic fragrances. She researched inventories, tailors' bills, recipes, wardrobe lists, doctors' accounts, custom duties, and other sources, so that those interested could experience first-hand the smell of Henry VIII's perfumed shirts, historic Indian shawls saturated with patchouli, and fragrant Japanese wedding *kimonos*.[20] The links between memory and beautiful aromas are extensive.

A different form of remembering is discussed by De Perthuis in her brilliant and empathetic essay "Darning Mark's Jumper. Wearing Love and Sorrow," in which she deals with a particular form of memory and how a deeply personal article of used clothing was to become uniquely valuable.[21] She draws on multiple levels of emotional meaning by sharing her moving account of darning her dying partner's well-loved jumper. Its meanings engendered remembrance of their previous life together, their subjectivities, and eventually their separation. The garment was so well worn it was as "distressed" as its wearer and his companion. The author claims the garment, which embraced her memory of him, was both priceless and worthless. It represented comfort and warmth for him and at the same time, in material terms, it lacked monetary worth as it was second hand. It was not whole, and had been repaired by her, but in that repair lay the repository of her love and later memory. It highlighted the questionable practice of discarding old for new in a commodity-focused society. The act of darning and making whole such "distressed" clothing has no material value as such, other than remembrance.

Birth and death haunt clothing and memory. The christening robe typically preceded by the wedding gown in Western culture are events that call up reminders of the joys of new life. The historic shroud, unlike personal "pre-loved" clothing, jewelry, and related items is the opposite—a sign of mourning, sorrow, and loss. In a short account of his grief at the death of his father, in Kerala, India,

Anthony Palliparambil faced the dilemma of showing respect for his father's memory through dressing the body. Stallybrass has described the painful decision that surrounds clothing the body of a loved one for burial.[22] What personal value did Anthony's father place on fashion and what were the wider social expectations of his interment? For instance, what clothes should his son choose on his behalf for the burial ceremony? A new shirt and tie were socially expected but did not reflect his father's habits. In terms of his own dress, was wearing fashionable clothing appropriate even for attending a funeral? Fashion is a celebration of life, so the author asks exactly when is it appropriate to resume to care about one's own appearance, once the mourning period is over.[23]

# Boundaries

Ethnographic articles of clothing made by Europeans occupy a special area for consideration well beyond the current discussion of memory in Western cultures. European collections of ethnographic body supplements occupy a different register of recollection, largely as they are put together by those outside the cultural space of the original peoples. This said, it is important to understand Indigenous oral cultures around the world have their own reasons and methods for remembering.

For some First Nations cultures, such as Australia's Aboriginal people, forms of memorizing are non-literate codes or "songlines."[24] It is an extraordinary skill to acquire and to remember, through song and dance, thousands of complex details of "country" and cultural practices. These include the relationships of stars to landmarks, animal behavior, signs of changing weather, and the location of plant species and water holes, all of which are essential to life in terms of food, water, and shelter.[25] They include memorizing culturally relevant activities, body painting, and designs for ceremony, as well as types of body supplements, accoutrements, and ornamentation, associated with complex ritualistic practices and all connected primarily with the relationship they have with their land.

Importantly, as Indigenous cultures have lived and moved across country by day, people would sing the songs looking for sustenance, trade possibilities and places of ceremony.[26] Memorizing culturally relevant ceremonial activities and body supplements over time has had implications for cherishing particular rituals and adornment. It has been embedded in social and temporal value systems and their associated items, all highly selective activities.

In institutional anthropological collections on display, what the wearer or group felt about garments or ornament is never publicly recorded, only what an anthropologist or keen amateurs wrote about their "curiosity" value, the supposed function, who perhaps made the items, out of which materials and where they were found. The emotion recorded was that of the finder only, the intense

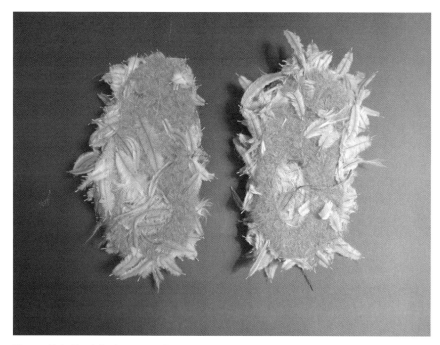

**Figure 7.4** Aboriginal sorcery slippers of the Pitjantjara people from the Gibson Desert, Western Australia. (Credit: Kim Akerman.)

pleasure of acquiring a rare item. A further issue was that collectors, often nineteenth-century explorers or government employees, frequently created labels for Indigenous artifacts that were misleading, if not occasionally erroneous. In Australia and Africa, colonial officials asserted their authority or ownership by writing on the actual object or pinning information on a label, perhaps with what is now considered dubious accuracy.[27]

Any observable wear—such as wrinkles and patina—are part of the built-in memory of artifacts themselves, as Sampson has noted about Western footwear. But in these Aboriginal sorcery slippers (*jinakarbil,* Pitjantjara) from the Gibson Desert in Western Australia, personal evidence or memory of wear is deliberately absent. These felted emu-feather soles with netted rabbit-fur yarn uppers leave no trace (no tread) of the shaman, the equivalent of Aranda *kurdaitcha* boots (Figure 7.4).[28]

# Emotions: Keeping Personal Dress

Western clothes worn by individuals are often kept, but they are also frequently discarded for many reasons. Why is it that only some dress is considered worth keeping, but not all? Some items are thrown out when the desire or emotion attached to them wears off, plus the dimming of sheer aesthetic attractiveness and their physical state of wear. Then of course the owner's personal boredom, dislike, failure to care for or perhaps the fact that these clothes do not enhance their idea of themselves or shape their own sense of self-identity or even match their change in weight. There are differences between wearing one's own dress, keeping it but never wearing it, dressing up in someone else's dress or disposing of it. "Fast fashion" means that tastes change incredibly quickly and there is the further issue regarding its disposal. It has become a serious ecological concern and the ethics of waste has becomes an issue. But essentially, keeping memories alive, or potentially recreating them, seems to lie at the heart of the retention of certain items of dress and not others.

Garments tend to be particularly cherished by owners if they have stories to tell or vivid memories to recall. To dispose of a wedding gown can be difficult for some, although there are plenty for sale second hand on clothing websites. Garments worn may be accurately or inaccurately remembered, linked to important social events, even associated with significant relationships and emotional moments in the past. Memory and the emotions are clearly important reasons why dress is kept and perhaps handed down at the request of a former owner.

The preservation of personal items like christening robes and the tiny shoes of babies can mean that those things—what one might call "memory objects"— can become filled with an *excess* of memory.[29] They are over treasured, kept as mementoes or relics, sometimes passed down to a family member, or memorialized to reinforce a family history that may never have existed quite as recalled. (See Focus 5a) In many cultures, such as ancient Egypt, the dead were buried wearing or alongside meaningful articles of clothing and ornament, which were understood to be for reuse in the afterlife. It is possible that grave goods in ancient burial graves may have served the same use. Shoes are particular cultural symbols that evoke memories of great intensity as they almost "stand in" for an absent person.[30] There is something very poignant about a single shoe of a child, which can be especially expressive of loss. Useless on its own, it may signal something incomplete about the life of the small wearer, the memory object of a life unfulfilled or incomplete.

There are other forms of memory that are less personal but which have greater philosophical import. Individual connoisseurs and collectors in the past have arbitrarily collected clothes and pictorial images from other cultures to illustrate costume history and enhance their "cabinets of curiosity." Collectors such as the German patrician Christoph Kress III, who lived in Nuremburg in the sixteenth century, amassed numerous examples of "foreign" clothes in the last decades of his life. This was part of an intense curiosity about other lands but he was keen to memorialize the exotic, in particular the dress of peoples in the Ottoman

**Figure 7.5** Cesare Vecellio, "Armenian Nobleman," from his wood-engraved costume book *De gli habiti antichi et moderni di diversi parti del mondo*, first edition in Italian, 1590. (Credit: Heritage Art/Heritage Images via Getty Images.)

Empire.[31] The acquisition of predominantly "Indian," "Moorish," and "Turkish" articles of dress was different from collecting keepsakes and family heirlooms; indeed, it was a sophisticated attempt to prevent the loss of the historic past as seen in records of costume books like this representation of "An Armenian Nobleman" from the famous 1590 illustrated book by Cesare Vecellio (Figure 7.5). These books were partly to show the owner's knowledge and connoisseurship and to boost their reputation as cultivated, worldly travelers. Yet they were also part of a globalized yearning to cherish and keep alive the cultural aesthetics of a foreign culture.

# Institutional Keeping

The idea of placing clothes into institutional care in a museum is a Western concept, and not necessarily relevant to those societies beyond its boundaries. Institutions such as dress museums have a cultural role to play as keepers of historical memories and emotions beyond those of a personal nature. Before the establishment of the great European public museums during the eighteenth century, many valuable garments were gathered into collections. These were located occasionally in private homes but especially in churches and palaces, using little in the way of collecting criteria, to the extent of even making up attributions. The Christian church has, for instance, been the repository of vestments, liturgical wear, and relics for centuries. (See Focus 5a) These were likely religious, even royal, memorabilia considered valuable for their embroidery or rich jewels, and their presumed association with alleged persons of significance.

The Cathedral Museum in Uppsala, Sweden, has a fine collection of very early textiles, burial regalia, and partial vestments. For a time, it housed the quite problematic and incomplete (but exceptionally rare) pure gold and silk gown of Queen Margrethe I of Denmark, Norway, and Sweden, who died in 1412. This medieval gown was credited with special powers for women in childbirth, and thus considered a relic. It has been carbon-dated to about 1400. Recently restored, it has been returned to the Christiansborg Palace in Copenhagen. Made of rich brocaded fabric, using the complex lampas technique, its precise history and use is somewhat unclear.[32] Even so it is a reminder of, or memorial to, the significant life of an important woman in the Middle Ages. The value of, or reason for, collecting and keeping garments like this lies in how emotions can be stirred by proximity to a garment of great antiquity and historical rarity. Memorializing wearers of the past, primarily through religious vestments and royal robes, has not been unusual in religious and other public institutions, especially as surviving medieval garments are so rare.

I suggest that the belief an historic garment is original, its likely association with a significant historical person or event, and the fact that its technique of making is no longer practiced, have been important factors behind institutional decisions to keep garments like that of Queen Margrethe. Criteria today for public acquisitions are not subjective and need to be justified. But the urge to acquire or retain an original garment in terms of its imagined closeness to a person of renown can sometimes be strong. These garments embody heightened emotions and, like relics, are sheltered from disposal. The question for any public acquisition of fashion or dress is what and when is a garment original? To be an original is to be either the very first of its kind, a garment genuinely belonging to a known owner or highly unusual. Mixed emotions are produced in the presence of an "original" item clothing, especially if it is very old. Clothes hanging in a private wardrobe carry with them the acquisition rationale of their owner and are later infused with their memory. When it comes to keeping and collecting clothes on behalf of institutions, the issues are different.

Until the twentieth century, some institutions took items from owners who were unable to care for them, or curators felt they had some obligation to keep historical items. Few small museums had collecting policies and accepted dress and ornamentation without much consideration for the future. When clothes were deliberately gifted, and accepted by these early museums, they often lacked reliable documented evidence of personal association with wearers, or their custodians. Today, institutions collect and keep significant clothing for many reasons, especially high-quality art-like garments or those with a sound provenance. If garments have no known source, they are freed from defined authorship and specific historical time. Even so, if they are pristine and aesthetically fine garments, with no observable flaws, they are more easily welcomed into a museum than less well-kept clothes.

But associated feelings and meanings are not attached to a garment forever. If feelings can no longer be recalled or are not documented, the space can be filled with new meanings, emotions, and purposes. All dress is fragile, difficult to conserve and subject to deterioration. If the owner is still alive, memories might be documented or found in association with a diary or letter, but how accurate can these be? Garments are volatile so the question is, who should take care of another's memories?

In colonial times, items were simply taken away from subject people but today, with new concerns regarding appropriation, many historic items and collections are now being repatriated. But where does memory sit in relation to a "collection," and who defines and names multiple items as a collection? Perhaps a dress/fashion collection implies a number of similar items, or maybe it is just a collective noun describing a chosen set of garments acquired by someone for personal reasons or tastes. Is a "collection" similar to that contained in a physical wardrobe, or is it purely conceptual? Perhaps the term has been applied retrospectively and arbitrarily by an outsider? A collection is not a flawless, unproblematic entity. It can be an inconvenient composition of dress, memory, emotion, and time. And emotions associated with collections can be troublesome.

An exhibition of shoes, part of the collection of Imelda Marcos, now on display in Marikina, a shoe-making city in the National Capital Region of the Philippines, evokes memories not of pleasure but mostly of hate and anger, a further aspect of emotional memory. Imelda was the extravagant wife of Ferdinand Marcos, a Filipino politician, kleptocrat, President (1965–86) and dictator (1972–81). His wife, the so-called "steel butterfly," was obsessed with collecting shoes, for personal, political, and strategic reasons. When Marcos was overthrown in 1986, Imelda's clothing, including over 2,700 pairs of shoes, were seized from the President's official residence, as a symbol of the couple's decadence. When activists and rebels overran the palace, they were said to have been horrified at the sight of the shoes they found in her closet. Like Marie Antoinette's wardrobe, many disappeared.

The remaining nearly 800 pairs of shoes (European and local brands) were relocated to the Marikina Shoe Museum and several hundred remain on view.[33] That the "collection" is located in the shoe-making hub of the Philippines is convenient for tourism but inappropriate given the extreme poverty and homelessness that exists there. Perhaps what visitors look for are some forms of heightened emotions that derives from seeing such extravagance in the midst of extreme poverty. Is that so different from the feelings of the poor who stormed Versailles, and in a frenzied attack destroyed the clothes set aside by Marie Antoinette for viewing at the height of the French Revolution?

According to Bide, high-status historical clothes in museum collections—and indeed those of the lower classes, if they survive—are more than just examples of how a society dressed in the past. They bear the detailed marks of lives and wearing, evoking personal memories and emotions that expand our understanding of interactions between wearers and their clothing.[34] The tiniest marks of wear and tear, or even stains, can demonstrate prior use, detail aspects of individual lives, and stimulate memories of personal activities in the past. Using observed information of how a garment has been worn over time and occasion gives museums the opportunity to create more complex and densely considered displays.

At times, the museum display of clothing can, according to Ellen Sampson, "sit between the shrine and the cabinet of curiosities: artifacts, taxonomized, decontextualized and made static, or at odds with the 'fleshy' and often messy practices of wearing clothes."[35] These words highlight the inevitable problems confronting those who exhibit Western dress and fashion. In terms of time and cultural remembering, the instability of collections of garment holdings and their display shows that generalizing about emotion and clothes of any particular historical moment needs careful consideration. Subjective as opposed to object-based meanings are entangled as part of the irregular interchange within embodied wear. Concepts like "out of date" would suggest there has previously been a single, overarching progress of time uniformly applied to outfits, resulting in meanings that are too straightforward. Given how intensely personal clothing can be, it is important to acknowledge an uneven and temporal mix of emotions circulate about clothing and its ownership, past and present.

Use-wear information, which includes the concept of cultural memory, needs to take a different temporal route from the historical orthodoxy of displaying garments as developmental sets of dates. Instead, as Bide suggests, there needs to be a response to different types of wear and tear as it is brought to light through embodiment. I suggest, by focusing on the relationship between how a garment has been made or acquired, worn and used, plus memories of wearers themselves, museums should be encouraged to create displays which disrupt historical orthodoxies, and reveal how echoes of past wearing and their meanings continue to challenge fashion cultures of the present.

A new generation of display of sartorial memories has moved away from the literal attention to the finesse of small details of use wear and period style. Fashion installations are posing daring questions about past and present wearing, about dress and the emotions, sustainability in a world of excessively rich and desperately poor, quality, and deterioration. They have moved out of former zones of comfort. New examples discussed in Focus 7a reveal how close attention to time and memories, anchored in material objects themselves and how they have been worn and used, can show the way toward new approaches to the study of fashion history.

## Focus 7a
## TIME: DISPLAYING SARTORIAL MEMORIES

Well-respected scholars working on the history of dress agree that fashion is an embodied art linked to the social world.[36] This Focus explores how sentiment and memories demonstrated in exhibitions of fashion and dress have enhanced understanding of the embodied nature of wearing over time. From the later part of the twentieth century, experimental museum curators began to reconsider the display of historical and contemporary clothing beyond conventional social history and themed approaches. These have been based largely on chronological histories of style, clustered around defined decades. Alternatively, exhibitions have focused on changing silhouettes and retrospectives celebrating contemporary haute couture, some said to be flavored by commercialism.[37] But at the beginning of the twenty-first century, new interest in the history of emotions began to enliven dress studies, showing garments could be better understood through close engagement with the feelings they engendered. Soon, radical questions began to be asked about the sequestering of clothing in museums where the relationship with the body appeared to no longer exist.

Exhibitions started to be more performative, open to the complexities of dress as vehicles of memory, imperfection, and reflective of changes in sentiment. Many curators began to allow the emotional power of ahistorical narratives to create new ways of experiencing fashion. Suggestions that fashion and dress, separated from original users, was decontextualized and static, flowed through to the critique of exhibitions, showing value could be found in the disorderly and the imperfect.[38] Offering novel kinds of interpretation was felt a more accessible method of engaging viewers. Even the suggestion of curating the immaterial nature of fashion digitally was flagged.[39]

Imaginative displays of dress using non-linear methods began to allow the power of emotional narratives to link objects, creating important new synergies and connections. In these progressive forms of exhibition, spectators were confronted by irregular, less didactic and surprising issues of temporality. Judith Clark's controversial "Malign Muses/ Spectres," ModeMuseum Antwerp 2004–05 (Spectres: When Fashion Turns Back, V&A, 2005) (Figure 7.6) was a significant installation of "provocative boundary pushing."[40] Here, fashion was displayed in a phantasmagorical manner, playing magical

**Figure 7.6**  The Merry Go Round Display in "Spectres: When Fashion Turns Back" installation, Victoria and Albert Museum, London, 2005. (Credit: Chris Jackson/Getty Images.)

games with past and present, remixing them, presenting it all through the magic of shadow lantern silhouettes, huge rotating cogs, and optical peephole devices to let viewers see garment details. Context was discarded.[41]

Some years ago, Riello suggested: "the history of fashion is not only written about, but it is in the gallery of fashion or in an exhibition, 'that the object is truly at the center of the narrative."[42] He also talked briefly about how fashion is didactically and emotionally conveyed through objects (garments), suggesting that: "Through its materiality, the object conveys its own history and value." These are important ideas. Obviously archival documentation is required for research but emotions need to be stirred by the value fashion has embedded in its material nature, and its role as a conduit of memories. In fact, unusual relationships and juxtapositions that occur purposely or inadvertently between garments and wearers, foster novel ways of thinking about clothing and associated memories.

Trends toward exhibiting fragile and tattered clothing began to appear such as the 2017 exhibition at the Fashion Space Gallery, London College of Fashion, entitled "Present Imperfect: Disorderly Apparel Configured." Reviewing this display, Sampson argued flaws were at the heart of this exhibition of women's fashion, showing imperfect garments embracing both what they are and what they once were.[43] She comments that fashion in a show like this almost makes the viewer feel as if they were *inside* not out, looking at the very structure of its building. Interestingly, I know of no men's fashion exhibits that have shown clothing as damaged, torn, or partial in quite this way.

Bodies respond to clothes as clothes do to bodies. Reused items can be as much part of a fashion installation or exhibition as the pristine. Garments are volatile; they likely do not retain their original social use and can indeed outlive the physical body. As discussed in Chapter 7, people throw clothes out or give them away over time, especially those that appear old fashioned or dated, perhaps worn out, or never used. But *imperfect* garments are imbued with significant small details of individual lives in their marks of wear. Clothes are made for bodies, not exhibitions. Emotions, desires, and values are embedded in these material subtleties which cannot be replicated fully in an exhibition, unless through metaphor, written text, or showing less-than-complete garments.

"Tattered and Torn," an installation on Governors Island, New York, was set up in an historic, run-down residential building with peeling paint, using nineteenth-century fashions deaccessioned from a number of collections.[44] It challenged both the idea of good taste and the value of beautifully crafted outfits worn by elite nineteenth-century women. Somewhat shabby and tarnished, the models had probably also been deaccessioned, for fashions in body shape change over time as do clothes themselves. Exhibition models cannot accurately replicate the living.

In relation to dress exhibitions that have dealt with questions about time and memory, I consider in particular tribute exhibitions to the artist Frida Kahlo (who died in 1954). These have centered on some of the contents of her well-known "memory" room in her home La Casa Azul, Coyoacán, Mexico City, where a collection of her personal clothing and other items were housed initially. It contained the mirrored bed that enabled her to paint self-portraits while lying down (Figure 7.7). After her death, Diego Rivera—her lover and husband—had the room locked, a testament to the emotional link between the two artists, ensuring it remained closed as a memorial keeping-place for her intimate clothing and memorabilia until fifteen years after his death.

Following its opening, the room was seen to hold some of Kahlo's "traditional" Mexican garments, including her *traje de tehuana*—which was, for Kahlo, her quintessentially Mexican trademark and appeared in many of her paintings—as well as her medical apparatus and other personal ephemera. Her brilliantly colored embroidered *huipil* (loose-fitting tunics) and *enagua* (full skirts) not only hid Kahlo's disability but showed her close identification with Zapotec women of the Tehuantepec Isthmus, from where her mother came.[45] The house was subsequently remade into a museum to honor Kahlo's memory, although it contains many other items including Rivera's pre-Columbian artifacts.

The concept of this memorializing has been considered by a number of exhibitions and reviews. The first exhibition held Kahlo's house was "Appearances can be Deceiving. The Dresses of Frida Kahlo," which later would be shown at the Brooklyn Museum. Aragón's review points out the complexity of her garments as not simply ethnic (national) and modern (Western), they were also exotic and political.[46] In 2018, London's Victoria

**Figure 7.7** Frida Kahlo, wearing Mexican dress and in bed at her home, La Casa Azul, Coyoacan, Mexico City. 1952. (Credit: Gisele Freund/Photo Researchers History/Getty Images.)

and Albert Museum held a larger, more comprehensive exhibition of many of her garments and related memorabilia, called "Frida Kahlo. Making Herself Up." One issue it raised was whether her illnesses, clothes, and personal effects were a more powerful manufactured memorial than her dramatic art. Alongside her striking clothes, photographs and emotive photographs taken of her wearing these garments (she had a large collection), her make-up, and even undergarments all added to this memorialization of her as an exotic celebrity. Was it possible that exhibition viewers *did* engage more with the curious relics of her life, illnesses, and striking appearance, than her artistic achievements? One review argues it perpetuated a mythologized and paternal *mestizo* hegemony at the expense of the actual disparate nature of Mexican Indigenous people.[47]

A number of quite different exhibitions and installations have treated the topic of memory and emotions in more tangential ways, introducing a new dynamic of understanding clothes via sentiment. A moving example was the sound, movement, and vision installation of clothing entitled "Personnes" by French photographer and film-maker Christian Boltanski, exhibited in 2010 in the vast nave of the Grand Palais, Paris

(Figure 7.8). Here, viewers were shown how perceptions of dress can be altered by confronting impermanent arrangements of clothes and how this impermanence calls into question issues of temporality, memory, material value, and the spatial. The intention was to emotionally challenge previous, more static, methods of exhibiting historic and contemporary clothing.

The title of the exhibition was ambiguous. Literally translated into English, it means "people," but the original French means "nobodies." It consisted of sixty-nine separate collections of dejected goodwill donations of old, disused, and decaying garments of all kinds. These thousands of discarded garments were set up in piles like rubbish heaps or mass graves, but with no display models. They thus had emotional resonances with Nazi collections of prisoners' clothes stacked in concentration camps. This was the equivalent of a vast "memento mori" recalling discovery of murderous war crimes against the innocent in so many countries around the world. A metal claw hung from a crane and hoisted up random garments before letting them fall arbitrarily. It was a random "collection" or cemetery of dress, with very different connotations than an intentional or neatly arranged wardrobe or clothing diary of a middle-class man or woman.

**Figure 7.8** Monumenta 3rd edition, Boltanski's "Personnes" installation, Grand Palais, Paris, 2010. (Credit: Raphael GAILLARDE/Gamma-Rapho via Getty Images.)

Artist/curators like Boltanski have taken new and thoughtful approaches to their exhibitions of dress. One of these was "Repair and Design Futures," a multi-disciplinary exhibition in 2018–19, curated by Kate Irvin.[48] Centered on issues of time, emotions, and clothing, it was dedicated to the metaphor of mending well-worn everyday working clothes by using patches and darning. Garments dating from about the 1800s until the twenty-first century were inspired by the temporal aesthetic of the "patched together." Pieces of fabric came from different sources, showing that a garment can grow piece by piece. Clothes were hung with amulets and all forms of detritus for magical purposes, showing that nothing need go to waste.

Linked to the exhibition was Kate Fletcher's book *Craft of Use*, which shows her ongoing concern with the sustainability of clothing, as opposed to merely the consumption of novelty.[49] The exhibition demonstrated the visual and emotional role of mending and repairing textiles and garments, challenging the idea of finding and applying a "date" to an article of dress. It celebrated the worn, the reuse of fabric, and the environmental implications of throwaway garments. She describes the tending of clothes through mending as a way of remaining near to material objects, and a way to modify and keep close to personal feelings and tastes. The exhibition included Japanese *boro* garments, outer coats originally worn by peasants, made of patchworked indigo-blue fabrics, such as denim (Figure 7.9). Considered of little value at the time, but now

**Figure 7.9** Japanese *boro* garments. "Boro Stoff des Lebens" exhibition, 2015, Museum of East Asian Art, Cologne. (Credit: Brill/ullstein bild via Getty Images.)

regarded as aesthetic marvels, they reach out beyond class, and are a mix of textile pieces from the past and present that cohere sympathetically.

In acknowledging the importance of time to understanding dress, we need to take from Healy the suggestion that "the best" condition and "ideal" image should not govern museum acquisition policies of a designer's work.[50] What Healy suggests as a replacement is the complete reverse of the pristine, show-stopping, theatrical-style fashion show, particularly the retrospective exhibitions orchestrated by Diana Vreeland at the Costume Institute in New York.[51] Her 2006 curatorial project, "'Noble Rot: An Alternate History of Fashion," was visual evidence of her display of the "poetics of decay" in broken-down, disheveled, and disintegrating clothing.[52] Museums, she suggests, need to intervene in the usual presentation of flawless fashions and radically challenge this practice by demonstrating the irreversible alteration of clothing over time.[53] Powerfully bridging the gap between past and present, the approach in this project made connections between time past, memory and emotions, creating affecting versions of the history of dress. This was no orderly time line. It was a tangled mix of components and feelings that rewrote the conventions of exhibitions prior to the next stage of digital media that would move exhibitions from the emotional and internal psyche, to the collapsing of the physical with the virtual.[54]

## Focus 7b
## FASHION: NO PRESENT WITHOUT A PAST

Desire for novelty seems to be a human compulsion, not just confined to Western fashion and whose origins are not fully understood.[55] Nor is it feasible to speak of a moment when fashion was "born," as signs of its developing stages have been suggested in thirteenth-century France, but also described as taking effect as early as the eleventh century.[56] Any idea that Western fashion started at a specific date, and is unique, is not supported by most scholars, a view expressed as early as 1994 by Craik in *The Face of Fashion*.[57] Kaiser claims fashion as a concept should be released from bounded times and places and replaced with concepts of transnational networks. She prefers "the metaphor of entanglement" between polarities and identities. Here, bodies and the materials which fashioned them, are open to wide influences and interactions of style.[58] Cultural memories play their part in these stylistic interconnections.

The place of haute couture as the driving force of novel sartorial creativity needs careful analysis. Understandably, if they are to survive in the highly competitive global industry of high fashion and ready-to-wear, designers must constantly use their creativity to find novel ways to stimulate consumption. Major week-long catwalk shows of their wares are no longer restricted to the great cities of the world—Paris, London, New York, Milan, and Tokyo. Fashion Weeks are held all over Asia, India, and Africa too, part of networks in which we see complex flows of ideas and materials from numerous sources.

These ideas are distributed via the constantly evolving digital technologies that have transformed global accessibility. Walter Benjamin's well-rehearsed model of bourgeois fashion is that it has a flair for quoting its own prehistory, but its novel aesthetics are captured within the economies of the ruling class. It is always a spring into the past under the control of the same ruling class. This aptly describes the haute couture designer, frantically looking for inspiration partly amongst a compendium of historic styles (be it the Middle Ages, the Italian Renaissance, British eighteenth-century dress or further afield). Clearly for Western high fashion, the present needs a past in order to survive. But what exactly is "the past," and when does it begin? Inevitably, it is viewed through the lens of the present.

Fashion is neither trivial or ephemeral. Such labels devalue its constant creative turnover and mark it out as the opposite of supposedly timeless "traditional" dress. Certainly Asian, South American, African, and Oceanian cultures, prior to Western contact, did not conceive of "fashion," as their body supplements were seemingly ritualistic. In Polynesia, for instance, materials from which ceremonial dress and accessories are made, and techniques of making, are both believed to be symbolic and imbued with life force and cultural potency.[59] In West Polynesia, body supplements of great value were plaited from pandanus strips. As they were considered imbued with the owner's *mana* (supernatural power and effectiveness), they were worn for special ceremonies and—importantly—passed down the generations.[60] When customary cultures made wear for the body, in connection with their rituals, they tended to reproduce existing practices of body supplements and markings, but the belief that these were unchanging is misplaced.

Writing about Africa, Hansen and Madison suggest customary dress was never a timeless or static practice. They also argue globalization has transformed African dress into an ever-changing cultural process and that African designers themselves have in fact become style initiators.[61] In creating new fashion systems, designers and consumers are challenging the success and dominance of Western fashion, facilitating diversification with the increased availability of novel textiles which encourage innovation. The polarizing concepts of Western and non-Western dress are no longer meaningful. Past and present are under scrutiny.

This does not suggest historical dress and accessories were never the profound inspiration for high-end fashion although painted, etched, or photographed images of past fashions bring with them the characteristic style of the artist or photographer. (See Focus 8a) And modern fabrics and dyes are different, threads and linings are different, undergarments are different, and aesthetic concepts are of their own time. Being influenced by aspects of dress of the past is something quite apart from replicating it. While designers can be inspired by earlier clothes and textiles, their aims are different. The present always intrudes. The past is viewed via the lens of the present, thus a designer's choice of a favorable past lies only with aspects of it acceptable to the present. In this context, the past is "merely a realm to visit and to admire," not to recreate.[62]

An obsession with a particular past has been the pervasive fascination the West has had with Indian fabric designs and garments. Britain's colonial occupation of India, which ended so disastrously, did not shake the love for Indian design in the UK. The patterns on Paisley shawls are typical of the archetypical cross-cultural fascination with Indian designs. Motifs like the almond-shaped *boteh*, of ancient Persian origin, traveled from there to be absorbed into early Indian fabric designs, then to European nineteenth-century fashion, and finally the counterculture of the 1960s. This languid 1870 painting by James Tissot, "Jeune Femme en Bateau" (Figure 7.10), shows a young woman drifting pensively and directionless in a rowing boat, her white ruffled muslin gown partly wrapped in a warm Paisley shawl. It is a brilliant yellow ochre color, with russet *boteh* designs, which gestures to cultures of the past while the outfit is very much of the present. Yet to complicate the image further, the idea of drifting, without someone in charge, seems to represent a kind of nostalgia for a non-specific past, with an

**Figure 7.10** "Jeune Femme en Bateau," painting by James Tissot, exhibited at the Paris Salon, 1870. (Credit: Buyenlarge/Getty Images.)

ineffectual small dog and a bunch of fast-fading blooms facing a future that has nowhere to go.

The remembered creates a nostalgia and yearning to return to a time that is irrecoverable, a past that is imagined only. The late Richard Martin, former scholar, critic, and costume curator of the Costume Institute at the Metropolitan Museum of Art in New York, as well as one of the most significant fashion writers of his period, suggested that historical references transport wearers and viewers to another time. By wearing clothes that recall the past, we are allowed "to step into something more than raiment; thereby we step into the past." But he admitted that: "the wearer dressed in the medieval manner is servant not to a feudal image, but a complex modern sign of the Middle Ages."[63] Historical revival fashions, which reuse the past, are really a sign of the present.

What we mean by "the past" is difficult to define, but for Western consumers the very quality of long-lasting is appreciated in its difference from "fast" fashion. The appropriate "past" can be wistful feelings about earlier days that clearly bypass the conditions of the ultimate faux pas: being "out of date." So, the past is categorized by being both acceptable but not. The old is not necessarily venerable as it can be devalued further by "a copy" and the past is by no means wholeheartedly admired in comparison to the new.[64]

## Source Material

Past fashions, used to stimulate the new, have been found selectively in particular historical periods, especially classical antiquity. The seventeenth century was another favored period and a popular source that inspired eighteenth-century dressmakers, designers, and tailors of European dress. Rubens' famous portrait of Susanna Lunden, often called "Le Chapeau de Paille" ("The Straw Hat"), which shows the sitter wearing a hat with a broad, feathered trim (1622–5), was often used as a pictorial model. This "Rubens hat with feathers" was later renamed the "Gainsborough hat" and worn by both British and French upper-class woman. Another popular source was the work of seventeenth-century artist Anthony van Dyck.

The great British portrait painters of the day, like Reynolds, Gainsborough, Ramsay, and Romney, became adept (often with the help of artisanal "drapery painters") at representing wealthy sitters in so-called "Vandyke" (sic) fashions of the previous century. These could include Vandyke-style masquerade costumes and fancy dress.[65] Gainsborough painted many young sitters in composite Vandyke/Watteau/ *commedia dell'arte* costumes. His famous "Blue Boy" of *c*. 1770 (Figure 7.11) wears fancy dress in this style, with its slashed sleeves, lace collar, and feathered hat.[66]

The fashionable "historic" garments represented in these portraits painted for aristocrats, set against imagined environments, were immensely desirable at the time and beyond. Images like Gainsborough's "The Honorable Mrs Graham" (1775–7)

**Figure 7.11** "The Blue Boy," a portrait of Jonathan Buttall by Thomas Gainsborough *c*. 1770, Huntington Library, San Marino, California. (Credit: H. Armstrong Roberts/ ClassicStock/Getty Images.)

deliberately evoked the luxuries of court life, grand, stately homes, the privilege of land-owning, the aesthetics of the well-tended countryside, plus the values of lineage. These images do not represent crass revivalism or heavy-handed historicism. Rather, they build a dreamlike emotional bond between consumers and an enviable social period in the past. But the velvet or brocade suits of aristocratic men soon gave way to the sober finesse of British tailoring, which was more suited to democratic political developments of the time.

In the later part of the eighteenth century, as political and social upheaval accelerated in France, wealthy women's fashionable gowns began to break with the lavish, formal dress of the past. When, in 1783, Élisabeth Vigée Le Brun painted a supposedly scandalous formal portrait of Marie Antoinette, wearing simply a cotton *robe en chemise*, there was an outcry. Given that a chemise was an undergarment, this portrait was viewed as highly inappropriate when shown at the Académie Française but soon became popular as tastes changed under the influence of the informal simplicity of gowns popularized by the queen. Subsequently, delicate gowns with very high waistlines mirrored women's taste for all things classical. They echoed the garments on antique Greek statues and the taste for antique treasures their husbands brought back from the Grand Tour or later the Napoleonic Wars. As these gowns were thin and almost transparent, they needed the warmth of a shawl or shoulder covering, conveniently provided by cashmere shawls in plain, brilliant colors, often with Paisley motifs.

In the late nineteenth and early twentieth centuries in Europe, America, and Britain, a renewed nostalgia occurred among wealthy trade barons and wives, this time for the fashions of the century earlier. Patrons, especially Americans, commissioned British and Continental artists to paint their portraits, and those of their wives, wearing lush versions of the glorious fabrics and lightweight silk gowns found in portraits of the mid to later years of the eighteenth century. The new, landowning pseudo-aristocracy of wealthy industrialists and business moguls had amassed large fortunes and wished to have themselves, their families, and their vast landscaped properties immortalized in grand works of art. The broad painterly styles of the major portraitists of the time, like Singer Sargent, were suitable for presenting loose stylistic versions of the past. Echoing portraits of the previous century, they enhanced and revived the gleaming silks, filmy gauze neckerchiefs edged with antique lace, and pastel-colored gowns worn by upper-class ladies. Fanned by the popularity of masquerade ball designs of the past, this fascination for eighteenth-century-style portraits was partly a nostalgia for what was believed a simpler era.

The delight in the fashions, sentimental poses, hairstyles, jewels and other stylish fashions of the 1700s was not merely a fad for "olden days" dress. In these portraits, members of a newly rich mercantile culture deliberately sought to present the reassurance of their forebears, an ethos taken from the landed gentry of the previous century, to whose class they did not strictly belong. The wives, in turn, celebrated "the season" by giving lavish entertainments, including masquerade dress and fancy-dress balls, where replicas of seventeenth- and eighteenth-century costumes were a popular choice. Their dress, as portrayed with fleeting brushstrokes, was very different from overt copies found in the earnest historical revivalist paintings of much the same period.

Certain periods of historic dress have been more popular for inspirational referencing than others. Vivienne Westwood is a successful designer with a particular interest in clothes of the European past, using them to parody and disturb. She undermined the copying of historic dress to question the class-based styles of fine dressing. She absorbed the essence of portraits like François Boucher's glorious painting of "Madame de Pompadour Reading" (1758), reinterpreting it as an ironic crumpled silk gown for her 2003 "Anglophilia Collection."[67] On her 1990 exterior bustiers (not undergarments), of different Lycra fabrics, she printed the fronts with different sections of a lascivious painting of Daphnis and Chloe, also by Boucher.[68] One can read this as a critique of fashion's sexualization of women but also a subversion of historical fashions, sometimes laced with bitter humor (Figure 7.12). The bustier here is ironically combined with a very short skirt.

**Figure 7.12** Vivienne Westwood, "Bustier and Miniskirt" (Dressing Up Collection), Autumn/Winter 1991–2. (Credit: Indianapolis Museum of Art/Getty Images.)

Westwood has delighted in challenging the history of British fashion, with a random mix of references to dress of previous centuries, like her 1991 "Cut, Slash and Pull" collection (versions of sixteenth- and seventeenth-century garments) and the "mini-crin" of 1985, an absurd combination of a mid-nineteenth-century Victorian crinoline with the miniskirt of the 1960s.[69] Other daring designers have followed her lead and used anachronistic combinations of earlier styles. They have created "the latest thing" from random selections of earlier garments and tastes, to enrich and enliven the present. These are patchworked postmodern styles, quite different from the more serious nature of historical revivalism.

Couturiers continue to be inspired by fashions based on previous eras. A spectacular example is the work of extravagant Milanese designers Dolce and Gabbana. In December 2019, their Alta Mode designs were based on the costumes for twelve great Italian operas and inspired by Renaissance paintings. When the men's fashions (embellished rich brocades, feathered coats, and bejeweled gloves) were shown in the Pinacoteca Ambrosiana and adjoining library, one journalist said many existing artworks seemed to come alive on the catwalk. The resplendent companion fashions for women were shown in La Scala opera house and ornamented with gold, silver, crystal, and feathers, while audiences watched from opera boxes. This was not costuming for prima donnas but, in the words of the journalist, for customers to be "leading ladies in their own lives."[70]

# 8
# UNFIXED: TIME AND DRESS

Time is constituted by culturally specific spans of measured sequential duration. It has different characteristics and meanings across Eastern and Western cultures, from country to country. Complex and historical differences have existed worldwide between calendars, each structured in unique ways. As I have demonstrated, particularly in the West but not entirely, time is regarded as a major determinant of fashion's "newness." It is linked inseparably to social and commercial changes in the making, aesthetics, and distribution of garments. Western fashion has been widely regarded as more advanced than dress of many other parts of the world, its nature regarded as more stylistically progressive. This explanation has long dominated the master narrative of fashion's histories. The concept of a sequential time line is still prevalent, especially in popular accounts.

For literary scholar and fashion theorist Vinken, fashion is the art of the perfect moment, the eternal present which, in this instant, almost effaces yesterday, with no thought for tomorrow.[1] So it is not an art of memory or nostalgia. But at the moment of realization of "the now," fashion is already part of yesterday. A marked change in the relationship of the history of fashion to time occurs as it moves beyond perfection, erasing traces of time. By fixating on the eternal present, it extinguishes its own mortality and becomes what she terms "postfashion." But here it makes itself into a "new art of memory."[2] This is not a memory of material "stuff," but rather it becomes a sign of mortality, an index of a discontinuous past, preserving only its traces. At this moment we see fashion's flaws and irregularities, its lustre has faded and it presents a quite different aesthetic. Vinken's text now suggests fashion is tied to time in a relationship that is highly unsettled.

The purpose of this book has been to analyse orthodox assumptions about the history of clothing and build on scholarship that previously took little sustained account of the nature of time. The theory of relativity of time and space that shook the notion of historical development in the early twentieth century, affected historical understanding of linear progress more generally. It is now possible to see dynamic networks and complex pathways in dress, where elements of "unfixity" account for fashion's disparate rather than cohesive character. In simple terms, the tie that "goes" with a suit, or dress that "goes" with matching hat and gloves is no longer part of stylish fashion. "Good" taste has given way in recent times to intentional mixing of designs, formerly described as "clashing," which perhaps is itself a new form of crosscultural taste. If there is something termed "good," taste, it is no longer of consequence but nor is "bad" taste. [3]

This repositioned view of fashion and dress accepts pluralities of discourse and diversity in the complex narratives of clothing.[4] Devoucoux has argued that dress studies could well follow the model of archaeology where in its acceptance of plurivocality it is challenging former beliefs in homogeneity and the "old master narratives" of art history. He goes so far as to suggest that a new dynamic be applied which incorporates methods from cultural anthropology and textile archaeology, using "smaller space-time contexts with thematic foci": in other words, a diversity of "clothing worlds" to replace homogeneity. He proposes that critics introduce a concept of fashion archaeology in order to create a new dynamic for the study of clothing.[5]

One of the most high-profile fashion designers in Paris is Alessandro Michele, who was named creative director of Gucci in 2015. He has had a long history of designing for numerous established haute couturiers and is the Italian master of including in his work widespread appropriations taken from past and present sources—his world is kaleidoscopic, where everything goes with everything. He is "a situationist of pastiche, an inexorable maker and undoer of lavish spatiotemporal twines."[6] His creative impulses use historical ideas to create extreme and edgy looks, making the "out-of-date" vulgarity of some fashions desirable. His love of pastiche showed in the outfit he wore to the gala opening of the Heavenly Bodies Exhibition in 2018 (Figure 8.1). While he claims one of his passions is history, this is not necessarily novel given the work of other designers like Westwood or Viktor & Rolf. In an interview soon after he was appointed to his creative directorship, he confessed to liking to mix old and new, saying; "I'm not interested in the future—it doesn't exist yet—but I'm really interested in the past and the contemporary. I put everything together."[7]

Is this merely a catchy journalistic comment suggesting he has no real interest in an authentic past either? Or is the real question around how fashion's claim to newness might fit with Michele's view that the future does not yet exist? Is the contemporaneity of fashion just a progression through a previous future? Perhaps this is a form of 'head in the sand" that fails to understand how the complexities of increasing fashion consumption, and its links to newness, contribute to issues of sustainability, a major and urgent global challenge. In fact an estimated 17 million tons of discarded textiles, including clothing, entered landfill in the US in 2018, which is an alarming statistic.[8] The situation in Ghana is worse.

Michele's profile displaces the older character of a fashion designer, the autocratic dictator (couturier) who emerged in the nineteenth century. Famed designers like Worth, as demonstrated by Breward, came to prominence due to a number of factors characteristic of modern consumerism and retailing methods.

**Figure 8.1** Alessandro Michele, Lana Del Rey, and Jared Leto dressed up for the gala opening of the exhibition "Heavenly Bodies: Fashion and the Catholic Imagination," The Costume Institute, The Metropolitan Museum of Art, 2018. (Credit: Neilson Barnard/Getty Images.)

These included the expansion of urban culture, as well as mechanization and the reorganization of labor; these factors combined to create an environment in which high-end fashion could thrive in communities outside the inner circles of various courts of Europe and beyond.[9]

But the digital world now embraced by fashion has left its aristocratic past to take its place in celebrity seating around the Paris catwalks. At the same time, it has moved to the shopping precincts of all the major cities in the world or their online equivalents. Customers are no longer simply the seriously wealthy. They occupy a wide range of cultural and financial levels on social ladders that are now more complex than a sequence of single defined steps. These cohorts are more difficult to specify than in earlier decades, although their stylish dress still marks out aspirational social positions, values, and financial worth.

The speed of global transmission of fashionable style, the result of digital social media, has created a fast changing landscape for fashion.[10] Our image-saturated world has altered the parameters of style. The intense spatiotemporal acceleration of new ideas has now spread rapidly via increasingly networked groups of customers. The "influencers" on Instagram and other platforms are now as important as many designers, further destabilizing the definition of "fashion."[11] Observers and customers increasingly crowd to shopping centers to socialize, but they buy online. Rocamora categorises this shift, in terms of speed, as the "new fashion times."[12]

Success of image-based design dissemination relies more and more on the extremism of digital manipulation and air brushed photographic fictions, far from clothes in a wardrobe. As Evans explains, a great deal of contemporary fashion circulates obliquely as a commodity, not as worn, but as "an image, an idea, or a conceptual piece."[13] Image is not a representation of an original but has become a new kind of commodity, consumed digitally in a novel kind of way unlike the object itself. The latter, hanging on a rack, lacks the verve of fashions exhibited in galleries or featured in magazines.

# Fast Fashion: Digital Fashion

The "new" and the "latest" are still major drawcards at the heart of customer desires for fashion in the middle to upper echelon of many social economic groups around the world. The demands for exorbitantly priced garments and accessories are still linked to the skills and grandiose practices of haute couture. But these pricy methods operate within a framework that is losing custom. The highest-quality design and handwork (exclusive couture) has become economically unsuited to the fast-moving commerce of a globalized world. It serves relatively few clients.

It is the digitization of the production, marketing, and consumption of fashion that has disrupted traditional temporality in how clothes are made, sold and worn. The seasonal pace of the high-fashion industry continues, but any acceleration demanded of traditional working practices cannot be sustained if haute couture is to match the fast turn-around of less exclusive wear. Prêt-à-porter (ready to wear) copies high fashions and reproduces them rapidly for less affluent clients at much reduced cost. The length of time needed to produce these garments, straight from catwalk to final point of sale, has decreased rapidly. It is the new digital technologies that emerged in America in the 1970s that spawned the Quick Response (QR) techniques that allowed the gap between catwalk and finished products to be reduced.[14] It was also a response to consumer demands for instant product availability.

On-line marketing of middle- to low-range fashion was a further disruption to the traditional tempo of ways clothes had been made, used, and sold. Ready-made fashions have been a feature of the new "massclusivity" of the clothing market, a term in use by the later 1990s, describing firms such as Zara and H&M.[15] Catwalk designs were communicated instantaneously to salespersons and online shoppers all over the world. These new products were also the result of hasty methods of production, employing low-paid clothing workers housed in substandard conditions in Asia, Central America, and in parts of

Europe. Sometimes called "fast" fashion, quick-response orders have disrupted the previous methods of making exclusive, middle-range, and even everyday fashions.

Eminent curator and academic José Teunissen suggests the old fashion system is no longer working and what the speed of fashion demands is unsustainable. The Hollywood dream is outdated. In her view, fashion will have to come up with a new model. It cannot go on producing new trends every six or so weeks, and which are out of date immediately after launch. Instead, it will have to devise a new visual language that does not rely on luxury and connects designers and customers directly. The "straitjacket ideal of young, slim, white and rich men and women is about to be replaced by a more open and inclusive aesthetics that celebrates nature and new ideas of gender and people."[16] To a degree, this has begun to happen.

Fashion has split into discrete cohorts in a number of ways. Over the past number of years, some couturiers have altered their remit and now consider themselves lifestyle designers, mixing textile design, fashion and interior design, thus complementing their profits and gaining space in overlapping spending practices. Twenty-first-century upper-end fashion is no longer tied exclusively to a group or class. Responding to change, a numbers of designers have been regarding fashion as a practice more cerebral than purely aesthetic. Here they can challenge aesthetics and comment on their own work, rather than just designing elite garments for the rich. What is interesting is that the eclecticism, finesse, glitz, extreme creativity, and visual spectacle of stage effects on the catwalk continue to be the hallmark of fashion. In the frenzy to innovate the new in garments, many couturiers have stepped up to remodel the spectacle of the catwalk.

The performance of fashion has become a theatricalized segment of time where onlookers are mesmerised by stage direction, the impossibility of themes, and skilled spotlighting. The curious Viktor & Rolf 2015 autumn and winter collection, for instance, based on contorted picture frames, was performance art, with garments unwearable in daily life. It shows fashion can be intellectual and experimental, and that its concepts are multidimentional. The challenging novelties of fashion are, to an extent, being upstaged by even more challenging catwalk extravaganzas. Westwood, Margiela, and Viktor & Rolf are some designers whose products are counterintuitive, their aesthetics and meanings irregular and unstable.

The concept of linear time lines has also been questioned seriously in a number of exhibitions of fashion. Here, standing back from conventional sequences and historical time, curators have used theatrical frameworks and flexibility of associations to demonstrate new ways of looking at dress. In the words of Greer and Barbieri; "The emphasis is less on scenery and props and more on the spatial, temporal, and sensorial relationships between the physical objects and the perceiving subject."[17] "Remixing It: the Past in Pieces," one of the installations associated with "Spectres: When Fashion Turns Back" (ModeMuseum, Antwerp, 2004–05, and the V&A 2005) was a case in point. Relativitiy is echoed in this new genre of unconventional fashion exhibitions. (See Focus 7a)

It is interesting that the familiar fashion "time line" was reinterpreted in the important New York exhibition "About Time: Fashion and Duration, a Century and a Half of Fashion 1870 until the Present" (Metropolitan Museum of Art, 2020–1).[18] Using the exquisite collections of fashion in the Museum, the exhibition overview explained an unfolding time line around two adjacent galleries, set up as giant clockfaces of 60 minutes, divided into one-minute segments. Yet it also stressed temporal associations in designer garment styles that conflated past, present, and future (Figure 8.2).

Using Henri Bergson's philosophy of the two faces of time—the first objective and pragmatic, and the second, *la durée*, meaning more disruptive, lived time, was integrated into the exhibits. One gallery used a familiar linear time line,

**Figure 8.2** A 1948 Christian Dior dress and a 1977 Norma Kamali dress on display near indicative marks of a large clock in the "About Time: Fashion and Duration" exhibition, The Costume Institute, The Metropolitan Museum of Art, 2020–1. (Credit: Taylor Hill/Getty Images.)

stressing progress, the second a disrupting linear time line with garments behind, suggesting a more philosophical view across the years. Garments in the first were practically all black, referring to the familiar trope of fashion history expressed by the silhouette. A standout exception was a white Viktor & Rolf garment from their spring 2020 collection, made in a patchwork style of handmade lace fabrics. This was surplus left from previous collections, gesturing to a new era of making do with less, the need for sustainability, collaboration, and the possible future of fashion.[19]

# The Role of the New

As we have seen, Vinken defines fashion as "the art of the perfect moment"—the more ephemeral, the more perfect—but while seemingly giving form to the moment, its realization is simultaneously its destruction.[20] This is the puzzle that infuses twenty-first-century fashion and dress, which has entered a phase of increasing uncertainty and instability. Fundamental to the meaning of fashion has been the priority given to fleeting ideas that are the mainstay of the "new." The overwhelming desire for the transient lies, as ever, at the heart of social and commercial purchases of dress that characterize modern mainstream consumer culture in Europe and the US, as well as Asian, African, and Pacific urban markets.

But clearly any attempt to discuss fashion must now bear in mind the conundrum that has emerged surrounding making, marketing, and meaning in a global environment saturated with digital information. Routines of wearing have come under pressure and temporal diurnal conventions are being altered. Technology is waiting round the corner for its chance to shine. New research, looking at nations outside Europe and the US, in particular those in Africa, shows "fashionability" is a term more suited to the mix of today's trends than "fashion."

There is an experiential dimension here as well.[21] The demi-god couturier has given way to active participation of wearers, creating what is a personal performativity in civic dress. African styles, for instance, have no relationship to the conservatism of either "classic" fashion or "timeless" garments (See Focus 8a). Their designers are fully aware of international fashionable style, yet the "distinctly local" has begun to challenge universality of design with improvised fashion events and the originality of style seen here at Dakar's open-air Fashion Week in 2020 (Figure 8.3). While "the hallmark of fashion everywhere is change," as Hansen says, the innovative nature of stylish dressing in Africa is complex—the fashions systems of which demonstrate "localized notions of modernity"—are influencing the global.[22]

At the heart of fashion at the present time lies the underlying thread of uncertainty, combined with a sense of new opportunities as cultures juggle with

**Figure 8.3** A model presents a striking creation at the 2020 open-air Dakar Fashion Week. Due to coronavirus restrictions, it was held under baobab trees, at Nguekhokh, 60km from Dakar, Senegal. (Credit: Fatma Esma Arslan/Anadolu Agency via Getty Images.)

issues of class, identity, economic inequality, taste, and eco-responsibility. The expansion of technologies now available to designers has given them multiple opportunities to experiment with new ideas. Quinn's book *Textile Futures* (2010) is a fascinating account of some of these innovations and the ability of designers to create aesthetically interesting, high-performance sustainable fabrics.[23] Communication technology is being integrated with optical fibers, and experiments with three-dimensional techniques are disrupting traditional cutting and sewing methods. These inventions will create an entirely revitalized fashion landscape.

# The Not so New

The scenario of a fracturing economic world and the Covid pandemic has apparently made little difference to mainstream Western fashion. New middle-of-the road fashions, produced almost on a daily basis, still contribute to what is regarded politically as the vital need for ceaseless consumerism as the quest to maintain economic growth continues. On the other hand, some high-fashion designers have accepted, to a degree, the concept of repurposing and recycling as their personal commentary on sustainability. There is a certain irony in designer products where "new" imperfections of decay have been created in pricy denim trousers with knee and thigh areas artificially torn and frayed.

Recycling has certainly entered the spectrum of fashionable taste, but one must not forget the actual nature of distressed clothes as these play a significant part in the day-to-day lives of the underclasses. In fact, the global mix that clearly consists of clothes of many qualities, is a living symbol of the uncertainty of Western culture's sartorial existence. Lou Taylor's extremely insightful essay "From Farm, to Dump, to Poverty Chic" narrates the history of poor farmworkers' clothing in Normandy from 1900 and its six stages of life.[24] These stages consisted of working people wearing clothes until they were almost unusable, bartering the residue for other goods, then left-overs being purchased by wholesale rag dealers and finally some being used for paper-making. By the 1950s, many of these clothes were left to rot as they had no monetary value. Recycling was impossible, even into paper. Finally in 2010, some of the piles of rotting garments were salvaged by secondhand dealers and later the fashion system also found a way to reinvent these impoverished garments for their relatively elite customers. Other garments were sanitized or aged artificially as "poverty chic," or what Taylor calls "bogus brand-new 'vintage denim clothing'."[25]

# Lineage: Keeping the Past in a Throwaway World

Despite its dependence on the new, the past is essential to fashion. (See Focus 7b) Whilst the out of date is despised by some, it is a major resource for others. At the high end of the market, increasingly toward the end of the twentieth century, some couturiers began to look to their own past for design inspiration and as a way of managing their legacy. As scholarly libraries have jettisoned the practice of retaining handwritten archives, including sketches, so designers have foreseen that their long-term reputation might diminish. At a time when the long-term nature of high fashion has itself been under threat, and the endless novelty demanded by fast fashion has changed the design climate, couturiers have been finding ways to consolidate their own histories. In addition, a number of designers of standing have considered eclectic reuse or reissue of their own garments to further publicize their work.

In a conscious desire to challenge the current "unfixity" in their industry, they have begun to collect physical examples of their work and create repositories of their historical documents to establish their own design genealogies. This is a counter to the idea of fashion's ephemerality. These archives keep the public alive to a designer's creativity and assist when major retrospective exhibitions of their work are held. A number have set up in-house data bases, partly to deter copyright infringements, but also to note and record their past achievements.

From 1964, Yves Saint Laurent kept prototypes of his garments shown on the catwalk. These were mainly for his own use, much like research notes. Since 1985, Soizic Pfaff, head curator of the Christian Dior Archives, has been seriously building up Dior's legacy of dresses, fabric swatches, hats, shoes, and some sketches, all in pristine accommodation off the Avenue Montaigne in Paris. A form of elegant tribute to Dior and his achievements, the archive is maintained immaculately but not a public collection as such. It is a serious research facility housing over 300 haute couture gowns for the study of Dior's designs from the past until the present day.[26]

In 2017, a Yves Saint Laurent Museum was opened in Paris to show his works to the public, and in the same year the Yves Saint Laurent Museum (mYSLm) was opened in Marrakesh, Morocco. The latter houses thousands of garments and accessories, as well as sketches. It is both a research facility and museum showing how much North Africa inspired the designer. These examples are apparently attempts to manage the legacies of designers and counter the almost directionless nature of haute couture, the future of which seems unclear.

# Sustainability

In the modern world, exclusive couture has become increasingly unaffordable to vast numbers of global citizens. At the same time, much scholarly research is being done in relation to responsibility in the fashion and textile industries. Low-cost Western clothes are discarded all too easily and the pleasures attached to them shortlived. The West is a throwaway society and the obviously novel can lose its verve, sometimes becoming a liability rather than an advantage. Burgeoning consumption of poorly made clothing and desire to make rapid changes from one outfit to another is increasingly a worldwide problem, perhaps best noticeable in the attire of the middle-range consumer.

Part of the difficulty is the short-term lifespan of cheap fashions that are discarded thoughtlessly and ending up in landfill. Charity shops worldwide are filled with customers looking for secondhand clothing and in less affluent areas vendors sell used clothing on the street. The situation in the cities of Accra in Ghana, and Libreville in Gabon, are particularly dire. The former has become an unregulated dumping ground of "mountains" of unwanted secondhand clothing; around 50 tons arrives each day, much of it exported in good faith from UK charity shops [27] Most is too soiled to sell. It is left in heaps and spills into the

**Figure 8.4** Youngsters search through trash, including textile waste, at the Mindoubé dump in Libreville, Gabon, 2021. (Credit: STEEVE JORDAN/AFP via Getty Images.)

rivers, while piles of garments are burned, in turn polluting the atmosphere. Libreville has a similar story: here, textile waste is mixed with unwanted electronic and other goods that demonstrate the problems of clothing over-production (Figure 8.4).

As the prices of everyday fashions generally diminish, there is a greater consumption of low-cost garments, which wear out rapidly, creating untold waste-disposal issues. *Genuinely* sustainable clothing is not cheap which means that in order to turn profits, companies need to reduce the living wages of their workers [28] Some design companies are beginning to capitalize on these supposed credentials and reuse materials, though it is questionable how effective reuse is on a large scale. A lot of slick promotion seems to indicate that the clothing market is listening to concerns around sustainability, but this seems largely advertising hype rather than any radical rethink.

One example of "virtue signaling" can be found in Patagonia's 2019 opening of its Worn Wear store in Boulder, Colorado, which produces thousands of jackets, sweaters, and bags, upcycled from old garments, for its ReCrafted line. The aim has been to find a youthful, athletic market for one-of-a-kind old clothing, and to reduce waste from the fashion industry.[29] This aesthetic of pseudo poverty appeals to those concerned about the environment and the brand's use of old clothes has apparently been extremely successful. Unfortunately, garments are slow to make and so sustain profitability.

Some company experiments with eco products, like Levi Strauss's Project F.L.X. (Future-Led Execution), are debatable. They sell hard-wearing stylish denim jeans in three versions of 501s (Denim Flex 360). Instead of many washings, the company washes each pair once, cutting down on waste.[30] A laser tablet then whitens or darkens the trousers, burns holes, and cuts and frays the fabric. The customer contributes to the final surface of the garment they are buying and, within reason, can personalize them with additional details. This plays with the idea of product individuality for the consumer, but it's not clear how these garments are eco friendly.

Recycling, reuse, or renting seems, at this point, the only solution until new fabrics are invented. Closed-looped technology recycles purchased clothing, reduces used material to a pulp, reforms it to fiber, and remakes the textile so that a new garment can be produced. This is an attractive prospect for sustainability advocates, as there is no waste and nothing goes to landfill. If the fabric is strong, a garment can loop endlessly from garment factories to stores, to purchasers, to textile recyclers, and back to the factory. An example is the company For Days, which in 2018 set up a take-back system. Once garments were dirty or unwearable, they could be returned to the company, which recycled them, and the wearer received a new one.[31] Apparently this did not prove to be a sustainable system and other options were canvassed. One reason for this was that the company had not been clear about how many times a garment could be recycled. In some cases, huge machines can be used to crumble used polyester clothing and reform it into fiber, which is then remade into fabric before being computer designed and remade. Again it is not clear how effective this is and how many times a garment can be recycled. H&M's unwanted garment-to-garment recycling loop is in its infancy.[32] At present, this is certainly nothing like a profitable enterprise for a fast-fashion company.

# How and When Will It End?

Today, dress around the world, and especially in urban areas, has an ostensible commonality of appearance that is part of the globalized nature of production and consumption. This commonality is characterized by a sense of overall sameness, occasionally interspersed with a certain lack of conformity, that shows urban fashion is to a large degree a personal phenomenon. High-street and upper middle-class Western apparel is gradually taking the place of haute couture, the latter now marketed largely via the realm of sensational aesthetics of fashion photography. Former distinctive routines of dressing, and etiquette for different times of the day and different events, are slowly disappearing. There is now minimal social unease for consumers about what to wear on different occasions and, within economic constraints, they have considerable choice about their decisions.

Generally fashion has become less formalized, its features multidimentional and personally experiential. There are fewer obligations for specific forms of social dressing. The polarity between traditional versus modern in dress is no longer applicable except on rare ceremonial occasions. Seasonal color schemes and existing narratives have been destabilized while the former historical synthesis of design and product has been undermined. Methods of how clothes have been made, sold, and worn are changing. Clear-cut terminology for dress is variable and differences between categories of garment, ornament, and trimmings are known by brand rather than by terms that are now largely obsolete. Much stylish dressing worldwide has been given over to groups with their own sense of individual fashionability.

Within the wide parameters of European style, especially among the young, there is a strong sense that their age and interests are made evident by their dress. In places like the Pacific, some small cultural groups outside the density of urban areas are also tied concurrently to certain customary and ethnic practices. Here body supplements and modifications remain, or are being reinvented for events beyond what is fairly homogeneous clothing for urban life. With regard to customary clothing, meaning is still centered on the symbolism of garments, body marking, and ornamentation, not the values central to commodities of Western origin. Processes such as wrapping the body with barkcloth in Tonga or making skirts and bags with plant fibers in, say, Hawaii or Papua New Guinea continue to have their place alongside everyday Europeanized dress. These link with longstanding social relationships, exchange values, and clan identities; they may cater to tourism but are not necessarily considered "fashion" as such.

If we use time as a central method to explain the differences between traditional and modern clothing in any system of attire, it becomes clear that no aspect of dressing can be described with precision. I concur with Sampson's view that all garments are maps of singularity, of acts performed on them by their makers and with them by their wearers.[33] A garment is both of a time and a material manifestation of "the passage of time." It is my view that all clothing is made up of multiple temporal inconsistencies. Every body supplement, bodily ornament, and modification has its own parameters. It is not possible to say that any particular piece of clothing is (for example) fully German, Italian, or Canadian. Nor that it is in or out of fashion. Its fabric may be Indian cotton, its makers from Greece, its marketing via the US but sold in Milan or Iran. Prior to the moment of wearing, it could have had many former lives and will have others in the future. These depend on the designer, the maker, and the history of fabric manufacture, as well as the construction methods and trimmings of the garments, not to mention the shape of bodies to be clothed.

Vinken claims that fashion made, worn, and displayed on the streets of the world's great cities, is the visible expression of the zeitgeist. The time of fashion is the moment: "the Now at the threshold of an immediate future."[34] But is this so? It's not possible to deny high fashion is primarily a practice found in densely populated city areas but does it epitomize the spirit of the times? Everyday fashions exist outside the great cities, yet where do they sit in terms of the temporal spirit? In addition to this, to which moments in time do fashion's various material components such as fabrics, linings, buttons, and stitching and so on belong? I suggest Vinken's unified zeitgeist theory cannot be substantiated fully. Every garment has its own myriad components, each with its own historical narrative and temporal differences. I suggest that fashion is a relative phenomenon.

The impact of time can be detected in all cultures, in their garments, their accessories, and the fabrics from which their dress is made. But in many societies beyond Europe, value is not placed exhaustively on the present. Habits of the past are respected in garments and body ornament, especially for ritual purposes. Value is accorded primarily to tradition, and a slow move toward change in the use of modern materials. But this is not in any way absolute. On the other hand, there is more to modish dressing than merely design novelty and perfection of execution. For instance, the global complexities of the fashioned and ornamented body, across manifold ethnicities, can encompass irregular practices, unfixed or unexpected differences, even parody. Routines come under pressure and in Western dress, temporal conventions of etiquette may be altered or out-paced.

If we take a negative view of the world post-COVID-19, it seems likely that we face an unpredictable economic and trading future. Many issues surrounding sustainability, poverty, and austerity could inform a new landscape for dress and fashion. One certainty is that the present methods of over-production of apparel and rapidity of stylish change cannot be maintained.[35] But it is my view that the innate creativity of the new generation of designers will confront the continuing demands made on dressing by devising modern technologies of textile production that will allow new forms of sustainable consumption. It seems time has caught up with society everywhere, but there are surely alternatives. The profound, almost limitless, examples of human inventiveness that we see in the extraordinary range of body supplements, accessories, and modifications represented in ancient rock paintings of the deep past cannot be allowed to be replaced by an austere future.

If we look beyond Western cities, in certain parts of Africa, for instance, there is "a cultural performance economy at play," which takes delight in creating novel styles for street wear from available goods.[36] Even the poor search for identity on a daily basis via this extraordinary clothing largely made from cast-off garments. Outfits are individually crafted, many by local tailors, using brilliantly colored African prints, bright accessories, outrageous hairstyles, and used clothing. This dressing is very different from the conventional city styles of business workers.

People of the lower urban classes in Freetown, Sierra Leone (of which there are sixteen different ethnic groups), are particularly vibrant dressers. Their streetwear and desire for novelty is entirely different from that of Continental Europe (see Chapter 4). The love of putting together ingredients from new and old clothes, and designing outfits personally, is not a global understanding of fashion in the European sense. What defines the dress of men and women in these urban cultures is its intense creativity, revitalization, and startling inventiveness.

It is impossible to predict whether the political and social practices of wearing will continue unchanged into the future, and if personal desires can play as large a part in the production of body coverings as they currently do. Even so, dress is something that is part of our embodiment. Clothing gives immense aesthetic pleasure, it expresses cultural vitality and the joys of social existence. It walks right next to us everyday and is a consolation in difficult times. It is an uneven montage of components pieced together to create the individual appearances we so crave. It is made up of all the possible forms of relativity of ideas, beliefs, tastes and pleasures of life. The creativity at the heart of all dressing is crucial to a world crying out for a renewal of aesthetic expression and vitality.

## Focus 8a
## CAN FASHION BE "TIMELESS"?

Fashion, like all forms of dress, has a relationship to time, but can it be time*less*? This implies a value that is everlasting. Literary scholar and fashion theorist Vinken, endeavouring to define fashion, has in fact suggested that it exists in the eternal present, a perfect moment, almost a "now" outside time.[37] This almost seems a kind of timelessness. Others see it differently, suggesting it is a social expression confined to a moment or short duration of time, but of the moment, not outside.

Time is an intensely variable socio-cultural phenomenon as well as a mathematical, astronomical concept. It has not always been regarded as a universal reference.[38] Until recently, most theorists and historians of fashion have regarded the creativity evident in fashion as a Western phenomenon and its focus linked fundamentally to the new. Yet paradoxically, over the years, it has been the West that has labeled some of its culture's dress as virtually unchanging—"classic" and "timeless," These terms are sometimes used interchangeably but seem inconsistent. Is there an explanation for this apparent discrepancy?

It has been common to regard the ancient dress of classical Greece as fixed in style but to continue to call Chanel suits "classic." Admittedly "classic" is slightly different from "classical," the latter used from the sixteenth century onward to describe the much-admired art, artifacts, and high standard of learning of the ancient Greeks and

Romans, as well as scholars who sought to keep its qualities alive. The term "classic" may have originated from a widely held, but now refuted, belief that garments in ancient Greece and Rome being unchanging were not to be regarded as fashion.[39] Yet as this book shows, no dress within any clothing system exists without change, hence the problem of terming body supplements "timeless."

## Classical Dress

Long-held views of the unvarying nature of ancient clothing have been challenged by many recent scholars of classical antiquity reassessing the dress of the Greeks and the Romans. A significant problem for any study of ancient dress has been the lack of original garments, although quantities of textile fragments have survived. Information has come mainly from the dress of marble statuary, often of mythical beings like this statue of the goddess Athena (Figure 8.5), as well as idealized portraits, funerary reliefs, and painted vases. But we now know luxury dressing was common amongst specific social groups, use of colored fabrics not uncommon and, for women in these patriarchal societies, elaborate self-adornment like hairstyles were important signifiers. So idealized clothing, as represented in imagery for public consumption, needs to be set against new historic knowledge of the complexity of dress worn in real life. This research challenges previous stereotypes.[40]

**Figure 8.5** This statue of the goddess Athena wearing a *peplos* is a late version of an original statue from the end of the fifth century BCE. The statue in the image is dated to late first century BCE–early first century CE. (Credit: Universal History Archive/ Universal Images Group via Getty Images.)

Welters and Lillethun outline changes amounting to what they term the "fashion impulse" evident in ancient and Hellenistic Greek, and Roman dress.[41] In Greece, fabric was woven to an individual's shape, and different styles of draping were used and kept in place with buttons, pins, and various ties. The female Doric *chiton* (sixth and fifth centuries BCE), varied in width and was woven on narrow looms.[42] It was worn close to the body, whereas later Ionic style textiles were woven on wider looms, making lighter and more voluminous garments. The garments of Roman women appear to have changed little in basic shape but there was much leeway in use of colored textiles.[43] Our understanding of the term "classical" dress needs to be reconsidered.

Recurring over the centuries have been persisting references to classical antiquity appearing alongside European fashions. Examples are the prevalence of seventeenth-century portraits of aristocrats wearing versions of Roman armor and mantles, along with their shoulder-length wigs. The simple, high-waisted styles of women in the late eighteenth and early nineteenth centuries are further evidence of the tenacity of fashion's classical references. Sensual white, body-revealing garments, sometimes called Empire styles, with high waistlines (and little delicate puffs of sleeves) were adored by Josephine, wife of Napoleon, and many others. They were borrowed to a large extent from the apparent simplicity of garments worn by women in antiquity. These thin, plain gowns were widely popular, gesturing to the new cultural regime in France, and adopted elsewhere, whilst hairstyles were a key antique reference as well.

At the time the word "Neoclassical" was used to describe style in the visual arts and architecture, it was complemented by this revival of the "classical" that we see in clothing. Yet fashion is never simply a copy of dress from the past. It is impossible to match dress worn by, say, the mythological characters depicted on vases and sculpture, with items of everyday wear. References to classical dress have been primarily ideas intended to match the present, with the purity and heroism of some imagined past.

## Modern Classic

The term "classic" means something different in today's Western fashion. It has now become a modern generalization about dress, a term given to long-lasting, stylishly streamlined fashions. It is applied to garments believed to have the enduring qualities of classical art and which show a marked degree of fine design and skillful crafting. The label is often attached to exclusive garments or accessories in mint condition, being so suited to purpose they continue to be made year after year with only slight alterations. So, the term implies the superiority of fine hand craft and aura of prestige, but not necessarily a design associated with antiquity. It also signals a long-term investment or collectable, suitable for auctioning. An example is the rare "classic" Hermès Birkin handbag (named after actress Jane Birkin).[44] These vintage bags are not just an accessory but a symbol of status and a celebrity level of wealth.

The word is applied to the highly select Chanel- and Louis Vuitton-branded luggage and handbags and their prestigious qualities. Here, we see a modern use of the word, one that describes these enduring brands of fashionable clothing so flawless they appear to have no need for alteration, or to stray far from the original. Chanel's little black dress, published in American *Vogue* in 1926, drew associations between the black, mass-produced modernist Ford Model T that ceased manufacture in 1927. The color (black) of Chanel's garment, and its somewhat industrial-like modernist cut, varied little over the years, a supreme example of a long-lasting style. Both car and dress were considered exceptionally popular, both regarded as classic.

## "Timeless" Dress?

So-called "timeless" dress emerged from the proto-aesthetic tastes of the later nineteenth century and is a relatively modern term given primarily to the Western clothing of bourgeois women. The term has been linked to garments and accessories that seldom change, such as the single-string pearl necklace. However, it has also been especially attached to women's garments of great simplicity, with apparent visual links to the pleats, folds and draping of classical clothing. Worn without tight corsetry, and sometimes called "aesthetic" garments, these gowns challenged the excessively formal styles of tight-fitting Victorian dress, particularly of the mid to later nineteenth century, with a loose fullness of style. So, at times "classic" and "timeless" *can* be interchangeable.

The designer most widely associated with "timeless" dress was Spanish artist Mariano Fortuny, who opened his fashion house in Venice in 1906. He was a designer of textiles and almost iridescent silk garments for women, well known for patenting his unusual methods of treating and pleating silks. His full-length garments were svelte, their column-like body-hugging shape splayed out over the feet of the wearer. Their style differed little over the years, adding to the belief of their being timeless. Based on the Greek *chiton* and other prototypes, these garments were considered "outside fashion," subtly referencing historical garments of antiquity and the textiles of the Renaissance.

His work is aesthetically simple but gleaming, with rich colors. Individualistic and loosely styled, in overall appearance it clearly makes direct design links with Antiquity. Fortuny was also inspired by richly colored textiles from all over world but Italy in particular. He used these fabrics for lavish, half-length jackets in a wide range of rich stenciled velvets to complement the gleam of his gowns. Supposedly fashion-less, his gowns were favored by women with artistic and individualistic tastes (dancers, actresses, and movie stars). Customers also included "artistic" women who used them as tea gowns for informal afternoon gatherings at home. Later they accrued such prestige they began to be worn on formal occasions as well. They seemed antique, outside time, and highly original.

In Fortuny's case, "timeless" as a description probably has its origin in the belief that his original pleated fabrics and limited style range were a tribute to a changeless antique past. His most well-known design, the Delphos gown, was first created c. 1907 in collaboration with his wife, Henriette Negrin, a French textile and fashion designer (Figure 8.6). They named it after the famous bronze statue, the Charioteer of Delphi, dated to 478–474 BCE and discovered in 1896. The Delphos gown was registered as a patent in his wife's name in 1909, its value increasing by the cachet of keeping secret his method of textile treatment.[45] Murano glass beads, which weighed down the edges of the garment's lightweight silk, ensured a smooth fit and controlled movement, enhancing the uncorseted human form beneath.

Over the years, the style of Fortuny's gowns changed only slightly, accruing value like a fine work of art. They were so admired that his factory continued to reissue the garment type for a year after his death in 1949. This is testament to their being described as "timeless." His unique pleating device for lightweight silk fabric remains a secret but involves heat, pressure, ceramic rods, paint, sponges, and some stitching. It has never been replicated, although his fabrics continue to be produced in the same factory on the island of Giudecca in Venice, on original machines.

**Figure 8.6** Mariano Fortuny. Pleated dress displayed as part of the "Fortuny: A Spaniard in Venice" exhibition at the Palais Galliera, Paris, 2017. (Credit: PHILIPPE LOPEZ/AFP via Getty Images.)

While female garments in ancient Greece and Rome are supposed to have remained the same for centuries, Fortuny's links to antiquity cannot be defended seriously. That they were, may just have been a canny selling point. But certainly, his oeuvre appeared to be outside the relentless drive for novelty in high fashions of the early twentieth century.

"Timeless," like "classic," is a generalized adjective, often used somewhat loosely. While the two terms overlap, they can be used separately. Both describe garments that are in contradiction to European high-end fashions that have engaged intensely with change and the commercial advantages of constant novelty. They demonstrate an ethos of the past not its actuality. No garments or accessories are ever entirely timeless. This would suggest dress can stand entirely outside historical and temporal change, a concept that has been challenged in this book.

## Focus 8b
## REPLICAS: ENGAGING WITH TIME

In this Focus, I concentrate on replicas of original garments, their significance, and how useful they can be for fashion and dress historians. The issue of time is inevitably interwoven into the discussion. The topic links with an emerging trend in dress research explored in a special issue of *Fashion Theory*.[46] Here, the editors discuss what they term a "making" or "embodied" turn in recent scholarly writing, concerned with the making, wearing, and movement of bodies in garments. Their issue includes a series of essays on object-based modes of investigation into historical dress, and what this new research means to dress history. My discussion deals primarily with constructing replicas as a research method plus another important new methodology: the reconstruction of garments using digital media.

Before exploring these issues, we need a clear understanding of what we mean by an "original" item of clothing. In western dress, the term means a unique garment from the past that has survived, preferably without alteration or change (see Chapter 7 for further discussion). They are also considered original even if slightly altered, or with small repairs. For those interested in material culture and object-led research, working closely with clothes of the past like these, is of considerable value. The method offers unexpected insights into understanding the step-by-step processes involved in the design and making of garments, as well as providing documented evidence of the nature and complexity of fabricating historic garments.[47]

A number of researchers working in the area have closely scrutinized the term "replica" and the subtle differences between terms such as re-create, reconstruct, and re-produce.[48] So, how can a replica, re-creation, or even a reconstruction be of use in object-led research? Original dress is a rich repository of information about style and pattern making, use of fabric, its weave, perhaps added embroidery, padding, seam-stitching (by hand, machine or both) as well as types of sewing threads, linings, the practicality of fastenings, fitting, the way the garment was worn (did the wearer need assistance to put it on or take it off?), the class of wearer, perhaps its provenance, and some idea of date. Replicas are serious attempts to document the exact details of how clothes were planned and steps taken to arrive at an end product, how they were likely stored, mended, and even altered.

Bide, one of the new researchers concerned with primary evidence of the material nature of dress, looks beyond social history as such. By giving careful attention to the details of fabric and how interpretations and understanding of fashions differ, she suggests individual marks and irregularities of wear in original garments are significant. They remind the viewer of important relationships between different components of outfits, how they were worn, as well as how marks and small details can evoke past events and personal memories.[49] She is one of a new generation of serious scholarly researchers, given to "looking," who is increasingly interested in the rich evidential possibilities, techniques, and meanings that can be detected from primary evidence (in good or even slightly damaged condition).

## Replicas

The copying of historic European and US dress has had a dubious reputation in academic circles. As noted, terms like "re-produce," "re-construct," and "duplicate" are now used by scholars in this still-developing field. Each may have subtle differences but they are no longer terms of disparagement. Some years ago, the practice would have been dismissed as an academically inappropriate—even old fashioned—method of research. Academic replicas are not intended to reproduce garments in the sense of tricking the viewer. Replicas are not interpretations nor can they be a substitute for an original item. But there is a subtle difference between copying past dress and replicating it, as the latter is considered a way of opening up new knowledge.

What many regard as "dressing up" as they did in the "past" is often deemed acceptable by the present. An impression of an historical garment is fine for use on the stage, or in living history re-enactments, but quite different from a scholarly replica. Some museum practitioners in fact consider a copy is more practical for use on many levels. Wearing an original historic garment may cause deterioration but copies can be worn for demonstration purposes or as educational tools for the general public, not always with gratifying results. (See Focus 4b) A copy need not be treated as carefully as an original, and can be handled or packed more easily. It can be repaired with modern threads and requires less security.

Precision replication is another matter. It has its own value as useful research. It is a way of understanding historical sewing techniques, enhancing the precise knowledge of how long it took to make a garment and the order in which it was completed. It has the capability of accurately demonstrating how garments might have been made, looked, felt, and worn when new—even not so new. It informs researchers about how it affected a wearer's comportment and the difficulties that might have accompanied its wearing. It can regenerate historic weaving and sewing techniques, methods not found in contemporary fashion.

One example is the replication of a rare Iron Age Norwegian hunter's tunic, found on the edge of the Lendbreen glacier and radiocarbon dated to 230–390 CE. Curiously, the original garment was made from the wool of a traditional breed of sheep, mostly from the soft, inner so-called "under" wool of the animal, with only a small amount of waterproof outer or over-hair. Part of the task of replication was to discover how long it took to reconstruct the tunic. To collect and prepare the fiber, spin and weave it (on a reconstructed warp-weighted standing loom) and stitch the garment took 402 hours, an extraordinary amount of time.[5051] The significance of research into garments like this offers new ways to understand garments in the socio-cultural life of making and wearing.

## Historical Interest in Replication

Antiquarian interest in the history of British costume by people like James Planché, a prolific nineteenth-century dramatist and author, was at the forefront of the drive to create accurate historic, so-called "period costumes" for the theater.[52] His interest in writing for the theater did not last long, but his books created an important interest in the history of British dress, giving actors valuable information on how these "costumes" were worn. The view that original garments have value for historians has also been due in great measure to the extraordinary work of costume historian Janet Arnold and her four-book series on *The Patterns of Fashion*. These volumes, originally published between 1964 and 2008, consist of precision measurements and linear drawings creating accurate patterns of women's garments based on extant examples from c.1660–1860.[53]

Janet Arnold was also renowned for her knowledge that assisted in making theater costumes, especially for The Globe theater in London. The Globe has prided itself in using garments and other effects as near to Shakespearian originals as possible, in line with the general ethos of the theater. To replicate the "initial practices" of making and staging has been their goal. But of course, not all players wore historically accurate costumes at the time, and will have used their own dress as well.[54]

A Scottish Seventeenth-Century Replica

Two examples of replication are useful to study. The first is a replica of a crewel embroidered woman's jacket dated 1615–18, and now part of the Burrell Collection at Glasgow Museum. In 2018–19, the original jacket was copied in great detail and the colorful result is now on display in Culross Palace or Great Lodging (in the village of Culross), which was built for a merchant in the late sixteenth or early seventeenth century in Fife, Scotland (Figure 8.7). Eight crewelwork embroiderers, volunteers at the Palace, decided to remake the original and beautiful decorative jacket for display in the Lodging. Crewel embroidery is a form of wool thread embroidered on linen, the stiches generally the same as those in any embroidery. The co-ordinator of the project, June McAleece, and other embroiderers, decided to replicate the jacket as it was likely the kind of embroidery the original women of the house would have undertaken.[55] It took these skilled embroiderers two years to complete the project.

**Figure 8.7** The 2018–19 replica of a crewel embroidered woman's jacket, 1615–18, Burrell Collection, Glasgow Museum, on display in Culross Palace or Great Lodging, in the village of Culross, Fife, Scotland. (Credit: The National Trust for Scotland, Culross Palace and Garden. The embroidery by The Culross Needlework Group was co-ordinated by June McAleece.)

### Captain Cook's Waistcoat

The second example is a research project to replicate an unfinished eighteenth-century embroidered waistcoat by practicing embroiderer Alison Larkin.[56] She had several reasons to make a replica of this incomplete waistcoat, probably stitched for Captain James Cook in *c.* 1779 by his wife Elizabeth for him to wear to the court of King George III. After Cook's premature death, it was left to her family unfinished.[57] It is one of four waistcoats, three probably worn by him, that are housed in various institutions in Australia and New Zealand.[58] The original was displayed in an exhibition of Cook memorabilia at the 1886 Colonial and Indian Exhibition in London and the replica was intended for an exhibition at the Captain Cook Memorial Museum, Whitby, North Yorkshire in 2015.[59]

Larkin's main objectives were to research and recreate a piece of eighteenth-century historic embroidery, to document its techniques and stitches and in particular identify skills of a specific known embroiderer. The names of women embroiderers both amateur and professional are not known at this time, so association with the style of a named amateur, Elizabeth Cook, is useful.

The waistcoat is extraordinary as it is made of two large embroidered pieces of beaten *tapa* barkcloth, backed with fine linen and two pocket flaps. It is possible that the fabric was a gift to Cook from a chief when he visited Tahiti on his *Resolution* voyage of 1771–5. *Tapa* is a most unusual material to be used for European clothes at the time and was possibly symbolic of Cook's maritime achievements.[60] After European contact with the Pacific Islands, well-made *tapa* became a valuable trade item with European visitors.

Cook's unfinished waistcoat is considered an intriguing study in the use of sturdy *tapa* cloth as a base for a subtle design in fine English embroidery using silk, metalic thread, and spangles. The replica used materials closely approximating those available in the 1770s, and is constructed using eighteenth-century stitching methods. It shows what the waistcoat might have been like had it been completed, giving insight into how such a garment might have looked in its original state. Being replicated so long after Cook's death, it is also an example of the complexity of finding appropriate sewing materials to undertake the work. For instance, *tapa* is no longer made in Tahiti.

## Living History

In many European countries, the UK, US, and Australia, there are groups of people who belong to societies that practice activities including dressing in "historic" costumes as a way to reimagine life in the past.[61] These groups are involved with re-enactments of a particular chosen past, be it the Middle Ages, the eighteenth century or another time,

**Figure 8.8** Hardcore authentics. Civil War re-enactors, the Jones Family from Ohio, at the 150th Gettysburg Re-enactment, Gettysburg, PA, July 2013. (Credit: Mark Makela/Corbis via Getty Images.)

and their activities are often centered on presenting battles or important historical events (Figure 8.8). This obsession with a particular past is characteristic of "Living History" groups who recreate historic conditions in venues such as colonial Gettysburg in Pennsylvania.

Aside from dressing-up as part of these events, or replicating historic garments, there is concurrently a marked interest in reviving historic techniques of dress-, hat-, and shoe-making. While the arts of fine stitching have largely disappeared, except in tailoring and haute couture, the global mass-production of clothing and accessories, not to mention e-commence, has spawned attempts to reinstate older skills. There are a number of reasons behind this, especially appreciated by those who look for individuality in purchases. Quality, authenticity, and finesse can be easily identified by those who have the time and money to look for fine garments and accessories that use the skills and tools of past years.

## Reconstruction as Methodology

One of the most interesting current developments related to replication is the new methodological research project mixing archival, scientific, and practical hands-on work called "Refashioning the Renaissance: Popular Groups and the Material and Cultural

Signs of Clothing in Europe 1550–1650" underway at the School of Arts, Design, and Architecture at Aalto University in Finland. The project's goal is to develop a material and theoretical-based approach to understanding and visualizing Renaissance clothing that combines traditional textile, dye, and fiber analysis and costume conservation, plus modern digital and electron microscopic methods. One researcher in the group is Sophie Pitman, who has a particular interest in reconstructing historic garments by revisualizing them partially using digital modeling of clothing patterns, 3D printing, and much more. Importantly, much of the work is focused on garments of lower social groups worn during the Renaissance.[62]

Creating a replica of a garment aims to give the researcher important information about methods of clothing construction, about alterations, how different garments were worn, the maker/s of the garment, and why it may have deteriorated. It is a partial insight into the relationship between dress, the garment's embedded emotional history and shaping of the social self. Precise re-making of historic clothes is no longer seen merely as a prelude to theatrical dressing-up. As Davidson notes, the embodied, experiential nature of wearing in the past can best be understood by reconstructing garments. Now part of the accepted methodology of research, the replica will become increasingly viewed as important, with quantifiable and academically valid results.[63]

The pioneers of material clothing replication have changed dress history and fashion studies. All forms of clothing have their own particular histories and, like other garments previously discussed, they are part of the ebb and flow of different temporal components, often unrecognized by those that lack experienced observational skills. In the future, these new methods are likely to yield important new results and create a picture of historical social wearing unimaginable twenty years ago.

# NOTES

## Preface

**1** Lera Boroditsky and Alice Gaby suggest that there are also marked cross-cultural differences in spatial orientation in their comparative study, "Remembrances of Times East: Absolute Spatial Representations of Time in an Australian Aboriginal Community," *Association for Psychological Science* 21, no. 11 (2010): 1635–9.

**2** Penelope J. Corfield, "History and the Temporal Turn: Returning to Causes, Effects and Diachronic Trends 1," *Les âges de Britannia: Repenser l'histoire des mondes Britanniques: (Moyen Âge–XXIe siècle)*, J.-F. Dunyach (ed.) (Paris: Presses Universitaires de Rennes, 2015), 259–73. Copyright@P.J.Corfield (2015).

**3** Penelope J. Corfield, "What on Earth is the Termporal Turn and Why is it Happening Now ?," monthly blog 49, January 2015.

**4** Penelope J. Corfield, *Time and the Shape of History* (New Haven: Yale University Press, 2007).

**5** Although Coordinated Universal Time was implemented in 1972.

**6** Julia Kristeva, trans. Alice Jardine and Harry Blake, *Signs* 7, no. 1 (1981): 13–35.

**7** Giordano Nanni, *The Colonization of Time: Ritual, Routine and Resistance in the British Empire* (Manchester: Manchester University Press, 2012).

**8** Giorgio Riello and Peter McNeil (eds), *The Fashion History Reader: Global Perspectives* (Abingdon: Routledge, 2010), 3.

**9** Susan B. Kaiser, *Fashion and Cultural Studies* (Oxford: Berg 2012), 1–4.

**10** Kaiser, *Fashion and Cultural Studies*, 13.

**11** Ibid., 174.

**12** Ellen Sampson, "The Cleaved Garment: The Maker, The Wearer and the 'Me and Not Me' of Fashion Practice," *Fashion Theory: The Journal of Dress, Body & Culture* 22, no. 3 (2018): 341–60.

**13** Heike Jenss and Viola Hofmann, "Introduction: Fashion and Materiality," *Fashion and Materiality: Cultural Practices in Global Context*, Heike Jenss and Viola Hofmann (eds) (London: Bloomsbury Visual Arts, 2019), 4.

**14** *Object Lives and Global Histories in Northern North America. Material Culture in Motion c. 1780–1980* , Beverley Lemire, Laura Peers, and Anne Whitelaw (eds) (Montreal & Kingston; McGill-Queen's University Press, 2021), 9.

**15** Lou Taylor, "Fashion and Dress History: Theoretical and Methodological Approaches," *The Handbook of Fashion Studies*, Sandy Black, Amy de la Haye,

Joanne Entwistle, Agnes Rocamora, Regina A. Root, and Helen Thomas (eds) (London: Bloomsbury 2013), 29–31.

16  Jenss and Hofmann, 4.

# 1  About Time

1  There are a number of terms defining clothing that I will use at different points in this book. Two widely accepted as standard for dress history are those set out by Joanne B. Eicher, Hazel Lee Evenson, and Sandra Lutz in *The Visible Self: Global Perspectives on Dress, Culture and Society* (2nd edn., New York: Fairchild Publications, 2000), namely "body supplements" that cover or enclose the body and "body modifications" that can alter the body. Both classifications can be either temporary or permanent. Further terms I use with discretion are "body coverings," "clothes," "garments," "apparel," "attire," and "adornment." I reserve the term "costume" for theatrical dress and similar performances. I give special attention to the term "fashion" in Chapter 8.

2  Massey in Susan B. Kaiser, *Fashion and Cultural Studies* (Oxford: Berg, 2012), 190.

3  Ellen Sampson, "The Cleaved Garment: The Maker, The Wearer and the 'Me and Not Me' as Fashion Practice," *Fashion Theory* 22, no. 3 (2018): 1.

4  Alexandra Palmer, "Looking at Fashion: The Material Object as Subject," in *The Handbook of Fashion Studies,* Sandy Black, Amy de la Haye, Joanne Entwistle, Agnès Rocamora, Regina A. Root, and Helen Thomas (eds) (London: Bloomsbury, 2013), 272.

5  Jobling in Agnès Rocamora, "Introduction," *The Handbook of Fashion Studies,* Sandy Black, Amy de la Haye, Joanne Entwistle, Agnès Rocamora, Regina A. Root, and Helen Thomas (eds) (London: Bloomsbury, 2013), 160.

6  Kaiser, *Fashion and Cultural Studies*, 3.

7  Georgio Riello and Peter McNeil (eds), *The Fashion History Reader: Global Perspectives* (London: Routledge, 2010), 3.

8  Agnès Rocamora, "New Fashion Times: Fashion and Digital Media', in *The Handbook of Fashion Studies,* Sandy Black, Amy de la Haye, Joanne Entwistle, Agnès Rocamora, Regina A. Root, and Helen Thomas (eds) (London: Bloomsbury, 2013), 74.

9  "Sustainability," https://www.about.sainsburys.co.uk/news/latest-news/2017/06-04-2017 (accessed June 2, 2021).

10  Naomi M. McPherson, "Dressing the Body in Bariai," in *Berg Encyclopedia of World Dress and Fashion*, vol. 7, Joanne B. Eicher (ed.) (Oxford: Berg, 2010), 465–70.

11  I follow the style of abbreviations such as BCE, BP etc as they occur in the original articles I use for information.

12  Rosemary Joyce, "Life with Things: Archaeology and Materiality," in *Archaeology and Anthropology. Past, Present and Future,* David Shankland (ed.) (London: Bloomsbury, 2012), 129.

13  Penelope J. Corfield, "Thinking Long, Studying History," 94, *History*, Monthly Blog, October 1, 2018. "What's wrong with Prehistory?", 96, *History,* Monthly Blog, December 3, 2018.

**14** Isabella Rosner, "'A Cunning Skill Did Lurk': Susanna Perwich and the Mysteries of a Seventeenth Century Needlework Cabinet," *Textile History* 2 (November 2018): 140–63.

**15** Dr Maxim B. Kozlikin, head of excavations at Denisova cave. See: https://siberiantimes.com/science/casestudy/news/n0711-worlds-oldest-needle-found-in-siberian-cave-that-stitches-together-human-history/ (accessed May 15, 2019).

**16** Sibudu rock shelter. See: https://www.megalithic.co.uk/article.php?sid=26471 accessed 12.5.2019 and https://northcoastcourier.co.za/128553/exploring-life-70-000-years-ago-sibudu-cave-tongaat/ (accessed May 12, 2019).

**17** See the work of Professor Mikhail Shunkov, head of the Institute of Archaeology and Ethnography in Novosibirsk.

**18** Meg Andrews, "Beyond the Fringe: Shawls of Paisley Design," http://www.victoriana.com/Shawls/paisley-shawl.html (accessed August 20, 2021).

**19** C. H. Rock, "Paisley Shawls: A Chapter of the Industrial Evolution," Paisley Museum and Art Galleries, 1966, 9.

**20** Kaiser, *Fashion and Cultural Studies*, 173–4.

**21** See Olga Soffer, "Recovering Perishable Technologies Through Use Wear on Tools," *Current Anthropology* 45, June 2004: 407, and https://science.sciencemag.org/content/328/5986/1634 (accessed May 13, 2019).

**22** Linda Welters and Abby Lillethun, *Fashion History: A Global View* (London: Bloomsbury, 2018), 72–3.

**23** https://anthropology.net/2009/09/11/flax-fibres-dated-to-34000-years-bp-found-at-dzudzuana-cave-georgia/ (accessed December 19, 2021) and "Oldest known fibres used by humans discovered," *Harvard Gazette,* Sept 10, 2009, https://news.harvard.edu/gazett e/story/2009/09/oldest-known-fibers-discovered/ (accessed December 20, 2021).

**24** Deborah Durham, "The Predicament of Dress: The Polyvalency and Ironies of Cultural Identity," *American Ethnologist* 26, no. 2 (1999): 391.

**25** Roderick Ewins, "Fijian Dress and Body Modifications," *Berg Encyclopedia of World Dress and Fashion,* vol. 7, Joanne B. Eicher (ed.) (Oxford: Berg, 2010), 442–3.

**26** Philip Sykas, "Re-Threading. Notes Towards a History of Sewing Thread in Britain," in *Textiles Revealed Object Lessons in Historic Textile and Costume Research,* Mary M. Brooks (ed.) (London: Archetype Publications, 2000), 123.

**27** My thanks to Rebecca Evans for alerting me to her essay "Hidden Treasure in the Art Gallery of South Australia," *Textile Fiber Forum,* June 2017, 10–11.

**28** Kitty Hauser, "A Garment in the Dock; or How the FBI Illuminated the Prehistory of a Pair of Denim Jeans," *Journal of Material Culture* 9, no. 3 (2004): 295–313.

**29** Robyn Healy, "Immateriality," in *The Handbook of Fashion Studies,* Sandy Black, Amy de la Haye, Joanne Entwistle, Agnès Rocamora, Regina A. Root, and Helen Thomas (eds) (London: Bloomsbury, 2013), 336.

**30** http://www.nms.ac.uk/gallowayhoard accessed 13.5.2019 (accessed July 27, 2019).

**31** Jules Prown, "Mind in Matter: An Introduction to Material Culture Theory and Method," in *Winterthur Portfolio* 17 (1) 1982: 3.

**32** Penelope J. Corfield, "History and the Temporal Turn: Returning to Causes, Effects and Diachronic Trends," (2015), 2–18 in *Les Ages de Britannia: Repenser l'histoire* *des Mondes Britanniques (Moyen Âge—XXIe siècle)*, J-F Dunyach (ed.) (Paris: Presses Universitaires de Rennes, 2015), 259–73. Also an acknowledgement to copyright@P.J.Corfield (2015).

**33** Johannes Fabian, *Time and the Other: How Anthropology Makes its Objects* (New York: Columbia University Press, 2002).

**34** Kaiser, *Fashion and Cultural Studies,* 172–3.

**35** Norbert Elias, "An Essay on Time," in *The Collected Works of Norbert Elias* 9, Stephen Loyal and Stephen Mennell (eds) (Dublin: University College Dublin, 2007).

**36** Daniel Miller, Daniel, "Introduction," *Clothing as Material Culture,* Susanne Küchler and Daniel Miller (eds) (Oxford: Berg, 2005), 28. Quoted in Lou Taylor, "Fashion and Dress History: Theoretical and Methodological Approaches," in *The Handbook of Fashion Studies,* Sandy Black, Amy de la Haye, Joanne Entwistle, Agnès Rocamora, Regina A. Root, and Helen Thomas (eds) (London: Bloomsbury, 2013).

**37** https://www.smithsonianmag.com/history/the-cave-art-debate-100617099/ (accessed January 13, 2022).

**38** https://historyofinformation.com/detail.php?entryid=2494 (accessed January 13, 2022).

**39** The team was from the University of Birmingham. See: https://www.bbc.com/news/uk-scotland-north-east-orkney-shetland-23286928 (accessed March 19, 2020).

**40** http://africanrockart.org/wp-content/uploads/2013/11/Coulson-article-A10-proof.pdf (accessed August 10, 2019).

**41** Gemma Angel, "Tattooing in Ancient Egypt. Part 2: The Mummy of Amunet," https://blogs.ucl.ac.uk/researchers-in-museums/2012/12/10/tattooed-mummy-amunet/ (accessed May 2, 2019).

**42** Roderick Ewins, "Fijian Dress and Body Modifications," in *Berg Encyclopedia of World Dress and Fashion,* vol. 7, (Australia, New Zealand and the Pacific Islands), Joanne B. Eicher (ed.) (Oxford: Berg, 2010), 436.

**43** Ruth McDougall, *No.1 Neighbour. Art in Papua New Guinea 1955–2016* (Brisbane: Queensland Art Gallery, 2016), 106.

**44** David S. Landes, *Revolution in Time: Clocks and the Making of the Modern World* (Cambridge, MA: Harvard University Press, 1983), 8, 53.

**45** John Styles, *The Dress of the People: Everyday Fashion in Eighteenth Century England* (New Haven, CT: Yale University Press, 2007), 100–03.

**46** Now in the Chester Beatty Library, Dublin.

**47** Karen de Perthuis, "Darning Mark's Jumper: Wearing Love and Sorrow," *Cultural Studies Review* 22, no. 1 ( 2016).

**48** See Roslyn Russell and Kylie Winkworth, *Significance 2.0: A Guide to Assessing the Significance of Collections* (Canberra: Collections Council of Australia, 2009).

**49** *Catalogue of the Museum of London,* Numbers A5999 and A6000.

**50** June Swann, "Peeling Back the Layers: Alterations," *Textiles Revealed: Object Lessons in Historic Textile and Costume Research,* Mary M. Brooks (ed.) (London: Archetype Publications, 2000), 114.

**51** Georgio Riello, "The Object of Fashion: Methodological Approaches to the History of Fashion," *Journal of Aesthetics and Culture* 3 (2011): 3.

**52**  Jules Prown, "Mind in Matter: An Introduction to Material Culture Theory and Method," *Winterthur Portfolio* 17, no. 1 (1982): 3.

**53**  HPB/UF51 was found below the floors on level 3 during restoration works in 1980 before the main archaeological investigation. Numbers of torn scraps of presumably convict garments were also found under the floors.

**54**  A partial shirt (HPB/UF8114) was also found below the floors on level 3 in a dormitory during the main excavations in 1980–1.

**55**  See Hilary Davidson, "Fear or Fashion?: The Archaeology of Australian Convict Uniforms," "Страх моды? Археология униформы австралийских каторжников [Fear or Fashion?: The Archaeology of Australian Convict Uniforms]," теориямоды:

   *Одежда Тело Культура* [Fashion Theory: Clothing Body Culture] 55 (2020): 47–60.

   This is a Russian publication.

**56**  See the entry in the *Australian Dress Register* statement of significance, 2001, by Kylie Winkworth, Shinae Stowe (ed.) (2010).

**57**  According to Davidson in "Fear or Fashion?," four shirts were issued per year in 1825. This was later reduced to two.

**58**  See the ongoing research project *Deliberately Concealed Garments Project* set up in 1998 by Dinah Eastop, https://www.concealedgarments.org/ (accessed May 17, 2019).

**59**  Caroline Tynan, Sally McKechnie, and Celine Chhuon, "Co-creation of Value for Luxury Brands," *Journal of Business Research* 63, no. 11 (2010): 1156–63.

# 2  Deep Time: The Origins of Dress

**1**  Irene Good, "Archaeological Textiles. A Review of Current Research," *Annual Review of Anthropology* 30 (2001): 209–26.

**2**  Rosemary A. Joyce, "Life with Things: Archaeology and Anthropology," in *Archaeology and Anthropology Past. Present and Future*, David Shankland (ed.) (London: Bloomsbury, 2012), 124–5.

**3**  https://www.nytimes.com/1993/07/13/science/site-in-turkey-yields-oldest-cloth-ever-found.html (accessed June 24, 2021).

**4**  https://mnch.uoregon.edu/collections-galleries/great-basin-sandals

**5**  Michael Morrison review of Gavin Lucas, *The Archaeology of Time* (London: Routledge, 2005), https://australianarchaeologicalassociation.com.au/journal/review-of-the-archaeology-of-time-by-gavin-lucas/ (accessed September 5, 2021).

**6**  Beverly Lemire, Laura Peers, and Anne Whitelaw (eds), *Object Lives and Global Histories in Northern North America: Material Culture in Motion, c. 1780–1980* (Montreal & Kingston: McGill-Queen's University Press, 2021), 9.

**7**  Lynn Meskill, *Object Worlds in Ancient Egypt* (Oxford: Berg, 2004), 2–4, 20.

**8**  Tim Ingold, "No More Ancient: No More Human: The Future Past of Archaeology and Anthropology," in *Archaeology and Anthropology. Past, Present and Future,* David Shankland (ed.) (London: Bloomsbury, 2013), 78–81.

**9**   See "How it all Began" in James Laver's popular text, *Costume and Fashion: A Concise History,* first published in Great Britain in 1969.

**10**  Stella Souvatzi, "Space, Place and Architecture: A Major Meeting Point between Social Archaeology and Anthropology," in *Archaeology and Anthropology. Past, Present and Future*, David Shankland (ed.) (London: Bloomsbury, 2013), 177.

**11**  Souvatzi, "Space, Place and Architecture," 182.

**12**  Ingold, "No More Ancient," 78.

**13**  Meskill, *Object Worlds*, 186.

**14**  Maria Viestad Vibeke, *Dress as Social Relations. An Interpretation of Bushman Dress* (Johannesburg: Wits University Press, 2018), 16ff.

**15**  Olga Soffer, James M. Adovasio, and David C. Hyland, "The 'Venus' Figurines: Textiles, Basketry, Gender, and Status in the Upper Paleolithic," *Current* Anthropology 41, no. 4 (2000): 511–37.

**16**  Ibid., 524. Some dispute has arisen here about gender and the wearing and making of fabrics.

**17**  Elizabeth Barber, *Prehistoric Textiles: The Development of Cloth in the Neolithic and Bronze Ages with Special Reference to the Aegean* (Princeton, NJ: Princeton University Press, 1991). In her view, this was due to the time it took to produce.

**18**  Olga Soffer takes this view of tools as evidence of use as well. See "Recovering Techniques Through Use-wear on Tools: Preliminary Evidence for Upper Palaeolithic Weaving and Net Making," *Current Anthropology* 45, no. 3 (2004): 407–13.

**19**  https://scholarlypublications.universiteitleiden.nl/access/item%3A2732622/view (accessed May 29, 2021). This website has a lengthy article by Dietrich Mania, "The Earliest Occupation of Europe: The Elba-Saale region Germany," 85–101. This has substantial details of the tools found at the Neumark-Nord site but the oak tannin on one tool is not mentioned.

**20**  ABC, *News in Science*, "Bone Tools Found at Neanderthal Site," August 13, 2013. A good case is made for Neanderthals inventing this aspect of modern human technology. See: https://www.abc.net.au/science/articles/2013/08/13/3824539.htm. (accessed January 3, 2019).

**21**  https://www.livescience.com/55289-prehistoric-tattoos-made-with-glass-tools.html (accessed June 12, 2019).

**22**  Elizabeth J. Himmelfarb, "Prehistoric Body Painting," *Archaeology* 53 (July/ August/2000); 4, https://archive.archaeology.org/0007/newsbriefs/zambia.html (accessed June 13, 2019).

**23**  Marian Vanhaereny et al., " Middle Palaeolithic Shell Beads in Israel and Algeria," *Science* 312, (2006): 1785–8, https://halshs.archives-ouvertes.fr/halshs-00444906/ accessed (3.6.2021).

**24**  Ewen Callaway, "Neanderthals Wore Eagle Talons as Jewellery," *Nature News,* March 11, 2015, https://www.nature.com/news/neanderthals-wore-eagle-talons-as-jewellery-1.17095 (accessed July 3, 2019).

**25**  Ian Gilligan, "The Prehistoric Development of Clothing: Archaeological Implications of a Thermal Model," *Journal of Archaeological Method and Theory* 17, no. 1 (2010): 58.

**26**  https://www.sciencedaily.com/releases/2009/05/090514084126.htm (accessed September 2, 2021). It was recovered from caves in the Schelklingen region of

Germany. Excavation took place under the direction of Professor Nicholas J. Conrad, University of Tübingen.

27  David Reed, "UF Study of Lice DNA Shows Humans First Wore Clothes 170,000 Years Ago," Principal researcher and Associate Curator of Mammals, Florida Museum of National History. See: http://news.ufl.edu/archive/2011/01/uf-study-of-lice-dna-shows-humans-first-wore-clothes-170000-years-agohtml (accessed July 3, 2019). "Neanderthal finds at the Contrebandiers Cave, Morocco, suggest a different date of 120,000 years ago," www.theguardian.com/science/2021/sep/16/scientists-find-evidence-of-humans-making-clothes-120000-years-ago (accessed November 16, 2021).

28  Ian Gilligan, *Climate, Clothing and Agriculture in Prehistory: Linking Evidence, Causes and Effects* (Cambridge: Cambridge University Press, 2018).

29  Ian Gilligan, "The Clothing Revolution," *Aeon,* May 13, 2021, https://aeon.co/essays/how-clothing-and-climate-change-kickstarted-agriculture (accessed December 21, 2021).

30  Ingold, "No More Ancient," 81.

31  "Ron Pinhasi and the Shoe," Blog in PLoS One, https://blogs.plos.org/everyone/2010/06/09/pinhasi-shoe/ (accessed July 30, 2019).

32  Or 5580–5330 cal BP. I follow archaeological dates as expressed by the authors of individual research papers.

33  This shoe is earlier than the shoes of the so-called "iceman," Ötzi, found in the Alps.

34  Personal correspondence with Boris Gasparyan at the Institute of Archaeology and Ethnography of the National Academy of Sciences of the Republic of Armenia, director of the expedition studying the archaeological sites of the Arpa River valley.

35  Made like the Armenian shoe, they were worn until the 1950s on the Aran Islands of County Galway, Ireland. Similar traditional southeastern European regional leather shoes for both sexes called *opanke/opanci* are a form of folk dress.

36  The vast collections of shoes as a sign of remembrance at Auschwitz and at other Jewish museums (Sydney, for instance) are the great, moving reminders of unnamed victims in the Second World War.

37  Hilary Davidson, "Holding the Sole: Shoes, Emotions, and the Supernatural," in *Feeling Things: Objects and Emotions through History*, Stephanie Downs, Sally Holloway, and Sarah Randles (eds) (Oxford: Oxford University Press, 2018), 72–93.

38  https://pages.uoregon.edu/connolly/FRsandals.htm (accessed October 28, 2021).

39  The Great Basin includes most of Nevada, half of Utah, and sections of Idaho, Wyoming, Oregon, and California.

40  http://www.antiquities.org.il/warrior_eng.asp (accessed July 30, 2019).

41  Kim Akerman, "Shoes of Invisibility and Invisible Shoes: Australian Hunters and Gatherers and Ideas on the Origins of Footwear" [online]. *Australian Aboriginal Studies* 2 (2005): 55–64 (accessed July 4, 2019).

42  These sandals were purchased in 1973 by Kim Akerman, a scholar working in Perth, Western Australia.

43  Anna Salleh, "Earliest Human Footprints in Australia," *News in Science*, December 21, 2005, https://www.abc.net.au/science/articles/2005/12/21/1532698.htm?site=news&topic=latest (accessed September 23, 2021).

**44** Museum of Egyptian Archaeology UCL no. UC 28614 B1. R. M. Hall, "Garments in the Petrie Museum of Egyptian Archaeology," *Textile History* 13, no. 1 (1982): 34.

**45** Alice Stevenson and Michael W. Dee, "Confirmation of the World's Oldest Woven Garment: The Tarkhan Dress," 90, no. 349 (2016), http://antiquity.ac.uk/projgall/stevenson349 (accessed August 5, 2020).

**46** Stevenson and Dee, "Confirmation," 2016.

**47** Hall, "Garments in the Petrie Museum," 30.

**48** Ibid., 32–3.

**49** Jana Jones, "The Enigma of the Pleated Dress: New Insights from Early Helwan Reliefs," *Journal of Egyptian Archaeology* 100, no. 209 (2014): 224. My thanks to Jana for this reference.

**50** Jones, "The Enigma," 8.

**51** Elizabeth Riefstahl, "A Note on Ancient Fashions: Four Early Egyptian Dresses in the Museum of Fine Arts, Boston," *Boston Museum Bulletin* 68, no. 245 (1970).

**52** Daniel Devoucoux, "The Discovery of Materiality: Archaeological Clothing Finds, Representation, and Knowledge Formation," in *Fashion and Materiality. Cultural Practices in Global Contexts*, Heike Jenss and Viola Hofmann (eds) (London: Bloomsbury Visual Arts, 2020), 61–6.

**53** Lynn Meskell, *Object Worlds in Ancient Egypt. Material Biographies Past and Present* (Oxford: Berg, 2004), 219.

# 3  Context: What Does It Mean?

**1** They are also used in other historical disciplines.

**2** Beverly Lemire, "Introduction," *Object Lives and Global Histories in Northern North America: Material Culture in Motion* c. 1780–1980, Beverley Lemire, Laura Peers, and Anne Whitelaw (eds) (Montreal & Kingston: McGill-Queen's University Press, 2021), 10.

**3** Lemire, "Introduction," *Object Lives,* 9.

**4** See David Shankland, "Introduction: Archaeology and Anthropology. Past, Present and Future Divorce and Partial Reconciliation," *Anthropology: Past, Present and Future,* David Shankland (ed.) (London: Bloomsbury, 2012), 3–4.

**5** Rita Felski, "Context Stinks," *New Literary History* 42, no. 4 (Autumn 2011): 573–91.

**6** Peter Stallybras and Ann Rosalind Jones, "Fetishizing the Glove in Renaissance Europe," *Critical Inquiry* 28, no. 1 (2001): 118.

**7** Ibid., 116-17.

**8** The exhibition *Inside Out* (V&A 2020) included a wide range of bags, such as a seventeenth-century frog purse, a metal chatelaine *c.* 1863–85, with manifold attachments, and a mock Fabergé egg evening bag by Judith Leiber.

**9** See Michael Mel, "Bilas: Dressing the Body in Papua," *Berg Encyclopedia of World Dress and Fashion,* vol. 7, Joanne B. Eicher (ed.) (Oxford: Berg, 2010).

**10** Kimberley Chrisman-Campbell, "From Caterpillar to Butterfly and Back: A Waistcoat of the French Revolution," *Costume* 45 (1) 2011: 70–1.

**11** Philip A. Sykas, "Re-Threading: Notes Towards a History of Sewing Thread in Britain," in *Object Lessons in Historic Textile and Costume Research*, Mary M. Brooks (ed.) (London: Archetype Publications, 2000), 123.

**12** Daniel Miller, *Understanding Material Culture* (California: Sage, 2007), 24.

**13** *200 Years of Australian Fashion* Exhibition, National Gallery of Victoria, 2016. The gown is dated by the gallery to *c.* 1878.

**14** Silk gown, Newstead House, No. NID52587. See Catriona Fisk, *Connecting Threads: Tracing Fashion, Fabric and Everyday Life at Newstead House,* Brisbane Exhibition, 2016.

**15** A gown that flowed loosely at the back, with no visible waistline at the rear of the garment.

**16** Fisk, *Connecting Threads,* 99.

**17** James Laver, "The Triumph of Time," *Contemporary Essays,* Sylvia Norman (ed.) (London: Elkin Mathews and Marrot, 1933).

**18** Ira Morris, *The Glass of Fashion* (London: The Pilot Press, 1947), 73.

**19** For instance, Kelly Richman-Abdou, *The Illustrated Timeline Presents Women's Fashion Every Year from 1784–1970,* based on fashion plates. My Modern Met, 2017, http://fashionhistory.fitnyc.edu/ (accessed July 12, 2019).

**20** "Fashion and Remodelling Clothing 1914–810: A Reverse Chronology," https://www.ikfoundation.org/itextilis/fashion-remodelling-of-clothing.html (accessed August 4, 2021).

**21** Stella Souvatzi, "Space, Place and Architecture: A Major Meeting Point Between Social Archaeology and Anthropology?," *Archaeology and Anthropology Past, Present and Future,* David Shankland (ed.) (London: Bloomsbury, 2012), 182–4.

**22** Rosemary A. Joyce, "Archaeology of the Body," *Annual Review of Anthropology* 34 (2005): 139–58.

**23** Shankland, "Introduction," 124.

**24** Tim Ingold, "The Textility of Making," *Cambridge Journal of Economic Value* 34 (1) (2010): 91–102.

**25** Michael Carter, *Fashion Classics: From Carlyle to Barthes* (Oxford: Berg, 2003), 127.

**26** Dani Cavallaro and Alexandra Warwick, *Fashioning the Frame: Boundaries, Dress and the Body* (Oxford: Berg, 1998), 96.

**27** Carter, *Fashion Classics*, 95.

**28** Susan B. Kaiser, *Fashion and Cultural Studies* (Oxford: Berg, 2012), 172–3.

**29** Catalogue MAAS (Museum of Applied Arts and Sciences), A7880.

**30** The collection of items that apparently belonged to the Marsden family was donated by the estate of a relative, Eliza Hassall, to the Royal Australian Historical Society in 1919 and thence to the Powerhouse Museum in 1981.

**31** The wedding dress (A7881) is of light figured silk, probably dating to 1793; it was made, originally for Elizabeth Marsden's on her marriage to Samuel Marsden. It is believed to have been later remade (as it now appears) and worn by Elizabeth's daughter, Ann, on her marriage to Reverend Thomas Hassall in 1822.

**32** Tanya Evans, "The Use of Memory and Material Culture in the History of the Family in Colonial Australia," *Journal of Australian Studies* 36, no. 2 (2012): 217.

**33** The ball gown (A7882) is of muslin with woven vertical rib stripes and is claimed to be dated *c.* 1822.

My thanks to Laura Jocic for this important reference and her work on dress in early Sydney. Laura Jocic, "Anna King's Dress: Trade and Society in Early Colonial Sydney," in Jennifer Milam (ed.), *Cosmopolitan Moments: Instances of Exchange in the Long Eighteenth Century* [Special Issue 9.1], *emaj* (December 2017), https://emajartjournal.com/special-editions/cosmopolitan-moments/laura-jocic-anna-kings-dress-trade-and-society-in-early-colonial-sydney/ (accessed September 5, 2020).

**34** Jennifer Craik, *The Face of Fashion: Cultural Studies in Fashion* (London: Routledge, 1994), 73–4.

**35** The class differences in women's fashions in the 1920s, and the clothing problems of working women in particular, are addressed more fully in Elizabeth Wilson and Lou Taylor, *Through the Looking Glass: A History of Dress from 1860 to the Present Day* (London: BBC Books, 1989).

**36** See Liz Conor, *The Spectacular Modern Woman: Feminine Visibility in the 1920s* (Bloomington: Indiana University Press, 2004) for her excellent coverage of women's styles at this time.

**37** The novel by Victor Margueritte, *La Garçonne* (The Bachelor Girl) (Paris: Ernest Flammarion, 1922) was very influential for its noticeable descriptions of the fashions of young women in the 1920s, including very close-cut hair.

**38** Conor, *The Spectacular Modern Woman,* 219–21.

**39** See Conor, *The Spectacular Modern Woman* for her discussion of "The Primitive Woman in the Late Colonial Scene."

**40** Valerie Mendes and Amy de la Haye, *20th Century Fashion* (London: Thames and Hudson, 1999), 75.

**41** Margaret Maynard, "Where Do Flappers Fit In? The Photography of Modern Fashion in Australia," *ACH Antipodean Modern* 25 (2006): 276.

# 4 Cultural Exchange: Past and Present

**1** Marianne Vedeler, *Silk for the Vikings* (Oxford: Oxbow Books, 2014), 149.

**2** *Object Lives and Global Histories in Northern North America,* Beverley Lemire, Laura Peers, and Anne Whitelaw (eds) (Montreal & Kingston: McGill-Queen's University Press, 2021).

**3** James Bennett and Russell Kelty, *Treasure Ships: Art in the Age of* Spices, Exhibition Catalogue Art Gallery of South Australia, Adelaide and Art Gallery of Western Australia, Perth 2015–16: 225–8.

**4** John Vollmer, "Cultural Authentication in Dress," *Berg Encyclopedia of World Dress and Fashion: Global Perspectives,* vol. 10, Joanne B. Eicher (ed.) (Oxford: Berg, 2010), 72.

**5** Danae Tankard, "'Tell me they were in fashion last year'. Samuel and Elizabeth Jeake and Clothing Fashions in Late Seventeenth Century London and Rye," *Costume* 50, no. 1 (2016): 30.

**6**  Vollmer, "Cultural Authentication," 70.

**7**  *Ikat* is a Javanese word derived from Arabic. Jasleen Dhamija, "Rites of Passage and Rituals in India," *Berg Encyclopedia of World Dress and Fashion,* vol. 4, Joanne B. Eicher (ed.) (Oxford: Berg, 2010), 217.

**8**  *Treasure Ships,* 228.

**9**  Ibid., 229.

**10**  Ibid., 316.

**11**  Vollmer, "Cultural Authentication," 73.

**12**  Much later called the Paisley Pine. See Meg Andrews, "Beyond the Fringe Shawls of Paisley Design," *Victoriana Magazine,* http://www.victoriana.com/Shawls/paisley-shawl.html (accessed August 4, 2019).

**13**  Other names for the design were the *Indian bootur* and later called a *buta.*

**14**  Helen Hoyte, "The Story of Norwich Shawls," Costume and Textile Association, 2016, http://www.ctacostume.org.uk/norwich-shawls.html (accessed September 18, 2020).

**15**  https://www.theguardian.com/uk-news/2019/mar/15/paisley-from-paisley-enjoys-a-resurgence-with-help-from-hermes (accessed July 2, 2019).

**16**  *Art Gallery of South Australia*, catalogue no. 160.

**17**  *Treasure Ships,* 303.

**18**  There are suggestions that Catherine of Aragon brought Spanish blackwork to Britain on her marriage to Henry VIII.

**19**  *Treasure Ships,* 303.

**20**  Roy Dipak, "Fashion, Attire and Mughal Women: A Story behind the Purdha," *The Echo: A Journal of Humanities and Social Science* I, no. 3 (January 2013): 105–09.

**21**  Sonia Mukherjee, *Royal Moghul Ladies and the Contributions They Made* (New Delhi: Cyan Publishing House, 2001), 223–4.

**22**  See the special edition of *Textile History* 48 (1) (May 2017), *Entangled Histories: Translocal Textiles Trades in Eastern Africa* c. 800 CE to the Early Twentieth Century, Editorial Note, Marina Moskowitz and Vivienne Richmond.

**23**  *Treasure Ships,* 228.

**24**  Ibid., 225.

**25**  Ibid., 234.

**26**  https://www.kimonoboy.com/sarasa.html (accessed July 30, 2019).

**27**  Margaret Maynard, "Status 1805–1900," *200 Years of Australian Fashion* (Melbourne: National Gallery of Victoria, 2016), 13.

**28**  See Laura Jocic, "Anna King's dress. Trade and Society in Early Colonial Society," in *Cosmopolitan Moments: Instances of Exchange in the Long 18th Century,* Jennifer Milam (ed.), *emaj* (online journal), Special Issue December 2017.

**29**  Susan North, "Indian Gowns and Banyans—New Evidence and Perspectives," *Costume: The Journal of the Costume Society* 54, no. 1 (2020): 30–55. This is a detailed study including an exhaustive account of the various names of these garments.

**30**  The term banyan comes from Arabic and derived from the Gujarati word vaniyo for merchant, Vollmer, "Cultural Authentication," 73.

**31** Fennetaux, Ariane, "Indian Gowns Small and Great: Chintz Banyans Ready Made in the Coromandel, c. 1680-1780," *Costume* 55 (1) (2021): 49-50.

**32** North, "Indian Gowns and Banyans," 39-40.

**33** The readymade production process in India is discussed in great detail by Fennetaux "Indian Gowns" 2021.

**34** Laura Peers, "Crossing Worlds. Hide Coats, Relationships and Identity in Rupert's Land and Britain," *Object Lives and Global Histories in Northern North America,* Beverley Lemire, Laura Peers, and Anne Whitelaw (eds) (Montreal & Kingston: McGill-Queen's University Press, 2021), 56–82. Image, p. 61.

**35** Ibid., 65–70

**36** Elizabeth Kramer, *Kimono: A Modern History* (London: Routledge, 2014) in *Reviews in History* no. 1787 (Newcastle upon Tyne: Northumbria University: 2015).

**37** Lissant Bolton, "Dress of Vanuatu," *Berg Encyclopedia of World Dress and Fashion,* vol. 7, Joanne B. Eicher (ed.) (Oxford: Berg: 2010), 482.

**38** Margaret Maynard, *Fashioned from Penury Dress as Cultural Practice in Australia* (Cambridge: Cambridge University Press, 1994), 65.

**39** William Dalrymple, "White Mischief," https://www.theguardian.com/uk/2002/dec/09/britishidentity.india (accessed November 17, 2021).

**40** Robert Ross, *Clothing: A Global History—Or the Imperialist's New Clothes* (Cambridge: Polity Press, 2008).

**41** Elizabeth Kutesco, "Fashioning Brazil: Globalization and the Representation of Brazilian Dress in National Geographic since 1988," *Fashion Theory* 20, no. 2 (2016): 2–3.

**42** Margaret Maynard, *Dress and Globalisation* (Manchester: Manchester University Press, 2004), 19–20.

**43** https://www.abc.net.au/news/2016-03-15/sierra-leone-fashion-in-freetown-profiled/7245840 (accessed August 20, 2021).

**44** Laura Peers, "Crossing Worlds: Hide Coats Relationships and Identity in Rupert's Land and Britain," *Object Lives and Global Histories in Northern North America. Material Culture in Motion c. 1780–1980,* Beverley Lemire, Laura Peers, and Anne Whitelaw (eds) (Montreal & Kingston: McGill-Queen's University Press, 2021), 67–8.

**45** Francesca Fionde, "Fake Art History Hurts Indigenous Artists as Appropriators Profit" (2018), https://thediscourse.ca/urban-nation/fake-art-indigenous (accessed April 8, 2020).

**46** John E. Vollmer, "Cultural Authentication in Dress," *Berg Encyclopedia of World Dress and Fashion,* vol. 10, Joanne B. Eicher (ed.) (Oxford: Berg, 2010), 69.

**47** See the Australian National Indigenous Arts Advocacy Association (NIAAA). A "Label of Authenticity" was launched in 1999, dedicated to protecting Aboriginal and Torres Strait Islander art and design rights, but disbanded in 2002. See also Peter Shand, "Scenes from the Colonial Catwalk: Cultural Appropriation, Intellectual Property Rights and Fashion," *Cultural Analysis* 3 (2002).

**48** Tonye Erekosima, Victor Eicher, and Joanne B. Eicher, "Kalabari Cut-Thread and Pulled-Thread Cloth," *African Arts* 14, no. 2 (1981): 48–51.

**49** The Toi Iho Mainly Māori Mark for artist groups mostly of Māori descent, and the Toi Iho Māori Co-production Mark for Māori and non-Māori artists and businesses working collaboratively across artforms. See https://www.nzherald.co.nz/nz/news/article.cfm?c_id=1&objectid=10604660 (accessed August 11, 2019).

50  They immediately removed all references to #Dsquaw from their website and their Twitter, Instagram, and Facebook accounts http://www.ctvnews.ca/lifestyle/dsquared2-slammed-online-for-dsquaw-fashion-line-1.2262422 (accessed June 3, 2016).

51  In 2012, the Navajo Nation sued Urban Outfitters for violating the Indian Arts and Crafts Act of 1990 by misrepresenting garments as Native-made. In 2016, a federal judge in New Mexico ruled in favor of the Navajo Nation. The outcome was a collaboration between the two. https://www.theguardian.com/us-news/2016/nov/18/urban-outfitters-navajo-nation-settlement (accessed August 12, 2019).

52  https://www.theguardian.com/global-development-professionals-network/2015/jun/17/mexican-mixe-blouse-isabel-marant (accessed August 12, 2019).

53  https://www.vogue.co.uk/article/isabel-marant-embroidered-blouse-plagiarism-row-mexico-antik-batik (accessed January 10, 2021).

54  The case was settled for Marant with money from Antik Brand.

55  A slang word that is not easily translated.

56  http://supchina.com/2017/06/02/women-building-real-businesses-selling-homemade-knockoff-clothing-online-2/amp/ (accessed August 11, 2019).

57  The exhibition was also shown at the Nagoya/Boston Museum of Fine Arts (closed in 2018), the Setagaya Art Museum, Tokyo, and the Kyoto Municipal Museum.

58  It is a garment worn in *kabuki* theatrical performances. Marina Takagi, "The Kimono Protests: Race and Cultural Appropriation in Japonisme," https://www.academia.edu/47842804/The_Kimono_Protests_Race_and_Cultural_Appropriation_in_Japonisme (accessed November 4, 2021).

59  https://hyperallergic.com/223047/the-confused-thinking-behind-the-kimono-protests-at-the-boston-museum-of-fine-arts/ (accessed August 19, 2019).

60  See the 2020 V&A exhibition, "Kimono: Kyoto to Catwalk," which deals with the sartorial, social, and aesthetic impact of the *kimono* in Japan from 1660s until the present.

61  Terry Satsuki-Milhaupt, *Kimono: A Modern History* (London: Reaktion Books, 2014), 355.

62  Liza Dalby, *Geisha* (Berkeley, CA: University of California, 1983); Liza Crihfield Dalby, *Kimono: Fashioning Culture* (New Haven, CT: Yale University Press, 1993); Paul Van Riel, *Kimono* (Leiden: Hotei Publishing, 2001), with an introduction by Liza Dalby.

63  Sada Yacco performed at the Exposition Universelle in Paris in 1900 and then returned to Japan as a symbol of the free modern woman.

64  Ironically, members of Living History organizations are encouraged to do just this.

# 5  Rituals: The Role of Time

1  Linda Welters and Abby Lillethun, *Fashion History: A Global View* (London: Bloomsbury Academic, 2018), 27.

2  Elizabeth J. Himelfarb, "Prehistorica Body Painting," https://archive.archaeology.org/0007/newsbriefs/zambia.html (accessed October 14, 2021).

**3** Ian Gilligan, "The Prehistoric Development of Clothing: Archaeological Implications of a Thermal Model," *Journal of Archaeological Method and Theory* 17, no. 1 (2010): 8.

**4** The Textile Research Centre in Leiden has an excellent website showing religious and secular ceremonial garments.

**5** Stewart Gordon (ed.), *Robes and Honour: The Medieval World of Investiture* (London: Palgrave Macmillan, 2001).

**6** Joanne B. Eicher, Hazel Lee Evenson, and Sandra Lutz, *The Visible Self: Global Perspectives on Dress, Culture and Society* (2nd edn. New York: Fairchild Publications, 2000), 45. For the original concept, see *The Invention of Tradition,* Eric Hobsbawm and Terence Ranger (eds) (Cambridge: Cambridge University Press, 1983).

**7** Lou Taylor, *The Study of Dress History* (London: Berg, 2002) discusses her ideas on pp. 201ff.

**8** A tall headdress worn by Christian bishops in the Western church and senior abbots as a symbol of office, tapering to a point at front and back.

**9** Beverley Lemire and Giorgio Riello (eds), *Dressing Global Bodies: The Political Power of Dress in World History* (Abingdon: Routledge, 2002), 3.This point refers to the work of Leora Auslander (2005) in particular.

**10** The information on early Roman Catholic liturgical dress in New Zealand comes from Sandra Heffernan, "Liturgical Robes in New Zealand," *Berg World Encyclopedia of Dress and Fashion*, vol. 7, Joanne B. Eicher (ed.) (Oxford: Berg, 2010), 321–5.

**11** Ibid., 324.

**12** I acknowledge the assistance of Alex Borodin for information on the vestments in this image. The photograph was taken by Alexandra Kim.

**13** This is a wide-sleeved black garment worn by bishops, priests, deacons, and monastics in public over the inner cassock. It is regular outerwear.

**14** Imperial Romans had robes of state for ceremonial occasions, in addition to owning their own clothing.

**15** F. E. Brightman, "Byzantine Imperial Robes," *Journal of Theological Studies* 2, no. 7 (1901).

**16** Michael Edward Moore, "The Kings New Clothes: Royal and Episcopal Regalia in the Frankish Empire," in *Robes and Honor: The Medieval World of Investiture*, Stewart Gordon (ed.) (New York: St. Martin's / Palgrave, 2000), 95–135.

**17** Also King of the Franks in 768 CE, King of the Lombards in 774 CE.

**18** *Nobiles Officinae* Exhibition, April 1–13, 2004, Kunsthistorisches Museum, Vienna. https://www.khm.at/Archiv/Ausstellungen/nobiles/en/01/main.html (Accessed August 9, 2020).

**19** In 1945, Princess Elizabeth became the first female member of the royal family to join the Armed Forces in a full-time active role in the Auxiliary Territorial Service. She wore standard battle dress. See the Royal Collection Trust.

**20** In England originally ermine fur was reserved for royalty but now can also be worn by Peers of the Realm. It is normally white in winter with a black-tipped tail.

**21** The yeomen also attended on other ceremonial occasions, such as the Queen's Birthday Parade, when in the past she inspected her troops on horseback, in full dress uniform. Her Majesty's uniforms were designed by the equestrian tailor Bernard Weatherill.

**22** Democratic elections were set in motion, intended to diminish British power, although official connections are retained.

**23** Fanny Wonu Veys, "Ta'ovala and Kiekie of Tonga," *Berg Encyclopedia of World Dress and Fashion*, vol. 7, Joanne B. Eicher (ed.) (Oxford: Berg, 2010), 412.

**24** Most were kept in the Imperial Treasury Room (*Schatzkammer*) in Vienna from 1246. Subsequently the whereabouts of Treasury storage places were altered constantly.

**25** Rachel Stone, "The Emperor's New Clothes: Moral Aspects of Carolingian Royal Costume," paper presented at the International Medieval Congress (Leeds, July 2011), 1–10.

**26** Julie Codell, "On the Delhi Coronation Durbars, 1877, 1903, 1911," *BRANCH*. https://www.branchcollective.org/?ps_articles=julie-codell-on-the-delhi-coronation-durbars-1877-1903-1911 (accessed October 25, 2020).

**27** https://www.ghanaweb.com/GhanaHomePage/NewsArchive/Full-independence-speech-of-Dr-Kwame-Nkrumah-886726 (accessed April 19, 2019).

**28** https://journals.openedition.org/etudesafricaines/20822?lang=en (accessed April 26, 2018).

**29** One example is the Silver Sandal Foot Reliquary, covered in precious gems from the Basel Minster Treasury, and now in the Swiss National Museum, Zurich, dated 1450. It is believed to hold the bones of a little boy murdered by King Herod.

**30** In Australia, various Acts have been passed to protect unlawful acquisition of remains of Indigenous peoples or their artifacts but it is an unresolved issue.

**31** He is remembered as the king who famously acquired the Crown of Thorns, as well as other holy relics from Byzantium, and had a spectacular shrine built in Paris, the Sainte-Chapelle. In 1480, the linen shirt/tunic was listed in the Chapelle's treasury inventories. In 1795, along with other relics, it was deposited in the Cabinet des Médailles of the Bibliothèque Nationale in Paris.

**32** Tina Anderlini, "The Shirt Attributed to St Louis," *Medieval Clothing and Textiles* II, Robin Netherton and Gale R. Owen-Crocker (eds) (Woodbridge: Boydell & Brewer, 2015), 50–1, https://www.jstor.org/stable/10.7722/j.ctt12879fj (accessed December 15, 2020).

**33** Catalogue A 27050, Museum of London.

**34** My thanks to Susan North for her expert information about Charles I's vest and other associated remains of the king.

**35** The suit of imported Chanel fabric was produced under instruction from Paris and fitted by the New York boutique Chez Ninon.

**36** Justine Picardie, *Coco Chanel: The Legend and the Life* (London: HarperCollins, 2020), 304–06.

**37** Jules D. Prown, "Mind in Matter: An Introduction to Material Culture, Theory and Method," *Winterthur Portfolio* 17, no. 1 (1982): 3–4.

**38** Felicity Bodenstein, "The Emotional Museum: Thoughts on the 'Secular Relics' of Nineteenth-Century History Museums in Paris and their Posterity," Conserveries mémorielles 9, http://cm.revues.org/834 (accessed December 15, 2020).

**39** A white silk shoe said to have belonged to Marie Antoinette, and "provenanced" to the queen's first chamber maid, was sold at Osenat Auction House, Versailles, in 2020 for €43,750.

**40** Sylvia Kleinert, "Aboriginal Dress in Southeast Australia," in *Berg Encyclopedia of World Dress and Fashion*, vol. 7, Joanne B. Eicher (ed.) (London: Berg, 2010), 27.

**41** It is appropriate in Australia to term Aboriginal people members of clans, language groups, or even nations.

**42** This site has a detailed discussion of skin cloaks and their meanings: https://museumsvictoria.com.au/article/the-timeless-and-living-art-of-possum-skin-cloaks/ (accessed September 9, 2021).

**43** The cloaks were sometimes called "robes," "capes," and occasionally "dresses." Sometimes robes were made of buffalo skin. One twined "robe" collected by Cook is in the Museum für Völkerkunde in Vienna.

**44** These were elaborate gift-giving ceremonies of groups of Indigenous peoples. They came together on special occasions, mostly on the northwest coast of Canada and the US. Gift exchanges were events involving status, with attempts of two groups competing to show who was the wealthiest. It was also a time to have interclan discussions, feast, and reaffirm family ties.

**45** They were not woven on looms but twined with supported free-hanging warp threads. Aldona Jonaitis, *Art of the Northwest Coast* (Seattle: University of Washington Press, 2013), 138–9.

**46** Information from the State Library of Queensland.

**47** Kleinert, "Aboriginal Dress," 27.

**48** Patricia Te Arapo Wallace, "Introduction to Maori Dress," *Berg Encyclopedia of World Dress and Fashion*, vol. 7, Joanne B. Eicher (ed.) (London: Berg, 2010), 254.

**49** Ibid., 257.

**50** This is a Māori finger-weaving technique.

**51** Now in the Usher Gallery, Lincoln, UK.

**52** Queen Elizabeth II owns a Māori cloak given to her in 1950. She has worn it when in New Zealand.

**53** The organization Te Roopu Raranga Whatu o Aotearoa, the national Māori weavers' collective, aims to preserve and foster the skills of making and using original materials.

**54** Indigenous women Vicki Couzens and Lee Darroch found two deteriorating cloaks in the Melbourne Museum: the "Lake Condah" cloak from south-western Victoria, dated 1872, and the "Maiden's Punt" cloak from near Echuca, dated 1853. Vicki Couzens researched and replicated the first cloak with Debra Couzens, while Treahna Hamm replicated the second with Lee Darroch.

**55** Possums have to be acquired from New Zealand as they are now protected in Australia.

**56** An example is Sorry Day, May 26.

**57** Established with Regional Arts Victoria in 2004, under the artistic direction of Vicki Couzens (a Gunditjmara woman from Victoria).

**58** It was based on the traditional Yorta Yorta possum-skin cloak "found" at Maiden's Punt (Moama) now a town on the Murray River.

**59** When he met the Leader of the Opposition, he deliberately wore the cloak inside out and a plain grey "beanie."

**60** Deborah Bird Rose, "The Power of Place," and Christine Watson, "Ngantalarra, on the Nakarra Nakarra Dreaming Track," *The Oxford Companion to Aboriginal Art and Culture,* Sylvia Kleinert and Margo Neale (eds) (Oxford: Oxford University Press, 2000), 40–9.

# 6 The Wardrobe Story

**1** Wardrobes are used when these cultures absorb Westernized clothing or change city work clothes for leisure or village wearing but not for ceremonial outfits.

**2** I do not discuss the garments of children and teenagers.

**3** Margaret Maynard, *Fashioned from Penury: Dress as Cultural Practice in Colonial Australia* (Cambridge: Cambridge University Press, 1994), 140–1.

**4** This is an exception in terms of historical interest. Matthew Storey and Lucy Storey, "Queen Victoria: An Anatomy in Dress," *Costume* 53, no. 2 (2019): 256–79.

**5** Else Skjold, "'Biographical Wardrobes: A Temporal View on Dress Practice," *The Journal of Design, Creative Process and the Fashion Journal* 8 (1) (2016): 135–48, https://research.cbs.dk/en/publications/biographical-wardrobes-a-temporal-view-on-dress-practice (accessed October 15, 2021).

**6** I. G. Klepp and M. Bjerck, "A Methodological Approach to the Materiality of Clothing: Wardrobe Studies," *International Journal of Social Research Methodology* 17 (4) (2014): 373–86, https://doi.org/10.1080/13645579.2012.737148 (accessed August 28, 2019).

**7** Kate Fletcher and Ingun Grimstad Klepp (eds), *Opening Up the Wardrobe: A Methods Book* (St. Charles, MI: Novus Press, 2017). The editors explicitly define their book as being more about social relationships with clothing, its meanings, and material effects, than physical containers.

**8** Ibid., 2–3.

**9** Ibid., 168 ff.

**10** Saulo B. Cwerner, "Clothes at Rest: Elements for a Sociology of the Wardrobe," *Fashion Theory* 5, no. 1 (2001): 80.

**11** Ibid.

**12** He also suggests clothes have private lives as part of the home, as wardrobe practices are more than communication. They include personal caring for clothes, washing, ironing etc. Ibid., 79–80.

**13** Ibid., 83, 86.

**14** https://shannonselin.com/2017/05/french-kings-rise-grand-lever/ (accessed June 20, 2019).

**15** King Louis IV established the post of Grand Maitre de la Garde-robe du Roi in 1669 to attend to his clothes.

16 Maria Hayward, "Dressing Charles II: The King's Clothing Choices 1660–85," *Appearances* 6 (2015), https://www.researchgate.net/publication/312910176_Dressing_Charles_II_the_king%27s_clothing_choices_1660-16852015 (accessed October 30, 2020).

17 In seventeenth-century Europe, the term "toilette" could be used to indicate both a garment and the finalizing of stylish dressing.

18 Pernilla Rasmussen, "Recycling a Fashionable Wardrobe in the Long 18th Century in Sweden," *History of Retailing and Consumption* 2, no. 3 (2016): 193–222.

19 Ibid., 210.

20 Ariane Fennetaux, "Sentimental Economics: Recycling Textiles in Eighteenth-Century Britain," *The Afterlife of Used Things,* Ariane Fennetaux, Amelie Junque, and Sophie Vasset (eds) (London: Routledge, 2015), 126.

21 Rasmussen, "Recycling," 193.

22 These garments may have been made of subserica—a mix of fibers. Kenneth D. Matthews, "The Imperial Wardrobe of Ancient Rome," *Expedition Magazine* 12, no. 3 (1970): 2, http://www.penn.museum/sites/expedition/?p=2111><12 (accessed November 6, 2020). This is a short but well-informed essay on Roman dress.

23 Alan Hunt, "A Short History of Sumptuary Laws," in *The Fashion History Reader: Global Perspectives,* Giorgio Riello and Peter McNeil (eds) (Abingdon: Routledge, 2010), 45.

24 Archival records for British monarchs are extensive. See Royal Household and Wardrobe Archives: http://www.nationalarchives.gov.uk/ The work of Janet Arnold on the clothing of Queen Elizabeth I is acknowledged, and that of Maria Hayward on Henry VIII.

25 The Great Wardrobe, which lasted for many years, was abolished in 1782.

26 Philip Mansel, *King of the World: The Life of Louis XIV* (London: Penguin, 2019), 5.

27 The UK National Archives AO3/912, 51.

28 Aileen Ribeiro, *Dress in Eighteenth Century Europe, 1715–1789* (London: B. T. Batsford, 1984), 126.

29 Ibid., 58–9.

30 Caroline Weber, *Queen of Fashion: What Marie Antoinette Wore to the Revolution* (New York: Picador, 2007), 149–50. It was held by the Comtesse d' Ossun, her wardrobe attendant 1782–92, and is now in the National Archives of France. Its precise function, either a record of account or for purposes of choice, is disputed.

31 Ibid., 12, 150, 160.

32 Carolyn Dowdell, "'No Small Share of Ingenuity': An Object-Oriented Analysis of Eighteenth Century English Dressmaking," *Costume: Journal of the Costume Society* 55, no. 2 (September 2021): 200.

33 Lou Taylor, "The Several Lives of a Collection of Rag Dump Clothing from Normandy (1900–55): From Farm, to Dump, to Poverty Chic," *Fashion Studies* 1, no. 1 (2018): 1–38.

34 A rare handmade full-size wardrobe using a Kinkara tea chest and "found" materials of the 1930s, made by an impoverished Italian migrant in regional Griffith, New South Wales, is now preserved in the town museum.

**35** The term *jhoot* is not possible to translate accurately into English, but seems to imply indeterminable wastage, prevarication.

**36** Mukulika Banerjee and David Miller, *The Sari* (London: Bloomsbury Academic, 2003), 57–8.

**37** Ibid., 47–51.

**38** Ibid., 54.

**39** Uploaded to Google's *We Wear Culture* in 2017.

**40** Viveka Hansen, "Wardrobes and Storage at a Manor House in 1758," iTextilis LXXX1, Nov 6 2017, The IK Workshop Society at The IK Foundation, https://www.ikfoundation.org/itextilis/wardrobes-and-storage-of-clothes.html (accessed November 13, 2020).

**41** An image of the Nizam's wardrobe can be found on: http://www.india-seminar.com/2008/585/585_narendra_luther.htm (accessed July 5, 2018).

**42** Except one *sherwani* (a formal coat-like garment similar to a frock coat), a top hat, two pairs of riding boots, a pair of pumps, and one pair of straw slippers.

**43** See the *Vogue Pattern Book* in the John Bright Collection, Bowes Museum, Barnard Castle, UK. Condé Nast published these in the US from 1909.

**44** Agnès Rocamora, "New Fashion Times: Fashion and Digital Media," *The Handbook of Fashion Studies*, Sandy Black, Amy de la Haye, Joanne Entwistle, Agnès Rocamora, Regina A. Root, and Helen Thomas (eds) (London: Bloomsbury Academic, 2013), 65.

**45** The bride price (bride wealth or bride token) is different from a dowry. Common in Africa, it is paid by the groom, or his family, to the bride's parents at the time of the marriage.

**46** Julie Hardwick, *Family Business: Litigation and the Political Economies of Daily Life in Early Modern France* (Oxford: Oxford University Press, 2009), 24–5.

**47** Kathryn Warner, "Isabella the Rebel Queen," 2016 https://www.goodreads.com/book/show/27109825-isabella-of-france (accessed September 4, 2019).

**48** Aileen Ribeiro, *Dress in Eighteenth-century Europe, 1715–1789* (London: B. T. Batsford, 1984), 59.

**49** Ibid.

**50** Caroline Weber, *Queen of Fashion: What Marie Antoinette Wore to the Revolution* (London: Aurum Press, 2006), 32.

**51** Ibid., 7.

**52** A teddy is an all-in-one garment composed of a camisole and panties. It is sometimes called a camiknicker.

**53** Clothing of calico was valued but not worn. Susanne Küchler and Graeme Were (eds), *The Art of Clothing*: *A Pacific Experience* (London: Routledge, 2005), xxvi.

**54** Annelin Eriksen, "Gender, Christianity and Change in Vanuatu: An Analysis of Social Movement in North Ambryn," (Abingdon: Routledge, 2007), https://www.crcpress.com/Gender-Christianity-and-Change-in-Vanuatu-An-Analysis-of-Social-Movements/Eriksen/p/book/9780754672098 (accessed September 4, 2019).

**55** Fanny Wonu Veys, "Barkcloth Wrapping in Tonga," *Berg Encyclopedia of World Dress and Fashion*, vol. 7, Joanne B. Eicher (ed.) (London: Berg, 2010), 415–17.

56 Saulo B. Cwerner, "Clothes at Rest: Elements for a Sociology of the Wardrobe," *Fashion Theory* 5, no. 1 (2001): 87.

57 *Australian Etiquette: On the Rules and Usages of the Best Society. Together with their Sports, Pastimes, Games and Amusements* (Sydney and Melbourne: D. E. McConnell, 1885).

58 There are many reproductions of this famous book. It is believed that representations of the dress are not entirely accurate, and more an aid to identifying different characters depicted.

59 Information gratefully acknowledged from Margaret Scott.

60 Margaret Maynard, "Indigenous Dress," *The Oxford Companion to Aboriginal Art and Culture,* Sylvia Kleinert and Margo Neale (eds) (Oxford: Oxford University Press, 2000), 385.

61 Pravina Shukla, "The Study of Dress and Adornment as Social Positioning," *Material Culture Review* 61 (Spring 2005): 4–16.

62 Her dates are quite unclear but *c*. 965–1010 CE is sometimes given. She was a courtier and poet. See Meredith McKinney, *Pillow Book of Sei Shōnagon,* translated with notes (London: Penguin, 2006).

63 In the early Heian Period, the layers could be up to twenty in number but were later officially restricted: see http://kasane.fuyuya.com/ (accessed January 21, 2021). The author describes the Grand Counselor arriving at Court in a soft cloak of a cherry-blossom combination, over deep-violet gathered trousers of heavy brocade.

64 McKinney, *Pillow Book,* 17.

65 Perhaps a formal dress for mass, a déshabillé in her chambers, and a gala dress for the evening. Caroline Weber*, Queen of Fashion: What Marie Antoinette Wore to the Revolution* (London: Aurum Press, 2006), 118–19.

66 Mukulika Banerjee and Daniel Miller, *The Sari* (Oxford: Berg, 2003), 66, 68.

67 Vibeke Maria Viestad, *Dress as Social Relations. An Interpretation of Bushman Dress* (Johannesburg: Wits University Press, 2018), 26. This study is based on the information from informants in the Bleek and Lloyd collections and the Louis Fourie collection, South African Museum and Museum Africa.

68 Philip Jones, "Aboriginal Dress in Australia: Evidence and Resources," *Berg Encyclopedia of World Dress and Fashion*, vol. 7, Joanne B. Eicher (ed.) (Oxford: Berg, 2010), 19–20.

69 Naomi McPherson, "Dressing the Body in Bariai," *Berg Encyclopedia of World Dress and Fashion,* vol. 7, Joanne B. Eicher (ed.) (Oxford: Berg, 2010), 469.

70 Fanny Wonu Veys, "Ta'ovala and Kiekie of Tonga," *Berg Encyclopedia of World Dress and Fashion,* vol. 7, Joanne B. Eicher (ed.) (Oxford: Berg, 2010), 412, 416–17.

# 7  Dress: Time and Cultural Memory

1  Edith Wharton, *A Backward Glance* (New York: Curtis Publishing Co., 1933), 1–2.

2  Joanne Entwistle, *The Fashioned Body: Fashion Dress and Social Theory* (Cambridge: Polity Press, 2015), 6.

**3** Ellen Sampson, "Creases, Crumples and Folds," *The Fashion Studies Journal* 5 (2017), www.fashionstudiesjournal.org/new-blog-2/2017/4/2/creases-crumples-and-folds-maps-of-experience-and-manifestations-of-wear-ikfoundation.org/itextilisl58hj (accessed September 22, 2021).

**4** Ellen Sampson, "The Cleaved Garment: The Wearer and the 'Me and Not Me' of Fashion Practice," *Fashion Theory* 22, no. 3 (2018): 341–60.

**5** Ellen Sampson, "Worn: Footwear, Attachment and Affective Experiences" (2016), Sampson/43627baf0cfb77706e8a0aaeae867d11238e5438 (accessed September 19, 2021).

**6** Peter Stallybrass, "Worn Worlds: Clothes, Mourning and the Life of Things," in *The Textile Reader,* Jessica Hemmings (ed.) (London: Berg, 2012), 70. First published in *Yale Review,* 1993.

**7** Kitty Hauser, "A Garment in the Dock; or How the FBI Illuminated the Prehistory of a Pair of Denim Jeans," *Journal of Material Culture* 9, no. 3 (2004): 295–313.

**8** Aileen Ribeiro, *A Visual History of Costume: The Eighteenth Century* (London: B. T. Batsford, 1983), 16.

**9** https://www.eyesofindia.com/blog/2015/04/general-info/trip-to-hodka-village.html (accessed July 20, 2021).

**10** Ariane Fennetaux, "Sentimental Economics: Recycling Textiles in Eighteenth Century Britain," in *The Afterlife of Used Things: Recycling in the Long Eighteenth Century,* Ariane Fennetaux, Amélie Junqua, and Sophie Vasset (eds) (Abingdon: Routledge Studies in History, 2014), 134–5.

**11** Carolyn Dowdell, "'No Small Share of Ingenuity': An Object-Oriented Analysis of Eighteenth Century English Dressmaking," *Costume: Journal of the Costume Society* 55, no. 2 (2021): 201.

**12** Stallybrass, "Worn Worlds," 74.

**13** Ibid., 69.

**14** Karen Hanson, "Dressing Down, Dressing Up: The Philosophic Fear of Fashion," *Hypatia* 5, no. 2 (Summer 1990): 107–21.

**15** Phillipa Snow, "The Clothes They Were Buried In," *Vestoj* 5 (2017), http://vestoj.com/the-clothes-they-were-buried-in/ (accessed October 20, 2020).

**16** The tight Jean Louis gown worn by Marilyn Monroe when she sang "Happy Birthday, Mr. President" to John F. Kennedy was sold at auction in 2016 for $4.8m (£3.9m).

**17** Dinah Eastop, "Textiles as Multiple and Competing Histories," in *Textiles Revealed: Object Lessons in Historic Textile and Costume Research,* Mary M. Brooks, (ed.) (London: Archetype Publications Ltd., 2000), 21.

**18** Mirabella Bella, *Ornamentalism: The Art of Renaissance Accessories* (Ann Arbor, MI: University of Michigan Press, 2011), 13–22.

**19** https://perfumesociety.org/perfume-house/jean-paul-gaultier/ (accessed May 3, 2020).

**20** Paper on perfumed textiles given at the Textile Society of America in 2008. https://digitalcommons.unl.edu/cgi/viewcontent.cgi?article=1104&context=tsaconf (accessed September 13, 2021) The first established perfume, with rosemary as a major ingredient, was for Queen Elizabeth of Hungary. Called "Hungary," it was produced in Paris in 1370.

21  Karen de Perthuis, "Darning Mark's Jumper: Wearing Love and Sorrow," *Cultural Studies Review* 22, no. 1 (2016): 59–77.

22  Stallybrass, "Worn Worlds," 76–7.

23  Anthony Palliparambil, Jr., "'Notes on Materiality, Ritual and Grief," *The Fashion Studies Journal* (Fashion and Mental Health Issue), July 7, 2021. Notional Issue 7, https://www.fashionstudiesjournal.org/ (accessed September 17, 2021).

24  See Lynne Malcolm and Olivia Willis, *Songlines: The Indigenous Memory Code*, July 8, 2016, https://www.abc.net.au/radionational/programs/allinthemind/songlines-indigenous-memory-code/7581788 (accessed October 31, 2019).

25  Karen Adams, a Wiradjuli woman, from central New South Wales, suggests song lines traced the journeys of ancestral spirits as they created the land. See also Alice M. Moyle, *Songs from the Kimberley* (Canberra: Australian Institute of Aboriginal Studies, 1977).

26  Lynne Kelly, *The Memory Code* (Cambridge: Pegasus Books, 2017). Kelly provides new insights into how oral societies around the world are able to store vast quantities of knowledge.

27  Judy Watson and Diana Young, *Written on the Body* (St. Lucia, Queensland: Museum of Anthropology, 2014).

28  Purchased by Kim Akerman in Perth 1964, from the Warburton Ranges, Gibson Desert, Western Australia. Information from the purchaser.

29  Ellen Sampson, "*Worn: Footwear, Attachment and Affective Experience,* 267–9, https://core.ac.uk/download/pdf/43099334.pdf (accessed 25.1.2021). This comes from the abstract of a PhD thesis presented to the RCA in 2016.

30  Ellen Sampson, "Memory: Movement and Materiality, the Shoe as Record," Abstract, conference paper, nd, https://northumbria.academia.edu/EllenSampson (accessed February 16, 2010).

31  Jutta Zander-Seidel, "Appropriating the World Through Clothing: Christopher Kress's Foreign Dress Collection," in *Fashion and Materiality: Cultural Practices in Global Contexts,* Heike Jenss and Viola Hofmann (eds) (London: Bloomsbury, 2020), 81, 85.

32  https://www.medieval.eu/royal-golden-dress-from-ca-1400-returns-to-denmark/ (accessed October 22, 2021).

33  Shirley Escalante, "Imelda Marcos Shoe Museum: The Excess of a Regime that Still Haunts the Philippines," 2016, https://www.abc.net.au/news/2016-10-02/imelda-marcos-shoe-museum:-the-excess-of-a-regime/7877098 (accessed September 22, 2021).

34  Bethan Bide, "Signs of Wear: Encountering Memory in the Worn Materiality of a Museum Fashion Collection," *Fashion Theory: The Journal of Dress, Body and Culture* 21, no. 4 (2017): 449–96.

35  Ellen Sampson, Review, "Present Imperfect: Disorderly Apparel Reconfigured," https://www.fashionstudiesjournal.org/4-reviews-2-1/2017/7/31/present-imperfect (accessed October 22, 2021).

36  Giorgio Riello, "The Object of Fashion: Methodological Approaches to the History of Fashion," *Journal of Aesthetics and Culture* 3 (2011): 1–7, Joanne Entwistle, *The Fashioned Body: Fashion Dress and Social Theory* (Cambridge: Polity Press, 2015).

37 Valerie Steele, "Museum Quality: The Rise of the Fashion Exhibition," *Fashion Theory* 12, no. 1 (March 2008): 12.

38 Ellen Sampson, "Present Imperfect: Disorderly Apparel Reconfigured," *The Fashion Studies Journal* 2 (August 2017), https://www.fashionstudiesjournal.org/reviews-2/2017/7/31/present-imperfect-nzxl2 (accessed August 13, 2021).

39 Robyn Healy, "Immateriality," *The Handbook of Fashion Studies,* Sandy Black, Amy de la Haye, Joanne Entwistle, Agnès Rocamora, Regina A. Root, and Helen Thomas (eds) (London: Bloomsbury, 2013), 325–43.

40 Christopher Breward, "Between the Museum and the Academy: Fashion Research and its Constituencies," *Fashion Theory* 12, no. 1 (March 2008): 91.

41 http://www.vam.ac.uk/content/articles/s/spectres/ (accessed November 8, 2021).

42 Riello, "The Object of Fashion," 3.

43 Sampson, "Present Imperfect."

44 http://www.artsobserver.com/2012/05/28/tattered-and-torn-an-exhibition-of-costumes-cast-off-by-museums/ (accessed September 20, 2021).

45 Katri Walker, Review, https://www.west86th.bgc.bard.edu/exhibitionreviews/las-apariencias-enganan-los-vestidos-de-frida-kahlo-appearances-can-be-deceiving-the-dresses-of-frida-kahlo-frida-kahlo-museum-casa-azul-coyoacan-mexico-city-on-permanent-display/ (accessed August 7, 2021).

46 Alba F. Aragón, "Uninhabited Dresses: Frida Kahlo, from Icon of Mexico to Fashion Muse," *Fashion Theory* 18, no. 5 (2014): 517–49.

47 Joanne Garcia Cheran, "An Indigenous Perspective on Frida Kahlo," July 4, 2021, Hyperallergic.com (accessed July 7, 2021).

48 It was shown at the Rhode Island School of Design and Brown University's Haffenreffer Museum of Anthropology.

49 Kate Fletcher, *Craft of Use: Post-Growth Fashion* (Abingdon: Routledge, 2016).

50 Robyn Healy, "The Parody of the Motley Cadaver: Displaying the Funeral of Fashion," *The Textile Reader,* Jessica Hemmings (ed.) (London: Berg, 2012), 89–98.

51 In 1971 she was appointed as Consultant to the Costume Institute, a curatorial section of The Metropolitan Museum of Art, New York.

52 Robyn Healy's "Noble Rot: An Alternate History of Fashion" was a project for the National Trust of Victoria in 2006.

53 Healy, "The Parody," 91.

54 Perline Yeo, "Exhibiting Transformative Fashion: Digital Interventions to Enhance Display and Interpretation," *Costume* 55, no. 1 (2021): 97–120.

55 Welters and Lillethun describe the compulsion for novelty as the "fashion impulse," and as endemic to human nature. Linda Welters and Abby Lillethun*, Fashion History: A Global View* (London: Bloomsbury, 2018), 29.

56 Sarah-Grace Heller, "The Birth of Fashion," in *The Fashion History Reader: Global Perspectives*, Giorgio Riello and Peter McNeil (eds) (Abingdon: Routledge, 2010), 34.

57 Jennifer Craik has repeatedly claimed that high fashion is not solely European and that there are many fashion systems. See *The Face of Fashion: Cultural Studies in Fashion* (London: Routledge, 1994), x–xi. This is reiterated in her book *Fashion: The Key Concepts* (2009).

**58** Susan B. Kaiser, *Fashion and Cultural Studies* (Oxford: Berg, 2012), 39.

**59** Susanne Küchler and Graeme Were, in "The Social World of Cloth in the Pacific Islands," *Berg Encyclopedia of World Dress and Fashion,* vol. 7, Joanne B. Eicher (ed.) (Oxford: Berg, 2010), 381–2.

**60** Adrienne L. Kaeppler, "Introduction to the Dress of the Pacific Islands," in *Berg Encyclopedia of World Dress and Fashion,* vol. 7, Joanne B. Eicher (ed.) (Oxford: Berg, 2010), 373.

**61** *African Dress, Fashion, Agency, Performance,* Karen Hansen and D. Soyini Madison (eds) (London: Bloomsbury Academic, 2013), 4.

**62** Lipovetsky was writing well before the new academic research interest in replicating examples of historical dress. Giles Lipovetsky, *The Empire of Fashion: Dressing Modern Democracy* (New Jersey: Princeton University Press, 1994), 249.

**63** These ideas come from one of the many essays written by Richard Martin. The actual source cannot now be found but these quotes were from pages 15 and 28.

**64** Lipovetsky, *The Empire of Fashion,* 23.

**65** Aileen Ribeiro, *Dress in Eighteenth Century Europe, 1715–1789* (London: B. T. Batsford, 1984) 186.

**66** Master Jonathan Buttle (not an aristocrat) by Gainsborough is now in the collection of the Huntington Library, Art Collections and Botanical Gardens, San Marino, California.

**67** Painter to the French Court. François Boucher's glorious portrait of "Madame de Pompadour Reading," 1758, Victoria and Albert Museum, 487–1882.

**68** In the collection of the V&A, T216-2002.

**69** The "Cut, Slash and Pull Collection" is sometimes called the "Cut and Slash Collection."

**70** Glynis Traill-Nash, "Off the Wall: Renaissance Art and Opera Inspire Duo," *Weekend Australian,* December 9, 2019: 3.

# 8  Unfixed: Time and Dress

**1** Barbara Vinken, *Fashion Zeigeist: Trends and Cycles in The Fashion System* (Oxford: Berg, 2005), 42. This is reframing the supposed cyclical nature of fashion.

**2** Ibid., 68–9.

**3** Renate Stauss and Ane Lynge-Jorien, Symposium Review: "The Death of Taste: Unpicking the Fashion Cycle," November 2006, *Fashion Theory* 12, no. 20 (2008): 261–6.

**4** See the comments that the term "fashion" needs redefinition, so far as to suggest it is nonprogressive. Heike Jenss and Viola Hofmann, "Introduction: Fashion and Materiality," in *Fashion and Materiality: Cultural Practices in Global Contexts*, Heike Jenss and Viola Hofmann (eds) (London: Bloomsbury Visual Arts, 2019), 5.

**5** Daniel Devoucoux, "The Discovery of Materiality: Archaelogical Clothing Finds, Representation, and Knowledge Formation," in *Fashion and Materiality: Cultural Practices in Global Contexts,* Heike Jenss and Viola Hofmann (eds) (London: Bloomsbury Visual Arts, 2020), 73–4.

**6** Angelo Flaccovento, *Vogue Italia*, 805 (September 1, 2017), 191.

**7** https://www.highsnobiety.com/p/alessandro-michele-gucci/ (accessed August 19, 2019).

**8** https://www.roadrunnerwm.com/blog/textile-waste-environmental-crisis  (accessed October 9, 2021).

**9** Christopher Breward, *Fashion* (Oxford: Oxford University Press, 2003), 22ff.

**10** See analysis of the speeding-up of society, communication, and fashion. Agnès Rocamora, "New Fashion Times: Fashion and Digital Media," in *The Handbook of Fashion Studies*, Sandy Black, Amy de la Haye, Joanne Entwistle, Agnès Rocamora, Regina A. Root, and Helen Thomas (eds) (London: Bloomsbury Academic, 2013).

**11** It is important to remember that popularity of apps like Instagram can themselves lose market share.

**12** Rocamora, "New Fashion Times," 63.

**13** Caroline Evans, "A Shop of Images and Signs," in *Fashion as Photography: Viewing and Reviewing Images of Fashion,* Eugénie Shinkle (ed.) (New York: I. B. Tauris, 2008), 22.

**14** Rocamora, "New Fashion Times," 66.

**15** Margaret Maynard, "Fast Fashion and Sustainability," in *The Handbook of Fashion Studies*, Sandy Black, Amy de la Haye, Joanne Entwistle, Agnès Rocamora, Regina A. Root and Helen Thomas (eds) (London: Bloomsbury Academic, 2013), 548.

**16** From a conversation about *The State of Fashion* exhibition she curated in 2018. https://www.thelissome.com/blog/2018/6/5/state-of-fashion (accessed December 3, 2020).

**17** Greer Crawley and Donatella Barbieri, "Dress, Time, and Space: Expanding the Field through Exhibition Making," in *The Handbook of Fashion Studies*, Sandy Black, Amy de la Haye, Joanne Entwistle, Agnès Rocamora, Regina A. Root, and Helen Thomas (eds) (London: Bloomsbury Academic, 2013), 57.

**18** See https://fashionhistory.fitnyc.edu/ for an example of a timeline and much more. (accessed August 19, 2021).

**19** https://www.metmuseum.org/exhibitions/listings/2020/about time (accessed July 4, 2020).

**20** Vinken, *Fashion Zeitgeist,* 42.

**21** Karen Tranberg Hansen, "Introduction," in *African Dress: Fashion, Agency, Performance,* Karen Tranberg Hansen and D. Soyini Madison (eds) (London: Bloomsbury Academic, 2013), 6.

**22** Hansen, "Introduction," *African Dress,* 5.

**23** Bradley Quinn, *Textile Futures: Fashion, Design and Technology* (Oxford: Berg, 2010).

**24** Lou Taylor, "The Several Lives of a Collection of Rag Dump Clothing from Normandy (1900–55): From Farm, to Dump, to Poverty Chic," *Fashion Studies* 1, no. 1 (2018): 1–38.

**25** Ibid., 20.

**26** Phil Backes, "The Unseen Archives of Christian Dior with Archivist Solzic Pfaff," January 9, 2018, https://www.dior.com/en_int (accessed July 24, 2020).

27 https://www.dailymail.co.uk/news/article-8044313/Shocking-report-reveals-cheap-clothes-resold-end-rotting-Africa.html (accessed March 20, 2022).

28 Maynard, "Fast Fashion," 542–3.

29 *The State of Fashion* (2020), 56 BOF McKinsey & Co., https://www.mckinsey.com/~/media/mckinsey/industries/retail/our%20insights/the%20state%20of%20fashion%202020%20navigating%20uncertainty/the-state-of-fashion-2020-final.pdf (accessed August 19, 2021).

30 Milanda Rout, "Follow the Thread," *Wish,* Feb 2019, 38–41.

31 T-shirt company For Days operates using this method. Emily Farra, "Zero Waste-Brand Wants to Reward You for Your Clothes," *Vogue,* February 24, 2021 https://www.vogue.com/article/for-days-closet-credit-system-closed-loop-commerce (accessed August 20, 2021) and https://www.vogue.com/article/for-days-upcycled-t-shirts-basics (accessed December 2, 2020). Customers need to become members and buy a number of new T-shirts (a kind of library for clothes).

32 https://about.hm.com/news/general-news-2020/recycling-system--loop--helps-h-m-transform-unwanted-garments-i.html (accessed February 4, 2022).

33 http://www.fashionstudiesjournal.org/2-visual-essays-2/2017/4/2/creases-crumples-and-folds-maps-of-experience-and-manifestations-of-wear (accessed September 3, 2021).

34 Vinken, *Fashion Zeitgeist*, 42.

35 Maynard, "Fast Fashion," 554.

36 Hansen and Madison, "Introduction," 9.

37 Barbara Vinken, *Fashion Zeigeist Trends and Cycles in The Fashion System* (Oxford: Berg, 2005), 68. This is reframing the supposed cyclical nature of fashion.

38 From 1884 until 1972, Greenwich Mean Time became the standard reference for the UK and a number of other countries, replacing age-old localized measures of time.

39 Linda Welters and Abby Lillethun, *Fashion History: A Global View* (London: Bloomsbury Academic, 2018), 157.

40 Mary Harlow and Marie-Louise Nosch, "Weaving the Threads: Methodologies in Textile and Dress Research for the Greek and Roman World—the State of the Art and the Case for Cross-disciplinarity," *Greek and Roman Textiles and Dress: An Interdisciplinary Anthology,* Antique Textiles Series 19 (Oxford: Oxbow Publications, 2014), 8, 19.

41 Welters and Lillethun, *Fashion History*, 29.

42 Ibid., 157–8.

43 *Roman Dress and the Fabrics of Roman Culture,* Jonathon Edmondson and Alison Keith (eds) (Toronto: University of Toronto Press, 2008), 11–12.

44 A secondhand diamond-encrusted Hermès bag, sold in 2018 by Christies for £162,500 in London, is said to be the most expensive handbag ever sold at auction in Europe.

45 The technique is discussed here: https://www.metmuseum.org/art/collection/search/83312 (accessed October 25, 2021).

46 Letter from the Editors, McNeil Peter and Melissa Bellanta, "Fashion, Embodiment and the 'Making Turn'," *Fashion Theory* 23, no. 3 (2019): 325–28.

**47** Alexandra Palmer, "Looking at Fashion: The Material Object as Subject," *The Handbook of Fashion Studies*, Sandy Black, Amy de la Haye, Joanne Entwistle, Agnès Rocamora, Regina A. Root, and Helen Thomas (eds) (London: Bloomsbury, 2013), 295.

**48** Hilary Davidson, "The Embodied Turn: Making and Remaking Dress as an Academic Practice," *Fashion Theory. The Journal of Dress, Body and Culture* 23, no. 3 (2019): 329–62.

**49** Bethan Bide, "Signs of Wear: Encountering Memory in the Worn Materiality of a Museum Fashion Collection," *Fashion Theory. The Journal of Dress, Body and Culture* 21, no. 4 (2017): 449–7.

**50** https://www.medieval.eu/recreating-a-norwegian-tunic-from-the-iron-age/ (accessed March 20, 2022).

**51** https://www.academia.edu/35628286/Reconstructing_the_Tunic_from_Lendbreen_in_Norway_Archaeological_Textiles_Review_no_59_2017_p_24_33_SFA_Center_of_Textile_Research_Copenhagen (accessed August 17, 2021).

**52** My thanks to Valerie Cumming for refreshing my memory about these early authors.

**53** Janet Arnold, *Patterns of Fashion: English Women's Dresses 1660–1860* (London: Wace and Co. Ltd., 1966). Janet Arnold's archive of resource slides is held by The School of Historical Dress.

**54** Another historian who helped foster replicas was Nora Waugh, an authority on historic garments. She assisted in designing costumes for Shakespearian plays at the Globe Theatre, but her reputation spread more widely via her general books on historic costume.

**55** Antonia Laurence-Allen, curator of Edinburgh and East, National Trust of Scotland, *Stitching the Past* (2019), https://www.nts.org.uk/stories/stitching-the-past (accessed November 30, 2020).

**56** Alison Larkin, "Replicating Captain Cook's Waistcoat: Exploring the Skills of a Named Embroiderer during the Eighteenth Century," *Costume* 51, no. 1 (2017): 54–77.

**57** The waistcoat, partially embroidered by Elizabeth Cook, was stitched on *tapa* cloth and linen, with silverplated thread and spangles. It is now in the Mitchell Collection, State Library of New South Wales, Sydney.

**58** Apart from the unfinished item, three others are complete (and possibly worn by Cook). They are an embroidered silk waistcoat *c*. 1755–65 (PC001529) in the collection of Te Papa Tongarewa Museum, Wellington, New Zealand. It came from a house visited by Cook and is believed to have been worn by him. A plain waistcoat with brass buttons, perhaps part of Cook's naval uniform, is in the State Library of Victoria, Melbourne, while another embroidered silk waistcoat currently in private hands in Australia.

**59** Bought by the New South Wales Agent-General in London, it entered the collection of the Australian Museum and in 1935 transferred to the Mitchell Collection.

**60** The *tapa* was apparently part of a collection of specimens collected during the different voyages of Cook in the South Pacific. *Tapa* is beaten cloth made on many Pacific Islands from the inner bark of the paper mulberry tree. It has been used for clothing and body wrapping especially for cultural rituals. The *tapa* for this replica though is modern *tapa*.

**61** It is interesting that drapery stores can sell paper patterns that help to recreate historic clothing. A case is Simplicity Creative Sewing Patterns 8578 for a women's 18th Century Gown, made in the USA. The pattern says it is ideal for theater productions, re-enactments, or as a Halloween or cosplay costume.

**62** https://cdmc.wisc.edu/2021/01/12/dr-sophie-pitman-to-join-sohe-as-cdmcs-rowland-distinguished-director/ (accessed March 28, 2022)

**63** Davidson, "The Embodied Turn" (2019).

# SELECT BIBLIOGRAPHY

Akerman, Kim. "Shoes of Invisibility and Invisible Shoes: Australian Hunters and Gatherers and Ideas on the Origins of Footwear." *Australian Aboriginal Studies* 2 (2005): 55–64.

Akerman, Kim. "Aboriginal Dress in the Kimberley, Western Australia." In *Australia New Zealand and the Pacific Islands. Berg Encyclopedia of World Dress and Fashion*, vol. 7, Joanne B. Eicher (ed.), 49–59. Oxford: Berg Publishers, 2010. (This article edited by Margaret Maynard.)

Appadurai, Arjun (ed.), *The Social Life of Things: Commodities in Cultural Perspective*. Cambridge: Cambridge University Press, 1986.

Banerjee, Mukulika, and David Miller. *The Sari*. London: Bloomsbury Academic, 2003.

Bella, Mirabella. *Ornamentalism: The Art of Renaissance Accessories*. Ann Arbor: University of Michigan Press, 2011.

Bennett, James, and Russell Kelty. *Treasure Ships: Art in the Age of Spice*. Exhibition Catalogue. Art Gallery of South Australia and Art Gallery of Western Australia, Adelaide: 2015–16.

Bide, Bethan. "Signs of Wear: Encountering Memory in the Worn Materiality of a Museum Fashion Collection," *Fashion Theory: The Journal of Dress, Body and Culture* 21, no. 4 (2017): 449–76.

Breward, Christopher, "Between the Museum and the Academy: Fashion Research and its Constituencies," *Fashion Theory: The Journal of Dress, Body and Culture* 12, no. 1 (2008): 83–94.

Chrisman-Campbell, Kimberly. "From Caterpillar to Butterfly and Back: A Waistcoat of the French Revolution," *Costume: The Journal of the Costume Society* 45, no. 1 (2011): 63–74.

Cliffe, Sheila. *The Social Life of Kimono: Japanese Fashion Past and Present*. London: Bloomsbury, 2017.

Codell, Julie. "On the Delhi Coronation Durbars, 1877, 1903, 1911." *BRANCH: Britain, Representation and Nineteenth-Century History*, (June 2012). Available online at: https://www.branchcollective.org/?ps_articles=julie-codell-on-the-delhi-coronation-durbars-1877-1903-1911 (accessed October 25, 2020).

Conor, Liz. *The Spectacular Modern Woman: Feminine Visibility in the 1920s*. Bloomington: Indiana University Press, 2004.

Corfield, Penelope J. "History and the Temporal Turn: Returning to Causes, Effects and Diachronic Trends 1." In *Les âges de Britannia: Repenser l'histoire des mondes Britanniques: (Moyen Âge–XXIe siècle)*, J.-F. Dunyach (ed.), 259–273. Paris: Presses Universitaires de Rennes, 2015. Copyright@P.J.Corfield (2015).

Corfield, Penelope J. *Time and the Shape of History*. New Haven: Yale University Press, 2007.

Crawley, Greer, and Donatella Barbieri. "Dress, Time, and Space: Expanding the Field through Exhibition Making." In *The Handbook of Fashion Studies*, Sandy Black, Amy de la Haye, Agnès Rocamora, Regina Root, and Helen Thomas (eds), 44–60. London: Bloomsbury, 2013.

Cwerner, Saulo B. "Clothes at Rest: Elements for a Sociology of the Wardrobe." *Fashion Theory: The Journal of Dress, Body and Culture* 5, no. 1 (2001): 79–92.

Dalby, Liza Crihfield. *Kimono Fashioning Culture*. New Haven, CT: Yale University Press, 1993.

Davidson, Hilary. "Holding the Sole: Shoes, Emotions and the Supernatural'. In *Feeling Things: Objects and Emotions through History*, Stephanie Downs, Sally Holloway, and Sarah Randles (eds), 72–93. Oxford: Oxford University Press, 2018.

Davidson, Hilary. "The Embodied Turn: Making and Remaking Dress as an Academic Practice." *Fashion Theory: The Journal of Dress, Body and Culture* 23, no. 3 (2019): 329–62.

de Perthuis, Karen. "Darning Mark's Jumper: Wearing Love and Sorrow." *Cultural Studies Review* 22, no. 1 (2016): 59–77.

Devoucoux, Daniel. "The Discovery of Materiality: Archaeological Clothing Finds, Representation, and Knowledge Formation." In *Fashion and Materiality: Cultural Practices in Global Contexts*, Heike Jenss and Viola Hofmann (eds), 59–77. London: Bloomsbury Visual Arts, 2019.

Eastop, Dinah. "Textiles as Multiple and Competing Histories." In *Textiles Revealed: Object Lessons in Historic Textiles and Costume Research*, Mary M. Brooks (ed.), 17–28. London: Archetype Publications Ltd., 2000.

Eicher, Joanne B. "The Anthropology of Dress." *Dress: The Journal of the Costume Society of America* 27, no. 1 (2000): 59–70.

Eicher, Joanne B., Hazel Lee Evenson, and Sandra Lutz. *The Visible Self: Global Perspectives on Dress, Culture and Society*. 2nd edn. New York: Fairchild Publications, 2000.

Elias, Nobert. *An Essay on Time*. 2nd rev. edn. Dublin: University College of Dublin Press, 2007.

Entwistle, Joanne. *The Fashioned Body: Fashion, Dress and Modern Social Theory*. Oxford: Blackwell, 2000.

Erekosima, Tonye Victor, and Joanne Bubolz Eicher. "Kalabari Cut-Thread and Pulled-Thread Cloth." *African Arts* 14, no. 2 (1981): 48–51.

Evans, Caroline. *Fashion at the Edge: Spectacle, Modernity and Deathliness*. New Haven, CT: Yale University Press, 2007.

Evans, Caroline. "A Shop of Images and Signs." In *Fashion as Photography: Viewing and Reviewing Images of Fashion*, Eugénie Shinkle (ed.), 17–28. New York: I. B.Tauris & Co. Ltd., 2008.

Evans, Caroline, and Alessandra Vaccari (eds), *Time in Fashion: Industrial, Antilinear and Uchronic Temporalities*. London: Bloomsbury, 2020.

Fabian, Johannes. *Time and the Other: How Anthropology Makes its Object*. New York: Columbia University Press, 1983.

Felski, Rita. "Context Stinks!" *New Literary History* 42, no 4 (2011): 573–91.

Fennetaux, Ariane. "Sentimental Economics: Recycling Textiles in Eighteenth-Century Britain." In *The Afterlife of Used Things*, Ariane Fennetaux, Amelie Junque, and Sophie Vasset (eds), 132–41. London: Routledge, 2015.

Fennetaux, Ariane. "Indian Gowns Small and Great: Chintz Banyans Ready Made in the Coromandel, *c*. 1680–1780." *Costume* 55, no. 1 (2021): 49–73.

Findly, Ellison Banks. *Nur Jahan: Empress of Mughal India*. New York: Oxford University Press, 1993.

Fisk, Catriona. *Connecting Threads: Tracing Fashion, Fabric and Everyday Life at Newstead House*. Brisbane: The Board of Trustees of Newstead House, 2016.

Fletcher, Kate. *Craft of Use: Post-Growth Fashion*. Abingdon: Routledge, 2016.

Fletcher, Kate, and Ingun Grimstad Klepp (eds), *Opening Up the Wardrobe : A Methods Book*. St. Charles Missouri: Novus Press, 2017.

Gilligan, Ian. *Climate, Clothing and Agriculture in Prehistory: Linking Evidence, Causes and Effects*. Cambridge: Cambridge University Press 2018.

Gordon, Stewart (ed.), *Robes and Honour: The Medieval World of Investiture*. London: Palgrave Macmillan, 2001.

Harlow, Mary, and Marie Louise Nosch. "Weaving the Threads: Methodologies in Textile and Dress Research for the Greek and Roman World—The State of the Art and the Case for Cross-disciplinarity." *Greek and Roman Textiles and Dress: An Interdisciplinary Anthology*. Antique Textiles Series 19. Oxford: Oxbow Publications, 2014.

Hansen, Karen Tranberg, and D. Soyini Madison (eds), *African Dress: Fashion, Agency, Performance*. London: Bloomsbury, 2013.

Hassan, Robert. "Globalization and the 'Temporal Turn': Recent Trends and Issues in Time Studies." *The Korean Journal of Policy Studies* 25, no. 2 (2010): 83–102.

Hauser, Kitty. "A Garment in the Dock; or, How the FBI Illuminated the Prehistory of a Pair of Denim Jeans." *Journal of Material Culture* 9, no. 3 (2004): 293–313.

Healy, Robyn. "Immateriality." In *The Handbook of Fashion Studies*, Sandy Black, Amy de la Haye, Joanne Entwistle, Agnès Rocamora, Regina Root, and Helen Thomas (eds), 325–43. London: Bloomsbury, 2013.

Healy, Robyn. "The Parody of the Motley Cadaver: Displaying the Funeral of Fashion." In *The Textile Reader*, Jessica Hemmings, (ed.) 89–98. London: Berg Publishers, 2012.

Himelfarb, Elizabeth J. "Prehistoric Body Painting." *Archaeology Newsbriefs* 53, no. 4 (2000). Available online at : https://archive.archaeology.org/0007/newsbriefs/zambia.html (accessed October 25, 2020).

Ingold, Tim. "Materials against Materiality." *Archaeological Dialogues* 14, no.1 (2007): 1–16.

Ingold, Tim. "No More Ancient; No More Human: The Future Past of Archaeology and Anthropology." In *Archaeology and Anthropology. Past, Present and Future*, David Shankland (ed.), 77–90. London: Bloomsbury, 2013.

Jenss, Heike, and Viola Hofmann. "Introduction: Fashion and Materiality." In *Fashion and Materiality: Cultural Practices in Global Contexts*, Heike Jenss and Viola Hofmann (eds), 1–11. London: Bloomsbury Visual Arts, 2019.

Jones, Jana. "The Enigma of the Pleated Dress: New Insights from Early Dynastic Helwan Reliefs." *The Journal of Egyptian Archaeology* 100, (2014): 209–31.

Jones, Philip. "Aboriginal Dress in Australia: Evidence and Resources." *Berg Encyclopedia of World Dress and Fashion*, vol. 7, Joanne B. Eicher (ed.), 17–26. Oxford: Berg: 2010. (This article edited by Margaret Maynard.)

Joyce, Rosemary A. "Archaeology of the Body." *Annual Review of Anthropology* 34 (2005): 139–58.

Joyce, Rosemary A. "Life with Things: Archaeology and Materiality." In *Archaeology and Anthropology. Past, Present and Future*, David Shankland (ed.), 119–32. London: Routledge, 2013.

Kaiser, Susan B. *Fashion and Cultural Studies*. Oxford: Berg Publishers, 2012.

Kopytoff, Igor. "The Cultural Biography of Things: Commoditization as Process." In *The Social Life of Things: Commodities in Cultural Perspective*. Arjun Appadurai (ed.), 64–92. Cambridge: Cambridge University Press, 1986.

Küchler, Susanne, and Daniel Miller (eds), *Clothing as Material Culture*. Oxford: Berg Publishers, 2005.

Küchler, Susanne, and Graeme Were (eds), *The Art of Clothing: A Pacific Experience*. London: UCL, 2005.

Küchler, Susanne, and Graeme Were. "The Social World of Cloth in the Pacific Islands." *Berg Encyclopedia of World Dress and Fashion*, vol. 7, Joanne B. Eicher (ed.), 381–5. Oxford: Berg, 2010. (This article edited by Margaret Maynard.)

Larkin, Alison. "Replicating Captain Cook's Waistcoat: Exploring the Skills of a Named Embroiderer during the Eighteenth Century." *Costume* 51, no. 1 (2017): 54–77.

Lemire, Beverly, Laura Peers, Anne Whitelaw (eds) *Object Lives and Global Histories in Northern North America. Material Culture in Motion c. 1780–1980*. Montreal & Kingston: McGill-Queen's University Press, 2021.

Maynard, Margaret. *Fashioned from Penury : Dress as Cultural Practice in Australia*. Cambridge: Cambridge University Press, 1994.

Maynard, Margaret. "Where do Flappers Fit in?: The Photography of Modern Fashion in Australia." *Australian Cultural History* 25 (2006). *Antipodean Modern*, Neil Levi and Tim Dolan (eds), 273–90.

Maynard, Margaret. "Fast Fashion and Sustainability." In *The Handbook of Fashion Studies*, Sandy Black, Amy de la Haye, Joanne Entwistle, Agnès Rocamora, Regina A. Root, and Helen Thomas (eds), 542–56. London: Bloomsbury Academic, 2013.

McNeil, Peter, and Melissa Bellanta. "Letter from the Editors: Fashion, Embodiment and the 'Making Turn'." *Fashion Theory: The Journal of Dress, Body & Culture* 23, no. 3 (2019): 325–28.

Meskell, Lynn. *Object Worlds in Ancient Egypt: Material Biographies Past and Present*. Oxford: Berg Publishers, 2004.

Milhaupt, Terry Satsuki. *Kimono: A Modern History*. London: Reaktion Books, 2014.

Mukherjee, Soma. *Royal Mughul Ladies and Their Contributions*. New Delhi: Gyan Publishing House, 2001.

Nanni, Giordano. *The Colonisation of Time: Ritual, Routine and Resistance in the British Empire*. Manchester: Manchester University Press, 2013.

North, Susan. "Indian Gowns and Banyans: New Evidence and Perspectives." *Costume: The Journal of the Costume Society* 54, no. 1 (2020): 30–55.

Palmer, Alexandra. "Untouchable: Creating Desire and Knowledge in Museum Costume and Textile Exhibitions." *Fashion Theory: The Journal of Dress, Body and Culture* 12, no. 1 (2008): 31–63.

Palmer, Alexandra. "Looking at Fashion: The Material Object as Subject." In *The Handbook of Fashion Studies*, Sandy Black, Amy de la Haye, Agnès Rocamora, Regina Root, and Helen Thomas (eds), 268–300. London: Bloomsbury, 2013.

Peers, Laura. "Crossing Worlds: Hide Coats, Relationships, and Identity in Rupert's Land and Britain." In *Object Lives and Global Histories in Northern North America. Material Culture in Motion c. 1780–1980*, Beverley Lemire, Laura Peers, and Anne Whitelaw (eds), 55–81. Montreal & Kingston: McGill-Queen's University Press, 2021.

Prown, Jules. "Mind in Matter: An Introduction to Material Culture Theory and Method." *Winterthur Portfolio* 17, no. 1 (1982): 1–19.

Quinn, Bradley. *Textile Futures: Fashion, Design and Technology*. Oxford: Berg, 2010.

Ribeiro, Aileen. *Dress in Eighteenth Century Europe, 1715–1789*. London: B. T. Batsford, 1984.

Riefstahl, Elizabeth. "A Note on Ancient Fashions: Four Early Egyptian Dresses in the Museum of Fine Arts, Boston." *Boston Museum Bulletin* 68, no. 354 (1970): 244–59.

Riello, Giorgio, and Peter McNeil (eds), *The Fashion Reader: Global Perspectives*. London: Routledge, 2010.

Riello, Giorgio. "The Object of Fashion: Methodological Approaches to the History of Fashion." *Journal of Aesthetics and Culture* 3, no. 1 (2011): 1–7.

Rocamora, Agnès. "Introduction to Chapter 'Spaces of Fashion'." In *The Handbook of Fashion Studies*, Sandy Black, Amy de la Haye, Agnès Rocamora, Regina Root, and Helen Thomas (eds), 159–63. London: Bloomsbury, 2013.

Rocamora, Agnès. "New Fashion Times: Fashion and Digital Media." In *The Handbook of Fashion Studies*, Sandy Black, Amy de la Haye, Agnès Rocamora, Regina Root, and Helen Thomas (eds), 61–77. London: Bloomsbury, 2013.

Sampson, Ellen. "The Shoe as Palimpsest: Imprint, Memory and Non-Contemporaneity in Worn Objects" (February 2013). Available online at: https://www.academia.edu/12489683/The_Shoe_as_Palimpsest (accessed October 25, 2020).

Sampson, Ellen. "The Cleaved Garment: The Maker, The Wearer and the 'Me and Not Me' of Fashion Practice." *Fashion Theory: The Journal of Dress, Body & Culture* 22, no. 3 (2018): 341–60.

Sampson, Ellen. "Creases, Crumples and Folds." *The Fashion Studies Journal* 3 (April 5, 2017). Available online : http://www.fashionstudiesjournal.org/2-visual-essays-2/2017/4/2/creases-crumples-and-folds-maps-of-experience-and-manifestations-of-wear (accessed October 25,2020).

Satsuki-Milhaupt, Terry, *Kimono : A Modern History*. London: Reaktion Books, 2014.

Shukla, Pravina. "The Study of Dress and Adornment as Social Positioning." *Material Culture Review* 61, no. 1 (2005): 4–16.

Soffer, Olga. "Recovering Perishable Technologies through Use Wear on Tools: Preliminary Evidence for Upper Paleolithic Weaving and Net Making." *Current Anthropology* 45, no. 3 (2004): 407–13.

Souvatzi, Stella. "Space, Place and Architecture: A Meeting Point Between Social Archaeology and Anthropology." In *Archaeology and Anthropology. Past, Present and Future*, David Shankland (ed.), 173–96. London: Bloomsbury, 2013.

Stallybrass, Peter. "Worn Worlds: Clothes, Mourning and the Life of Things." In *The Textile Reader*, Jessica Hemmings (ed.), 68–77. London: Berg Publishers, 2012.

Stallybrass, Peter, and Ann Rosalind Jones. "Fetishizing the Glove in Renaissance Europe." *Critical Inquiry* 28, no. 1 (2001): 114–32.

Steele, Valerie. "Museum Quality: The Rise of the Fashion Exhibition." *Fashion Theory: The Journal of Dress, Body & Culture* 12, no. 1 (2008): 7–30.

Stevenson, Alice, and Michael W. Dee. "Confirmation of the World's Oldest Woven Garment: The Tarkhan Dress." *Antiquity: A Review of World Archaeology* 349, no. 90 (2016). Available online at: https://www.antiquity.ac.uk/projgall/stevenson349 (accessed October 25, 2020).

Taylor, Lou. *The Study of Dress History*. Manchester: Manchester University Press, 2002.

Taylor, Lou, "Fashion and Dress History: Theoretical and Methodological Approaches." In *The Handbook of Fashion Studies*, Sandy Black, Amy de la Haye, Agnès Rocamora, Regina Root, and Helen Thomas (eds), 23–43. London: Bloomsbury, 2013.

Taylor, Lou. "Several Lives of a Collection of Rag Dump Clothing from Normandy (1900–1955): From Farm, to Dump, to Poverty Chic." *Fashion Studies* 1, no. 1 (2018): 1–38.

Vinken, Barbara. *Fashion Zeitgeist: The Trends and Cycles in the Fashion System*. Oxford: Berg, 2005.

Vollmer, John E. "Cultural Authentication in Dress," In *Berg Encyclopedia of World Dress and Fashion: Global Perspectives*, vol. 10, Joanne B. Eicher and Phyllis G. Tortora (eds), 69–76. Oxford: Berg Publishers, 2010.

Wallace, Patricia Te Arapo. "Introduction to Māori Dress." In *Berg Encyclopedia of World Dress and Fashion*, vol. 7, Joanne B. Eicher (ed.), 249–59. Oxford: Berg Publishers, 2010. (This article edited by Margaret Maynard.)

Weber, Caroline. *Queen of Fashion: What Marie Antoinette Wore to the Revolution*. London: Aurum Press, 2006.

Welters, Linda, and Abby Lillethun. *Fashion History: A Global View*. London: Bloomsbury Academic, 2018.

# INDEX

The letter *f* following an entry indicates a page with a figure.